## Praise for *The Godd*

"The defining characteristic of our age is the return of the Mother called by many names … Our salvation lies in knowing Her. *The Goddess Discovered* is a fine place to begin that knowing."

—Rabbi Rami Shapiro, award-winning author
and contributing editor at *Spirituality and Health* magazine

"Kaehr makes a point that our connection to early teachings may come to us from a place we never imagined—our past lives and ancestors. *The Goddess Discovered* is an engaging read, and the past-life regression and ancestral healing exercises should be a real help."

—George Noory, host of *Coast to Coast AM*
and *Beyond Belief* on Gaia

"I greatly enjoyed *The Goddess Discovered* and Shelley Kaehr's exposition on a universally captivating subject, the worldwide appeal of the goddess. Shelley authors many fine insights into the origin of the universal human traits."

—Raymond A. Moody, Jr, MD, internationally
renowned author of *Life After Life*

"In this informative and engaging work, Shelley Kaehr introduces the reader to the archetypal nature of the goddess as she appears across cultures and time... More than an encyclopedia of goddesses, Shelley provides practices for working with the goddess energies in our own lives and in exploring how the divine feminine manifested in our ancestral lineages and ways we can reconnect to that energy to heal self and planet now. This is a powerful, important, and necessary book."

—Nicholas S. Mather, PhD, Adjunct Professor of Philosophy
and Religious Studies, host of the *Rebel Spirit Radio* podcast

"A wonderful reference guide to continuously reflect on—essential to any sacred collection. Throughout this book, we are introduced to the multidimensional, multifaceted expression of the divine herself. Not only to connect with the goddess, but to ultimately embrace your inherent personal power within."

—Granddaughter Crow, author of *Belief, Being, and Beyond*

"A meticulously researched guide to the Divine Feminine as she appears in endless iterations around the world. This book is a treasure trove of Goddesses—listed for ease of reference by culture, archetype, function, and attributes. You will rediscover and learn new information about beloved, well-known goddesses as well as nearly forgotten deities. Complete with exercises designed to invite Goddess energy into your life, this book satisfies the inner yearning to reconnect deeply with the Divine Feminine."

—Rev. Wendy Van Allen, author of *Relighting the Cauldron*

"A masterful deep dive into world history, religion, and goddesses. Kaehr's theories of connectivity we feel toward our ancestors and through our past lives is supported by the magical energies of our universe. I highly recommend this book to all who wish to discover not only the Goddess, but a new appreciation for the diverse and fascinating world we live in."

—Bernie Ashman, author of *Sun Sign Karma* and *Sun Signs & Past Lives*

"The focus of Kaehr's book, besides thoroughly covering goddesses throughout history, is to urge us to personally connect with the ancient goddesses to understand how much we all truly have in common. What awaits the reader is a journey of release, understanding, renewed connection, and a deep dive into the soul healing we all crave in our modern world."

—Kac Young, PhD, ND, DCH, author of *Crystal Power*

"I have never experienced such powerful methods for activating the goddess/es that can speak to me—and help me become more of myself—as is shared by Shelley Kaehr. A must for those seeking conscious living and expression."

—Cyndi Dale, internationally renowned author of
*Advanced Chakra Healing* and many others

"In studying the past, you cannot escape encountering the Goddess, nor should you try. Kaehr's brilliant and incisive book illustrates why. Part encyclopedia, part exploration, part history lesson, and part how-to, her book is an essential element for those who wish to know more, understand more, and who even quest for the Goddess."

—Dan Baldwin, award-winning author

"A treasure trove for anyone interested in mythology, spirituality, and the divine feminine. This book presents an exhaustive list of goddesses unlike any I have ever seen before. The list spans different cultures and time periods…Kaehr draws on a wide range of sources, including ancient texts and contemporary research, to paint a comprehensive picture of each goddess."

—SynahMoon, author of *Tarot Cars Deck*

"This is the perfect balance between academia and mysticism…Despite the religious origins of goddess worship, no belief system is required to play here, just an imaginative and open mind. Discovery is a theme throughout this book as well as a concluding idea, and the forgotten past and sometimes marginalized peoples is made relevant again. *The Goddess Discovered* takes the lore and legend and helps the reader to relate to, meet, and apply goddess wisdom to one's own life. Venture into antiquity, connect with ancient worlds, or bring the 'collective sense of divinity' into the present in the many exercises and guided meditations provided."

—Julia Gordon-Bramer, author of *Tarot Life Lessons*

# THE GODDESS
# DISCOVERED

## About the Author

For over twenty years, Shelley A. Kaehr, PhD, has worked with thousands of people around the world, helping them achieve greater peace and happiness in their lives. Known as a renowned past-life regressionist and one of the world's leading authorities on energy healing and mind-body medicine, her award-winning books have been translated into multiple languages around the world.

A spiritual historian, Shelley enjoys creating content to help readers and students remember their soul histories and past lives. She coined the term *Supretrovie* to describe spontaneously induced past-life memories and strives to develop new methods to help people resolve challenging issues that arise from these influences. She created the groundbreaking Genealogical Regression, based on her award-winning international bestseller *Heal Your Ancestors to Heal Your Life*, to help seekers resolve inherited ancestral trauma. She believes we all have the power to rewrite our stories and create the life of our dreams.

Visit Shelley online at https://pastlifelady.com.

# THE GODDESS

# DISCOVERED

## Exploring the Divine Feminine
## Around the World

### SHELLEY A. KAEHR PhD

Foreword by Kris Franken

Llewellyn Publications
Woodbury, Minnesota

First Edition
First Printing, 2023

Book design by Samantha Peterson
Cover design by Shannon McKuhen

Llewellyn Publications is a registered trademark of Llewellyn Worldwide Ltd.

**Library of Congress Cataloging-in-Publication Data (Pending)**
ISBN: 978-0-7387-7176-2


Llewellyn Worldwide Ltd. does not participate in, endorse, or have any authority or responsibility concerning private business transactions between our authors and the public.

All mail addressed to the author is forwarded but the publisher cannot, unless specifically instructed by the author, give out an address or phone number.

Any internet references contained in this work are current at publication time, but the publisher cannot guarantee that a specific location will continue to be maintained. Please refer to the publisher's website for links to authors' websites and other sources.

Llewellyn Publications
A Division of Llewellyn Worldwide Ltd.
2143 Wooddale Drive
Woodbury, MN 55125-2989
www.llewellyn.com

Printed in the United States of America

## Other Books by Shelley A. Kaehr, PhD

*Beyond Reality: Evidence of Parallel Universes*

*Blast from the Past: Healing Spontaneous Past Life Memories*

*Familiar Places: Reflections on Past Lives Around the World*

*Heal Your Ancestors to Heal Your Life:*
*The Transformative Power of Genealogical Regression*

*Journeys Through the Akashic Records*

*Lifestream: Journey into Past & Future Lives*

*Meet Your Karma: The Healing Power of Past Life Memories*

*Past Lives in Ancient Lands & Other Worlds:*
*Understand Your Soul's Journey Through Time*

*Past Lives with Gems & Stones*

*Past Lives with Pets: Discover Your Timeless*
*Connection to Your Beloved Companions*

*Reincarnation Recollections: Geographically Induced Past Life Memories*

*Supretrovie: Externally Induced Past Life Memories*

# Contents

Contents

## Part Three
## GODDESS DISCOVERY AND GUIDED JOURNEYS

# Exercises

# Journal Prompts

# Disclaimer

This book is not intended as a substitute for consultation with a licensed medical or mental health professional. The reader should regularly consult a physician or mental health professional in matters relating to health and particularly with respect to any symptoms that may require diagnosis or medical attention. This book provides content related to educational, medical, and psychological topics. As such, use of this book implies your acceptance of this disclaimer.

Names and identifying details have been changed to protect the privacy of individuals.

# Acknowledgments

This book is dedicated to people of all ages, belief systems, and walks of life and would not exist at all were it not for the input and support of many people, including my incredible team at Llewellyn Worldwide, and especially the encouragement of my dear friend, Kat Neff. Thank you, Kat! My editor extraordinaire, Heather Greene, is absolutely fantastic and I am grateful for her visionary insight and feedback. Thank you both from the bottom of my heart! It's been such a joy working with Llewellyn on several books now. I am so very grateful to publisher Bill Krause, Terry Lohmann, Anna Levine, Sami Sherratt, Markus Ironwood, Lauryn Heineman, Aundrea Foster, Shannon McKuhen, Alisha Bjorklund, Kevin Brown, Leah Madsen, Sammy Peterson, and Angela Wix.

As always, I also extend my love and appreciation to my family and friends, including Jim Merideth, Pat Moon, and Paula Wagner, who mean so much to me. Special thanks to my friend George Noory for his encouragement and to everyone who supported my other Llewellyn projects, including Dr. Raymond Moody, Dr. Kac Young, and Cyndi Dale. I'd also like to thank my wonderful friends and students, particularly Janine, Theresa, Damaris, Maria, Lynn, and Maya, who inspired this project during the pandemic of 2020. Above all, I thank you and all my readers for diving into my books over the years. Thank you! May you find and embrace your inherent personal power and go forth to shine brightly in the world now and always.

# Introduction

Malta has quite a rocky history. Not only does this tiny archipelago bear the world record as the most bombed place on planet Earth thanks to a reported 3,000 air raids in two years and devastating military assaults during World War II, the spiritual history and monuments are some of the oldest sites in the world.[1] Inside Ħaġar Qim (meaning "standing stones") Temple, archaeologists discovered the Venus of Malta, a female figure in a pleated skirt with her legs tucked to one side. She is known also by "fat lady" thanks to her exaggerated thighs and arms and disproportionately small hands and feet. Venus of Malta is now housed in Malta's National Museum of Archeology. Another clay figurine known as the Sleeping Lady is another significant Maltese treasure discovered at the prehistoric necropolis ĦalSaflieni Hypogeum dating between 4000 to 2500 BCE. The 5,000-year-old statue features a full-figured woman reclining in a deep sleep with her head propped up on her arm. In the nearby Tarxien Temple also on Malta, archaeologists discovered a gigantic statue of a female in a pleated skirt.[2]

Malta isn't alone in the realm of rich archeological discoveries. The oldest known representation of a human figure is a mammoth ivory carving of a curvaceous woman called Venus of Hohle Fels discovered in Schelklingen, Germany, estimated to be 35,000 to 40,000 years old.[3]

---

1. Hudson, *UXB Malta*, 8.

2. Atkinson, *Malta &Gozo*, 52, 124–5, 172.

3. Kindersley, *Cultural Treasures of the World*, 14.

Excavations in Harappa and Mohenjo Daro in the Indus Valley yielded numerous terracotta figurines with breasts. Some scholars doubt these figures were intended to be goddesses due to their rudimentary forms, while others argue the presence of phallic symbols suggest that the Divine Mother's ability to give life was an important aspect of the spirituality of the early people of this region.[4]

The mysterious Sheela Na Gigs, stone carvings of naked women with enlarged vulvas dating back as early as the eleventh century, adorned medieval churches in Britain to the dismay of embarrassed clergy members who tried to hide them until they grabbed the attention of the scientific community 160 years ago.[5]

These are but a few of numerous examples of female carvings found in archaeological sites around the globe. The question remains: *What do they mean?* Why were they created in such abundance? More important, is it fair for academics to assume they represent goddesses? Are scholars doing their due diligence by defining the figures and prescribing them with the attributes of fertility and motherhood as though these are the only two possible qualities females can possess? Should we simply assume they prove the existence of a widespread phenomenon of goddess worship? Such menial conclusions are speculative at best, and this ambiguity speaks to a wider challenge that anyone has when delving into the study of world religions—appropriation.

When studying the ancient and living world religions explored within these pages, the best practice is to acknowledge the absolute fact that nobody alive today can fully comprehend the exact intentions and definitions for deities who are only known to us through archaeological evidence and fragments of occasional written proof. Nor can anyone outside any religion fully understand every single nuance behind a faith. Some of the world's richest belief systems were generationally passed down orally through storytelling, music, and dance. With that in mind, I approach this work with humble respect and absolute humility. Humanity has much yet to discover about the meaning behind the female images and the Goddess herself, which is among the main purposes for this book. Welcome to *The Goddess Discovered*!

---

4. Keay, *India*, 14.

5. Stevens, "Big Vagina Energy."

## Belief and Areas of Exploration

What comes to you during your lifetime is drawn into your experience at a soul level. If you are fascinated by the Goddess, there are likely two reasons why you are drawn to pursue these studies: past lives, ancestral influences, or both.

### Past Lives

People are drawn to the Goddess because of influences from past lives. Greek philosopher Plato described the phenomenon he called *anamnesis* or "soul knowing." According to Plato, at a soul level, people know who they were in the past and where they lived in prior incarnations. For those drawn to the pursuit of Goddess discovery, one reason why that happens is because the soul longs to return to the familiar and experience situations, circumstances, people, and even goddesses who were loved and adored in the past.

*Supretrovie* is the term I coined to describe the spontaneously induced past-life memories that happen to everybody whether they are consciously aware of it or not. Supretrovie happens when people are near artifacts and objects from prior lifetimes, including antiques or gems and stones, or the familiar feeling may occur while encountering familiar people or traveling into new places where the soul lived in the past. Supretrovie happens most often when one is engaging in learning or watching programming about new places, or in this case, while reading about familiar topics from the past. As you delve into *The Goddess Discovered*, you will experience various emotions and flashes of insight from the calling of your soul about your past lives. The study of world religions, spiritual practices, and learning the names and traits of specific goddesses that may not be familiar to you on a conscious level is bound to strike a familiar chord as you move through this material. When and how your Supretrovie will occur will be different for everyone. I feel certain that it will happen. My research and writings attempt to help you remember who you are because, like Plato, I, too, believe that everyone can access soul memories if given the proper protocols. Later in the book, you will discover your connections to the Goddess through an extensive past-life regression.

### Ancestral Connection

My primary theory as to why the Goddess continues to gain popularity goes right along with the societal trend away from large modern religious institutions toward more personal spiritual practices. Those urges are *built into your DNA*. Regardless of what religious denomination you may personally follow, your ancestors engaged in these practices long ago. As a collective, I am convinced our ancestors are calling us to a new way of being.

Science backs this up. Epigenetics is the ever-expanding scientific field that seeks to understand the interplay of outside influences as risk factors for disease. According to the Center for Disease Control, Epigenetics determines how your body reads your DNA sequence. While our DNA does not change, DNA can become chemically altered by various stress factors and environmental influences.[6] This means that nurture may be just as important as nature in determining your future health.

In a study from the National Institutes of Health National Library of Medicine, researchers found that descendants of Holocaust survivors had greater risks of anxiety, depression, and trauma.[7] Human beings are not *tabula rasa*—born as blank slates for the world to imprint on—but are in fact chemically influenced by the environment and therefore subject to inherited ancestral trauma. Hardships and calamities experienced by your ancestors leave energetic scars on your DNA that get passed down generation to generation.

Another 2008 study revealed special chemical markers present in children of people who were prenatally exposed to life-threatening starvation. During a World War II food shortage called the Dutch Hunger Winter of 1944 to 1945, thousands faced dire circumstances. Survivors' in utero offspring had DNA markers that were not present in their same-sex siblings born after this terrible time in history. Science proposed that people whose parents struggled with the stresses of hunger before their birth were significantly more likely to develop heart disease, diabetes, and schizophrenia than their siblings born during less stressful times.[8] Another scientific study suggests that up to 50 percent of our personalities and behaviors are brought straight through from our DNA.[9] The findings and data revealed by these groundbreaking studies validate the intuitive

---

6. Center for Disease Control, "What Is Epigenetics?"

7. Dashorst et al., "Intergenerational Consequences of the Holocaust on Offspring Mental Health," 1654065.

8. Heijmans et al., "Persistent Epigenetic Differences Associated with Prenatal Exposure to Famine in Humans," 17046–9.

9. Anthony, "So Is It Nature Not Nurture After All?"

feelings many people have had for decades about the importance of healing on behalf of their ancestors. What if you are picking up on feelings about goddesses that your ancestors had hundreds or even thousands of years ago? It's certainly possible.

All these findings would be wonderful if everything our collective ancestors experienced was positive and life affirming, but of course, that is obviously not the case. What can you do to transform the unwanted inherited influences from your DNA for the better? I'm a big believer in change and the ability of your body to heal if given the right circumstances. Twenty years ago, I developed the Genealogical Regression process to help clients heal challenging situations with parents and family members and consciously send light to ancestors to resolve ancestral energetic blockages from the past. Doing Genealogical Regressions and other kinds of ancestral healing that is becoming more prevalent and popular can help reshape the course of destiny, not only for yourself, but for future generations of your family. Later in the book, you will do Genealogical Regressions on both your mother's and father's side of the family and come to understand and transform ancestral patterns and discover how those energies connect to various goddesses from around the world whom your ancestors worshiped in early times.

## Goddess Archetypes and Themes

Aside from the role our ancestral DNA has in shaping our interests in spirituality, there are other possible explanations for our connection with the Goddess. Common themes exist within mythology and creation stories around the world. Humanity shares a universal thread of consciousness that exists between all people throughout time described by Swiss philosopher Carl Jung as a *collective unconscious* and the commonalities of thought between people called *archetypes*. Jung believed unconscious collective thought shared by all people is universal and gives us empathy to understand others. Jung noted that archetypes are pre-existent forms all people share without external conditioning.[10] These collective thoughts arise without any special effort and go beyond our personal sense of self. Jung believed these concepts were inherited by ancestors through the collective field and served to connect humanity as one.[11] Jung's philosophies suggest

---

10. Jung et al., *Memories, Dreams, Reflections*, 138.

11. Jung, *Archetypes and the Collective Unconscious*, 43.

that the millions, or perhaps *billions*, of people who worshiped goddesses and deities in the past may have influenced us on a collective level to do the same.

## Jungian Archetypes

Jungian archetypes figure prominently within the goddess pantheons because they represent the wider societal beliefs, concerns, and norms shared between all people from all walks of life. The following is a partial list of Jung's most prominent archetypes that figure into mythology and exploration of the Goddess.

**Child:** The child archetype is an innocent, helpless being delivered into a cold and harsh world. They simultaneously embody a divine creation, having crossed the threshold into physical form through stories of miraculous births. Themes of abandonment and rediscovery and the child as a god, goddess, or divine being are also common.[12]

**Creator:** The idea that people originated from a form outside of themselves is common across cultures. There is a creator in many mythoi who originated from another kind of creator who is self-made. For convenience's sake, he may embody the feminine tasks of creation and birth to construct and bring himself to life without the use of the female form.[13] In some mythoi, the divine creation began with a feminine energy.

**Hero:** Strong women who lived exemplary lives or were created in mythology serve as saviors for the sick and weak and are often tutelary or protective deities for entire cities, states, or nations. In Jung's view, the masculine version of the hero could take the form of a hunter who seeks lost treasure, a negative hero or villain, a king, or a child hero born of a Divine Mother.[14]

**Innocent:** The idea of an innocent untouched soul is a common archetype that takes several forms. The innocent maiden archetype represents the youth and vigor of early life. Often these maidens are perceived with great virtuousness and chastity, making them worthy of admiration and therefore worship since the earliest of times. Unbaptized newborns can also be

---

12. Jung, *Archetypes and the Collective Unconscious*, 167, 170, 179.

13. Jung, *Archetypes and the Collective Unconscious*, 228, 263–4.

14. Jung, *Archetypes and the Collective Unconscious*, 165, 171, 229, 255, 270.

perceived as vulnerable innocents, not yet protected by the spiritual forces by either the church or through protective spells or rituals of earlier times. The pure aspect of the innocent makes them the perfect victim of evil or dark forces. Crimes against the helpless are seen as more depraved and worthy of the harshest punishments.[15]

**Lovers:** Sensual love and marital relations between consorts and divine complements are common themes when studying goddesses. Often the pair represents opposite traits that bring divine balance into the world.[16]

**Magician:** Jung cites black magicians and white magicians who represent good and evil behaviors that all people experience. The black is an evil sorcerer, while the white is often the wise old man or sage who offers great depths of wisdom and prudent counsel.[17] In Goddess discussions, female sorcerers who either protect the living or intercede with the Underworld are incredibly common.

**Mother:** The personal mother is a primary force in the lives of all people as the instrument of human creation. Mother can take many forms. She can present as the youthful maiden or elderly grandmother. Her characteristics can be as a kind and sacrificial caregiver, or as a wicked denier of affections—an expression of sympathy, female authority, and wisdom, or she may take on a wider role for humanity as the lunar-influenced Earth Mother. Christians embodied the Divine Mother as Queen of Heaven or Mother Church.[18]

**Sage:** In Jungian philosophy, wise mystics who could be either male or female figure prominently in mythology.[19] These figures offer sage advice to humanity.

**Trickster:** Trickster figures who appear in various pantheons to test mortals and help them aspire to ideal behavior are found mostly with the gods. According to Jung, they represent the summation of inferior qualities found within individuals and collectively embody the archetypal shadow

---

15. Jung, *Archetypes and the Collective Unconscious*, 26, 90.

16. Jung, *Archetypes and the Collective Unconscious*, 63.

17. Jung, *Archetypes and the Collective Unconscious*, 34, 270.

18. Jung, *Archetypes and the Collective Unconscious*, 29, 81–2, 107, 184–6, 199.

19. Jung, *Archetypes and the Collective Unconscious*, 270.

tendencies found within all people. The shadow represents their personal deficiencies and foibles and, according to Jung, can be part of a greater collective that affects everyone. Where there is light, the shadow image exists as a counterpart.[20]

**Wise Old Man:** The elderly gentleman archetype could be a version of a white magician, depending on the context. He invests his years assisting others in navigating the choppy waters of life. He may appear in dreams as a typical grandfather, priest, teacher, doctor, or some other authority figure.[21]

You will encounter aspects of these archetypes within the pantheons explored in this book.

## Goddess Themes

People in the ancient world, no matter what area they came from, all shared similar hopes, dreams, and fears that are incredibly similar to the things we worry about today. As the concept of archetypes suggests, these early concerns were represented through common themes found in myths and expressed within the deities crafted and worshiped to assist people with challenges in life. Let's look at some of the main themes associated with goddesses you will find in this book.

**Death and the Afterlife:** Ensuring the afterlife would be welcoming and safe became an obsession for the people of early times. With death all around them, they constructed rituals to ensure their loved ones were welcomed into the afterlife. With no great understanding of where people went after death, the fear created the reverence that led to rituals and ceremonies designed to appease the goddesses and gods they encountered. Aspects of death that were worshiped included the following:

*Heavenly realms*
*Incentives to do good works on Earth*
*Underworld deities*
*Punishment for wrongdoings and the results of bad behavior*

---

20. Jung, *Archetypes and the Collective Unconscious*, 262, 270.
21. Jung, *Archetypes and the Collective Unconscious*, 216.

Thanks to the perils of the ancient world, every single aspect of death had to be acknowledged in hopes of appeasing unseen forces of destruction to stop wreaking havoc and to bless those energies that supported and sustained life.

**Food and Sustenance:** Without food, survival won't happen. All societies turned to the Goddess for help in providing food. In fact, many of the early fertility goddesses you may think only dealt with childbearing also represented the concept of fertility when it came to bountiful crops and food. Those deities overlook several areas:

> *Hunting*
> *Harvests*
> *Food*

Several goddesses help ensure a bountiful hunt or create plentiful harvests. In some cultures, people worshiped specific food items. Food became personified, such as grains and corn. The Maya, for example, believed that people came from maize and gave the ultimate importance to corn in their religious practices. This is not surprising since corn meant life could go on.

**Motherhood and Childbirth:** Concerns with childbirth, fertility, ensuring survival, and continuity of offspring were of paramount importance to every single living being since the beginnings of time. For that reason, all pantheons dedicated several deities to ensuring the successful continuity of life, who were represented in a variety of ways:

> *Divine Mother*
> *Fertility statues*
> *Childhood protection*
> *Maternal protectors*

Everybody understood the perilous activities associated with giving birth, surviving a pregnancy, and having a healthy child who could survive in the harshest of conditions, so they honored every single aspect of this sacred process.

**Natural World:** Early people learned to track the movement of the stars in the sky to predict behaviors and to lessen uncertainty. For that reason, they prescribed god qualities to the skies and other natural phenomena.

People created goddesses to represent the heavens and Earth, the sun and stars, rivers, streams, trees, and so forth. Doing so helped the ancient ones explain the natural world around them while attempting to exercise control over what is theoretically uncontrollable.

**Physical Health and Healing:** Shamans and healers learned to work with the natural environment to create remedies to help those who were ill and suffering. They prayed to goddesses to help intercede and save people from death and illness and learned the wisdom of herbs and other gifts found in the natural environment. Goddesses were useful helpers to act as intermediaries between the patient and the higher power who could intervene on their behalf to save lives and create wellness.

**Protection:** Beyond the protective embrace of a Great Mother, people often adopted tutelary deities who acted as spiritual guardians for specific geographical locations. These gods and goddesses watched over the cities and states and all inhabitants to protect them from wars, diseases, or invasions.

**War and Conquest:** Ancient peoples also had big concerns over attacks, and while the gods are often sent to protect the people, that's not always the case. Some societies also enlisted the help of powerful goddesses to ensure success in battle or to protect territorial borders and boundaries.

**Weather:** Crops needed rain to grow to create food so people could survive. In Egypt, people celebrated and honored the annual flooding of the Nile that kept the community alive. Too much of a good thing could be a problem in the case of flooding, yet droughts were also of concern. Citizens in different cultures around the world invoked deities to help maintain balance, save lives, and hopefully create a more hospitable and favorable environment for sustaining life.

**Women's Life Cycle:** Other feminine archetypes found in goddesses throughout history involve the life cycle of a woman and the various stages of the life cycle embodied within worshiped deities. The three main stages of life ancient people worshiped included the following:

*Maiden:* A girl in her prime, youthful and exuberant.

*Mother:* The creation process of bringing a child into the world. The term *creation* could be literal or metaphorical.

*Crone:* She is envisioned in old age, often called a hag, and can represent the final stage of life or serve as a fierce protective spirit to scare away evil spirits or other unwanted influences.

The triplicate of feminine divinity is also present within several Triple Goddesses who embody different aspects of any of the above archetypes. Some are portrayed as a single deity who shape-shifts through her various lifecycles into the Maiden, Mother, and Crone. Others such as the Diana Triformis, the Roman aspect of Diana, had three functions: Huntress, Mother, or Underworld deity. The Huntress embodies a fertility or Maiden-type energy. Divine Mother is equated with Luna the Moon, the feminine divine lunar energy, and childbirth. The Underworld or liminal deity represented the fragile spaces between life and death. Triplicate goddesses were common within many pantheons.

## How to Use This Book

To get the most out of this book, I include historical facts and cosmology of the regions explored at the beginning of each chapter. The goddess listings are uniform in nature and provide helpful information about each deity mentioned. Each entry will feature the following:

**Goddess Name:** The name will be a reflection of the most common found as many deities are known by other names or spellings.

**Keywords:** Simple archetypal words will be included to give you a quick sense of what the goddess embodies and represents.

**Category:** The category descriptions will vary and will be defined early on in each chapter. Some goddesses will be categorized by geographical location, while others may be grouped by mythological texts, codices, or other literature or written proof or attestation of the deity's existence.

**Also Known As:** When known, alternative names or spellings for the goddess will be included.

**Description:** Each goddess description will include basic facts about what is known about her and her worship.

**Recommended Reading:** At the end of chapters, I recommend good books on each subject so you can discover additional information should you choose to learn more.

**Additional Categories:** While categories will change with each of the chapters, there are archetypal goddess and deity types that are so common, they cross cultural barriers and are found in numerous pantheons. Where applicable, throughout the entire book, the following categories will be mentioned in addition to the individual chapter categories. I define them here to give you an idea of what to expect:

*Ancestral:* Deities who are considered sacred ancestors of the people who worship them.

*Chthonic:* This term comes from classical Greek mythology, yet it applies to groups around the world and refers to any deity or goddess who inhabits the Underworld, a mythical realm of the dead.

*Personification:* Numerous cultures throughout the ages personified occurrences in the natural world by giving them human traits and deified nonphysical ideals, inanimate objects, or states of being into immortal beings and goddesses. In these cases, I will share what the goddess represents through her embodiment of various states and conditions found in the physical world.

*Primordial:* Many creation myths begin with a dark universe and chaos emerging from that darkness. At times, these goddesses represent the first beings who existed before all others and emerged to form the universe, Earth, humankind, and all physical aspects of creation. This information will be shared along with any creation myths known.

*Tutelary:* Thematically I mentioned earlier the importance for protection of people and places in ancient times. *Tutelary* is a term that specifically defines goddesses who stand as guardians for entire empires, cities, or specific places. At times, these same guardians may be the personification of a physical place in addition to acting as guardian of an area or region.

No matter where you're from in the world, people go through certain kinds of challenges and share similar experiences that, over time, carve out deep impressions in our unified field of the All-That-Is. Those shared experiences are reflected in the goddesses worshiped throughout the ages and can be demonstrated through several common themes found in myths and pantheons around the world. I hope your Goddess Discovery is a joyful journey.

## Summing Up

I've been keenly interested in writing and creating content to help people identify who they truly are, either in past lives through their own soul experiences through time, or through the energies brought forth from their ancestors. I hope that by examining goddesses, you will awaken dormant soul memories or enliven ancestral energy that exists within your own DNA so you can live your life in alignment with who you truly are at the deepest level. We all need greater understanding of ourselves. Think of all the experiences your ancestors had or your own soul experienced in prior incarnations that you could invest in helping discover the proper solutions to the challenges facing humanity right now. When you consciously remember and awaken your inner light, the world transforms for the better.

Aside from your personal journey of discovery, another wonderful benefit received by engaging in the material in *The Goddess Discovered* is to learn more about the incredible people inhabiting our planet now and in the past. Investing time and energy in understanding and learning more about other cultures and religions creates greater tolerance and peace. Such studies help to remind us all that people around the world have far more in common than we realize.

There is much to explore on your journey to discover the Goddess. You're here for a reason. Something brought you to this material at a soul level. Will you explore your ancestral past? Will you discover your past lives, or will you simply learn about some of the fascinating world religions and belief systems practiced by human beings throughout history? Perhaps you'll find all of that and more. Like a wave in the ocean, the energy of the Goddess will help you discover more about your soul's journey through time and why your unique light and voice is so important at this moment in history.

*Part One*

# Goddesses of the Ancient World

Throughout history, people worshiped divine feminine energies. What goddesses will you like best? Which goddesses would you rather avoid? Those intuitive sensations may be highly influenced by your past lives. If you're familiar with your ancestry, keep that in mind as well as you look through the upcoming pantheons from the ancient world. There may be special feelings you'll have about the areas and goddesses your ancestors worshiped in the past. The exploration is a chance to understand your soul like never before and explore your history in a new and refreshing way that may inspire you further in the future.

## Chapter One
# Ancient Near East Goddesses

The ancient Near East includes some of the oldest regions in the world credited with world-altering inventions and the origins of civilization, including Anatolia (now modern Turkey), Egypt, the Levant (which includes modern-day Syria), Lebanon, Israel, Palestine and Jordan, Mesopotamia, and Persia. The goddesses of ancient Egypt and Mesopotamia will be discussed.

## Egyptian Cosmology

Egyptian cosmology varied by region. Several creation stories existed with different pantheons and deities playing different roles to suit the political climate and leadership at the time. Egyptian rulers often evolved and merged goddesses with earlier deities to create new deities to support their political ends. Rebranding spirituality helped the pharaoh build a perception of power and prestige. Belief systems differed greatly among the various nomes, or city states, of Egypt. Rulers shifted pantheons and creation myths to suit their purpose. If you lived in Heliopolis near modern-day Cairo, for example, you worshiped an entirely different set of deities based on a different creation myth than people who lived in Thebes near modern-day Luxor. Goddesses merged with others or were absorbed in later time periods to become the deities we know today.

Despite the differing beliefs concerning creation, all Egyptian mythology describes humanity emerging from an abyss of darkness and chaos and the attempt to maintain balance between order and chaos. Deities within the Egyptian pantheon were typically paired with consorts who embodied opposite qualities, such as masculine and feminine or the positive and negative aspects of external conditions found in the natural world. Death and the afterlife were also of utmost importance in early Egypt. Our understanding of how deities were worshiped comes from priceless funerary texts that gave scholars concrete proof about real Egyptian spiritual practices and customs:

1. **Pyramid Texts:** Written on the walls of the pyramids at Saqqara, these funerary texts date back to the fifth and sixth dynasties and are among the oldest in the world.[22]

2. **Coffin Texts:** Writings and spells on coffins that date back to 2100 BCE.[23]

3. **Book of the Dead:** Papyrus containing funerary material dating from the beginning of the New Kingdom around 1550 BCE. The literal translation of this material is "the Book of Coming Forth by Day."[24]

While our category is Egyptian, where possible I will include details about goddesses mentioned in these important documents.

## Mesopotamian Cosmology

Mesopotamia, located between the Tigris and Euphrates Rivers, is one of the oldest regions of human settlements in the world, a seat of innovation and expansion located in the area known as the Fertile Crescent that encompassed areas of modern-day Turkey, Iran, Iraq, and Syria.[25] Unfortunately, due to foreign invaders and conquerors, the people were under different rule and therefore, at times, worshiped different goddesses during two major periods:

1. **Sumerian Period 4100–1750 BCE:** Sumerians were the people of southern Mesopotamia who established one of the oldest cities in the world according to modern archaeologists: Uruk. The Sumerians believed Eridu to be the oldest city, founded by the god Enki as a utopia comparable to the Biblical Garden of Eden, described in a text known as the *Eridu Gen-*

---

22. Mercer, *Pyramid Texts*.

23. Allen, *Egyptian Coffin Texts*.

24. Budge, *Egyptian Book of the Dead*.

25. Kuiper, *Mesopotamia*, 11.

*esis*, the world's first official flood tale.[26] Like the Egyptians, Sumerians believed the world began from watery chaos and dedicated temples called Ziggurats to deities to protect them from a return to disorder. Within the Sumerian region in southern Mesopotamia, scholars recognize several periods of development: Early Uruk Period (4000–3500 BCE), Late Uruk Period (3500–3100 BCE), Presargonic Period (2700–2350 BCE), Akkadian Period (2334–2218 BCE), Sargonic and Gutian Period (2334–2113 BCE), and Ur III Period or Sumerian Renaissance (2112–2004 BCE).[27] During these various periods of history, goddesses were synchronized or merged and deity names changed.

2. **Babylonian Period 2000 BCE–312 BCE:** The most famous city in Mesopotamia became a great superpower under the leadership of King Hammurabi, who reigned from 1792 to 1750 BCE, thrived again under King Nebuchadnezzar II, and eventually succumbed after numerous attacks to a general formerly under Alexander the Great named Seleucus I Nicator, who claimed the region and established the Seleucid Empire after Alexander's death.[28] During Hammurabi's reign, all the previously worshiped deities were revalued, and the role of women, and therefore goddesses, diminished drastically after Hammurabi elevated the god Marduk over all others, and goddess temples were repurposed to serve the gods. Prior to this period, women had relative equality to men, but after this period, no longer. The decline of equality of the sexes seemed to correlate with the decline of the cities themselves.[29]

## Ancient Near East Goddesses

Goddess status and names in both Egypt and Mesopotamia shifted and evolved throughout history, heavily influenced by the rulers of the day who decided which gods and goddesses they believed would best build their brand, so to speak, and establish their authority as effective rulers. Rulers sought to control the belief systems of the people and become immortalized.

---

26. Hess and Tsumura, *I Studied Inscriptions from Before the Flood*, 129–42.
27. Van De Mieroop, *History of the Ancient Near East*, 21, 374.
28. Van De Mieroop, *History of the Ancient Near East*, 344–6.
29. Van De Mieroop, *History of the Ancient Near East*, 126.

## Ama-arhus

**Keywords:** Compassion, Mother

**Category:** Mesopotamian

**Also Known As:** Arad-Ama-arhus, Amat-Ama-arhus

A fertility goddess worshiped in Uruk, she emerged during the Seleucid period from 312 to 64 BCE, in the Macedonian Greek empire founded by Seleucus Nicator, Alexander the Great's former general.[30] *Ama* means "maternal," and cult worship of several goddesses with that name became common during this time.[31]

## Ammit

**Keyword:** Guardian

**Category:** Egyptian

In the Egyptian *Book of the Dead*, Ammit guards the scales of Ma'at while the deceased's heart is weighed against the feather in the Hall of Two Truths. With a crocodile's head, a lion's neck and mane, and the rear of a hippo, Ammit embodied the most feared animals to encourage people to live truthful lives. Ammit was called Devourer of the Dead because she ate the hearts of the wicked and cast them into the lake of fire.

## Amunet

**Keyword:** Air

**Categories:** Egyptian, Primordial

Amunet and her counterpart Amun represent the masculine and feminine primordial air that began the creation of the universe. Worshiped within the Ogdoad of Hermopolis in ancient times, they were called the Hidden Ones and were two of eight creation deities.

---

30. Jordan, *Dictionary of Gods and Goddesses*, 13.

31. Asher-Greveand Westenholz, *Goddesses in Context*, 131.

# Ašnan

**Keyword:** Harvest

**Categories:** Mesopotamian, Personification

**Also Known As:** Ezina

Creator god Enki placed her in charge of agriculture, acknowledging her as the power of the land and the good bread of the whole world in the myth *Enki and the World Order*. Enki created grain and used the name Ezina, a synonym for *grain*, making her a personification of food.[32] Her name was Ašnan during the Akkadian period and Ezina in the Sumerian period.

# Aya

**Keyword:** Dawn

**Category:** Mesopotamian

**Also Known As:** Nin-Aya, Sherida

Aya personified the dawn. The term *Nin* sometimes combined with her name as the *Nin*, a prefix used to denote deification status.[33] Aya is also associated with Sherida, a Sumerian dawn goddess.

# Bastet

**Keywords:** Protection, Fertility

**Category:** Egyptian

Bastet appeared in the *Pyramid Texts* and *Coffin Texts*. She evolved from a lioness into a domesticated cat. Protector for the deceased and guardian of pregnant women, mummified cat burials dedicated to Bastet were found at Bubastis and Saqqara. Bastet and war goddess Sekhmet shared a consort, creator god Ptah. Bastet's son with Ptah, Maahes, had a lion head and served as a protector in times of war.

---

32. Espak, *God Enki in Sumerian Royal Ideology and Mythology*, 109, 172.

33. Asher-Greveand Westenholz, *Goddesses in Context*, 7.

# Ereškigal

**Keywords:** Transformation, Death

**Categories:** Mesopotamian, Chthonic

Inanna's elder sister, Ereškigal ruled the Mesopotamian Underworld called the Netherworld. She served as the only woman to pass judgment on others in the afterlife. Her original consort, Gugalana, was replaced by Nergal, son of the wisdom god Ea. Nergal climbed down the ladders of heaven into the Netherworld, fell in love with Ereškigal, dethroned her, and took her place as ruler of the Netherworld.[34]

# Gula

**Keyword:** Healing

**Category:** Mesopotamian

During the Babylonian period, she became a powerful healer and physician goddess who replaced Nin-Isina with those same qualities of healing. Known as the Great One, Gula cut the umbilical cord and assigned destiny to the newborn.[35]

# Hathor

**Keywords:** Fertility, Sky, Sun

**Category:** Egyptian

Cow-headed goddess Hathor is one of the most important Egyptian goddesses. In the *Coffin Texts*, she is a mother figure and consort to Horus. The Egyptian *Book of the Dead* depicts her in her cow form. As one of the Eye of Ra deities, Hathor acted as a vicious defender and protector to her main consort, the sun god Ra. As the Eye of Ra, she personified Ra and acted as an extension of his power. At night, Ra disappeared to impregnate Hathor, who would emerge as the stars and later as the daytime skies.

---

34. Ponchiaand Luukko, *Standard Babylonian Myth of Nergal and Ereškigal.*
35. Asher-Greve and Westenholz, *Goddesses in Context,* 65.

# Hauhet

**Keywords:** Eternity, Infinity

**Categories:** Egyptian, Primordial

Hauhet personifies the unseen aspect of creation, eternity, and the infinite nature of the universe with her masculine counterpart, Heh. Both were members of the Ogdoad of Hermopolis as two of eight primordial beings who created the universe.

# Inanna

**Keywords:** Love, Fertility

**Categories:** Mesopotamian, Personification

**Also Known As:** Ištar, Ishtar

Goddess of love and heavenly light, Inanna personified the morning and evening stars and was one of the most important Sumerian deities of the Uruk period from 4000 to 3100 BCE.[36] Inanna was Ereškigal's sister who traveled to the Underworld and died for three days. Her servant, Ninshubur, persuaded the gods to bring her back to life so long as someone took her place. When Inanna discovered her husband, Dumuzid, never mourned her death, she named him as her replacement. Akkadians, Babylonians, and Assyrians called her Ištar or Ishtar.

# Isis

**Keywords:** Motherhood, Magic

**Category:** Egyptian

Mentioned in the *Pyramid Texts*, Isis is the all-encompassing mother goddess, healer, and bringer of good luck. As both sibling and consort to Osiris, she resurrected him and became goddess of magic and protector of the dead. The Divine Mother of Horus. Isis and Osiris were members of the Great Ennead of Heliopolis as creation deities in the former city of the sun.

---

36. Crüsemann et al., *Uruk*.

## Iusaaset

**Keywords:** Divine Mother, Creation

**Categories:** Egyptian, Primordial

Member of the Great Ennead of Heliopolis, Iusaaset is an obscure goddess from the original creation myth of Heliopolis associated with the Tree of Life. The Divine Mother who served as the Hand of Atum, she assisted creator god Atum in ejaculating humanity into existence.

## Kauket

**Keyword:** Darkness

**Categories:** Egyptian, Primordial

Part of the Ogdoad of Hermopolis, she is the feminine half of the pair of creation deities worshiped in Hermopolis. She and her consort, Kuk, represent the chaos and primordial darkness of the great void from which all life emerged.

## Lamma

**Keywords:** Protection, Guardian

**Categories:** Mesopotamian, Tutelary

**Also Known As:** Lammasu

Initially named Lamma in Sumeria, she became Lammasu in the Assyrian pantheon. Mesopotamians believed as long as the Lamma remained in the city, the area could not be destroyed by enemies. Some scholars speculate that rather than an individual goddess, the term might designate a deity who embodies the protective qualities of a guardian. The term *lamma* seems to be applied to any female tutelary, guardian, or protective deity.[37]

## Ma'at

**Keyword:** Truth

**Category:** Egyptian

*Pyramid Texts* and the Egyptian *Book of the Dead* feature Ma'at, who served in the Hall of Two Truths and weighed an ostrich feather against the heart of the

---

37. Asher-Greveand Westenholz, *Goddesses in Context*, 48.

individual who wished to ascend into the afterlife. If the scales were balanced, the person passed Osiris and entered the heavenly realms. She accompanied the sun god Ra (also known as Re) at all times and brought order and truth to light. The concept of Ma'at involves the obsession with balancing order and chaos and the desire for the peaceful middle ground. Her consort is sacred scribe Thoth.

## Mut

**Keyword:** Mother

**Category:** Egyptian

Mut is the Divine Mother and consort of Amun and mother of moon god Khonsu, collectively known as the Theban Triad. Mut replaced Amun's earlier consort from Hermopolis, Amunet, where Amun and Amunet functioned as a pair of primordial deities. Mut was one of many vulture goddesses who wore crowns of both Upper and Lower Egypt to signify her reign over the entirety of Egypt.

## Nanaya

**Keywords:** Fertility, Love

**Category:** Mesopotamian

Widely worshiped throughout Mesopotamia, she represented physical love, eroticism, and sensuality. She helped both content and scorned lovers. Her consorts were Nabu and Mu'ati. As Inanna's daughter, she is sometimes synchronized with Inanna/Ištar.

## Nanshe

**Keywords:** Justice, Fertility

**Category:** Mesopotamian

Sumerian goddess of divination and justice, she helped underdogs receive their just due, including orphans, widows, and anyone in difficult situations. She also reigned over fertility through wildlife and was particularly associated with fishing and birds. An ancient story called "Nanshe and the Birds" paid tribute to her stellar qualities. Nindara was her consort.

## Naunet

**Keyword:** Water

**Categories:** Egyptian, Primordial

Naunet is the female counterpart to Nun in the Hermopolis creation myth and part of the Ogdoad of Hermopolis. Both represent the primordial female and male aspects of the chaotic waters from which all life emerged. In one version of the Hermopolis creation myth, a cosmic egg emerged from the waters of a lake to give rise to humanity.

## Neith

**Keywords:** Mother, Creation

**Category:** Egyptian

Mother of sun god Ra, Neith is a fierce goddess and consort of Khnum, an early creator god. In the *Pyramid Texts*, Neith nursed a baby crocodile and is considered crocodile god Sobek's mother. She also guarded the canopic jars as protector of Duamutef, guardian of the deceased's stomach. She is one of the judges in the *Book of the Dead*, provider of mummy bandages and shrouds.[38] Neith is the official guardian for the city of Sais where she had been worshiped since 3000 BCE.

## Nekhbet

**Keyword:** Protector

**Categories:** Egyptian, Tutelary

The vulture goddess protected and acted as a tutelary deity for Upper Egypt. Nekhbet was half of the duo known as the Two Ladies along with her sister, Wadjet, who served a similar role for Lower Egypt. Vultures became common iconography on the headdresses of pharaohs interred in their tombs as a symbol of divine protection.

---

38. Mercer, *Pyramid Texts*.

# Nephthys

**Keywords:** Death, Protection, Afterlife

**Category:** Egyptian

Death goddess and member of the Great Ennead of Heliopolis, Isis's sister is consort to her brother, Seth (also known as Set), yet she seduced Osiris and gave birth to the jackal-headed mummification god Anubis. Nephthys has great healing powers. She helped Isis bring Osiris back to life after Seth killed him and became protector of the dead and one of the guards of the four canopic jars. Nephthys is known as mistress of the mansion or lady of the temple enclosure, referring to her house headdress, a symbol of her role as temple priestess.

# Ningal

**Keywords:** Divine Mother

**Category:** Mesopotamian

Great Lady or Divine Mother, with her consort, the moon god Nanna, she was the mother of goddess Inanna and sun god Utu. She was widely worshiped during all periods of Mesopotamian history and called mistress or mother of Ur.[39]

# Ninḫursaĝa

**Keywords:** Mother, Fertility

**Category:** Mesopotamian

Wisdom and water god Enki's consort and one of the most important Sumerian deities, she is a creation goddess featured in the myth of *Enki and Ninhursag*. After warning Enki of drought, Enki brought water to the land and fell in love with Ninḫursaĝa and they had a love affair, resulting in their daughter, Ninsar. Ninḫursaĝa acted as the Divine Mother who cared for many of the great leaders. Over time, she evolved into a birthing goddess.

---

39. Asher-Greve and Westenholz, *Goddesses in Context*, 49.

## Nin-Isina

**Keywords:** Queen Mistress of Isin

**Category:** Mesopotamian

**Also Known As:** BaU

Divine physician, a medical and healing goddess widely worshiped in Isin, Mesopotamia. The daughter of supreme god An, her consort was Pabilsag, who was the personification of the Sagittarius constellation. She was eventually synchronized with Gula and has also been noted as a healing goddess named BaU.[40]

## Ninkasi

**Keyword:** Beer

**Category:** Mesopotamian

Ninḫursaĝa created beer goddess Ninkasi, whose name has been translated to "Mistress Barmaid," to help heal Enki's ailing mouth. In the ancient *Hymn to Ninkasi*, the writer explained how she ferments the beer. Today, her name is used by modern brewing companies. Her sister, Siraš, was goddess of the brewing process.[41]

## Ninlil

**Keyword:** Mother

**Category:** Mesopotamian

**Also Known As:** Sud

She was a grain goddess who represented the city of Nippur in the form of serpents and stars.[42] In myth, Ninlil's mother warned her not to pursue a relationship with Enlil, god of wind and storms. She dismissed her mother's advice and became Enlil's official consort and mother of Underworld god Nergal, moon god Nanna, and warrior god Ninurta. Ninlil determined a person's fate and Enlil made every decision with her by his side.

---

40. Asher-Greveand Westenholz, *Goddesses in Context*, 63, 82, 86.

41. Asher-Greveand Westenholz, *Goddesses in Context*, 55, 168.

42. Monaghan, *Encyclopedia of Goddesses & Heroines*, 42.

# Ninmug

**Keyword:** Fertility

**Category:** Mesopotamian

In the myth *Enki and the World Order*, Ninmug is mentioned in lines 405–410 as an artisan deity and patron goddess of metalworks.[43] She is also among the many birthing fertility and mother goddesses.

# Nintinugga

**Keyword:** Healing

**Category:** Mesopotamian

Called Mistress Who Revives the Dead, she was among the several medicine and healing goddesses assigned to changing bandages and tending wounds. The cult dedicated to her was primarily located in the Sumerian city of Nippur.[44]

# Nisaba

**Keyword:** Wisdom

**Category:** Mesopotamian

A very early Sumerian goddess of learning, writing, and astrology, she was known as the August Scribe or Lady of Wisdom, a professor of great wisdom and a skilled mathematician, economist, and advisor. The traits ascribed to her were typically reserved for men in other cultures and time periods. Her consort was a minor god named Haya.[45]

# Nut

**Keywords:** Sky, Fertility

**Categories:** Egyptian, Personification

Member of the Great Ennead of Heliopolis, Nut personified the night sky. She is often depicted as a woman with her body stretching out over her consort, Geb, who personified Earth. The sun traveled through Nut's body by night and

---

43. Kramer and Maier, *Myths of Enki*, 213.

44. Asher-Greve and Westenholz, *Goddesses in Context*, 82.

45. Asher-Greveand Westenholz, *Goddesses in Context*, 19.

the stars by day. Nut may represent the Milky Way. She appears prominently in the *Pyramid Texts* as a cow and mother. She is also worshiped through sow amulets, suggesting she helped with fertility and rebirth.

## Sarpanit

**Keyword:** Fertility

**Category:** Mesopotamian

**Also Known As:** Zarpanītum

Babylonian goddess known as Mistress of Babylon, she was the main goddess in Babylon and consort to Marduk, the ancient Mesopotamian deity who evolved into patron of the city of Babylon. Her other epitaphs include Creatress of the Seed, leading her to be classified as a pregnancy and fertility goddess.[46]

## Satis

**Keywords:** Fertility, Hunting

**Categories:** Egyptian, Personification

Satis is an Eye of Ra deity who protected sun god Ra. She personified the Nile in Upper Egypt and served as a protector and maternal figure in the area around Nubia. A third of the Elephantine Triad with her consort, Khnum, and her daughter Anuket, patron goddess of the Nile, she served as a war and hunting goddess and contributed to the successful annual flooding of the Nile.

## Sekhmet

**Keywords:** Healing, War

**Category:** Egyptian

Sekhmet is an Eye of Ra deity and one of the Memphis Triad with her consort creator god Ptah and son Nefertem. The most important lioness goddess in Egypt and daughter of sun god Ra, Sekhmet breathed fire, representing the hot desert winds. She destroyed her enemies with plague or healed those worthy of salvation. Sekhmet is both builder and destroyer. Her name comes from the Egyptian word *sekem*, meaning "power" or "vitality from the sun."

---

46. Asher-Greveand Westenholz, *Goddesses in Context*, 80, 92.

# Serkat

**Keyword:** Healing

**Category:** Egyptian

Serkat is a consort to falcon-headed god Horus. A healing goddess with special talent to aid those who have been stung by venomous creatures, Serkat is associated with the scorpion. Likewise, because of her dual nature, she could also inflict punishments upon wrongdoers with that same venom. She protected and guarded the dead and served as one of the guards of the canopic jars of Horus. She eventually became a merged aspect of Isis.

# Seshat

**Keywords:** Wisdom, Knowledge

**Category:** Egyptian

Most people consider Thoth the official ancient scribe of Egypt, but in reality, Seshat, whose name means "She Who Is the Scribe," invented writing, and Thoth taught that skill to man. Some accounts have her as Thoth's daughter, while others consider him to be her consort. She held a palm frond with tick marks, representing the pharaoh's lifespan, and assisted with mathematical calculations and sacred geometry. Her spotted leopard or jaguar attire represented the stars, and priests worshiped in her temples.

# Sopdet

**Keyword:** Star

**Categories:** Egyptian, Personification

Sopdet is the personification of the star Sirius, the incredibly important astronomical marker to the early Egyptians. Because the annual appearance of Sirius on the horizon as a morning star signified the annual flooding of the Nile, Sopdet received praise to ensure the success of the flood. Sopdet's consort, Sah, personified Orion and later became conflated with Osiris, and Sopdet merged with Isis.

## Taweret

**Keywords:** Fertility, Protector, Childbirth

**Category:** Egyptian

A vicious and dangerous deity, Taweret is known as Great One or Lady of the Birth House and protects children during childbirth. Taweret stands on two legs, with the back and tail of a Nile crocodile, large human breasts, the arms of a lion, and the head of a hippopotamus. Early Egyptians observed female hippos aggressively growling to protect the young and began to worship them for protection to dispel darkness that would harm a child.

## Tefnut

**Keywords:** Moisture, Rain, Fertility

**Categories:** Egyptian, Primordial

Great Ennead member Tefnut served as primordial goddess of moist air alongside her counterpart, Shu, who personified dry air. Tefnut represented rain and moisture on the Nile and dew on the leaves after a rare rainfall. Considered a fertility goddess, she assisted with life-giving moisture to break the dry air cycle and bless the people with water. Depicted as a lioness with pointed ears, Tefnut is typically shown wearing a solar disk with Uraeus, a cobra, on her head and carrying a protective ankh, the symbol for eternal life.

## Tiamat

**Keywords:** Sea, Snakes

**Category:** Mesopotamian

A primordial water goddess who personified salt water; her consort, Apsu, personified fresh water. Tiamat became Marduk's main enemy in the Babylonian creation myth *Enuma Elish*. Marduk defeated her and split her body into two, creating heaven and Earth, the Tigris and Euphrates from her eyes, mist from her saliva, mountains from her breasts, and all physical features of the earth from her body.

# Uttu

**Keyword:** Weaving

**Category:** Mesopotamian

One of many consorts of creator god Enki, Uttu is goddess of wool, weaving, and looms. She was personified by a spider and known as the Conscientious Woman or Silent One.

# Wadjet

**Keyword:** Protection

**Categories:** Egyptian, Tutelary

This cobra-headed goddess from the Nile Delta region of Lower Egypt protected pharaohs who wore crowns featuring Wadjet's image and a sun disk in her honor. The vulture goddess Nekhbet served a similar role and acted as her counterpart for Upper Egypt. She was one of the Two Ladies who protected Egypt.

# Summing Up

Interacting with the goddesses of ancient Egypt and Mesopotamia allows us to tap into the consciousness of some of the earliest people on Earth.

The themes Mesopotamian worshipers concerned themselves with in honoring the deities—agriculture, fertility, childbirth, and protections from wars—did not change much at all over thousands of years of human history and remained the prevalent themes of the Egyptians and other early people, proving we all have much more in common than we might think. We likely share ancestry with these early people as well. Although our Ancestry.com accounts won't be able to verify that fact, there is a deep-rooted connectivity we can access when considering the Mesopotamians and the path they forged forward with innovations and ideas that still bless us to this very day. For modern seekers, Egypt is embedded into popular culture, yet by expanding our search to other early civilizations, we can gain knowledge of our collective humanity at a more profound level. I hope you enjoyed exploring this area through the vantage point of the goddesses the people loved and worshiped in ancient times.

## Recommended Reading

*Egyptian Mythology* by Geraldine Pinch

*The Complete Gods and Goddesses of Ancient Egypt* by Richard H. Wilkinson

*Goddesses in Context* by Julia Asher-Greve

*Invoke the Goddess* by Kala Trobe

*Chapter Two*

# Celtic Goddesses

*Celt* is a term used to describe many groups of people who inhabited the European continent in ancient times. The word *Celt* is likely brought to us by the Greek word for *fighter*, *Keltoi*, and refers to several groups of tribal clans whom scholars typically believe inhabited the area known in ancient times as Gaul: Ireland, Scotland, Wales, and Britannia. In reality, the oldest remains of the Celts were found in a burial site near Salzburg, Austria, where scholars believe several Celtic chieftains were buried around 700 BCE. The early dating on that burial is one of many reasons why scholars find challenges when attempting to clearly define the Celts.[47]

## Celtic Cosmology

Spiritually speaking, we know very little about the Celts because their practices were taught through oral traditions by Druid priests who believed that spiritual teachings should not be recorded in writing. What we do know is based on remnants of art, weaponry, votive offerings such as jewelry, pottery, weapons, grave goods found in sacred sites, and anything considered valuable. Historical accounts of the Celts left behind by Greek and Roman writers like Greek historian and politician Posidonius (135–51 BCE), who studied the Celts in Gaul; Pliny the Elder; Julius Caesar; and Strabo, Greek philosopher and author of *Geography*, one of the longest works in Greek literature, are also invaluable for

---

47. Allen and Reynolds, *Celtic Warrior*.

our current understanding of the Celts.[48] Much of what we think we know about the Celts comes from these classical sources, although these writers possibly only interpreted the Celtic beliefs based on their secondhand observations rather than having firsthand experience of the validity of Celtic practices. Another source of information about the Celts comes from Ireland. Much of those writings came after the spread of Christianity, meaning that the interpretations may not be accurate or could be influenced by the judgment of early Christians on their Pagan neighbors, deliberately distorted to establish the authority of the Church. There is simply no uniform religion, art, or practice that spans the vast geographical area where the Celts lived and worshiped, no written history or theology to cite. For those reasons, Celtic practices remain elusive.[49]

Evidence of Celtic goddess worship is absolutely implied in the discovery of the Sheela Na Gig carvings of naked women mentioned earlier in the book.[50] While their appearance implies an obvious connection to fertility, they may have also played a role in ancient Celtic folk religion as protective amulets or guardians for buildings as well as assisting with domestic harmony or acting as talismans to ward off the evil eye or to protect people against lustful thoughts or behaviors.[51] Celts worshiped nature in sacred oak groves, streams, and rivers that represented gateways between our world and the mystical Otherworld that existed beneath the sea or in the ground.

Knowledge about goddesses from the main geographic areas where the Celts lived, including Britannia, Ireland, Scotland, and Wales, comes to us through numerous literary and poetic sources, including the following:

1. **Mabinogi:** Refers to the first four tales or branches in the collection of British Middle Welsh stories based on oral traditions from the twelfth and thirteenth centuries.[52] The *Mabinogi* also featured the first mentions of legendary King Arthur in the tales *The Lady of the Fountain*, *Peredur*, and *Geraint and Enid*, all popularized by Lady Charlotte Guest, who published a

---

48. Kidd, *Posidonius*; Wernerian Club and Holland, *Pliny's Natural History*; Roller, *Geography of Strabo*.

49. MacCullough, *Religion of the Ancient Celts*, 2.

50. Stevens, "Big Vagina Energy."

51. Freitag, *Sheela-Na-Gigs*, 1, 80.

52. Ford, *Mabinogi and Other Medieval Welsh Tales*.

translation of the *Mabinogi* that influenced much of the popularity of the tales to this day.[53] The collection played an important role in helping scholars uncover the goddesses worshiped by these early clans.

2. **Mythological Cycle:** Irish legends and tales of Tuatha Dé Danann, beings from Irish mythology who live in the Otherworld, a supernatural realm described in Irish legends as the home of fairies and other theoretically mythological figures where mortal travelers with shamanic talents can visit.[54] They're linked to the domed tombs scattered around the Irish countryside, including Newgrange, a tomb and sacred site situated along the Boyne River north of Dublin, considered one of the oldest buildings in the world dating back to 3200 BCE.[55] Because Tuatha Dé Danann have the ability to interact with humans, they are perceived as the fairy folk of lore. They were banished from heaven and descended on Ireland.

3. **Ulster Cycle:** Medieval Irish sagas and mythological stories that include the Irish epic *Táin Bó Cúailnge or Cattle Raid of Cooley*, known as the *Iliad* of Ireland.[56]

4. **Welsh Triads:** Fragments of medieval manuscripts listed in triads, or sets of three, is a structure widely used in Welsh literature that may have origins with the Druids.[57] Writers believed grouping truths into threes would help people recall the teachings easier. Triads came in several categories: theological, bardic tales including songs, historical accounts, or proverbs.[58]

5. **Aislinge MeicConglinne:** A twelfth-century Middle Irish romantic epic written between 900 and 1200 CE. Translated in English to *The Vision of Mac Conglinne*, the tale is of unknown authorship and offers important references to Irish mythology.[59]

---

53. Jacob, "History of the Mabinogion"; Guest, *Mabinogion*.

54. Blamires, *Magic of the Celtic Otherworld*, 71.

55. George, *Newgrange Burial Chamber*, 4.

56. Dunn, *Ancient Irish Epic Tale Táin Bó Cúailnge*.

57. Lloyd, *History of Wales*, 122.

58. Barnes, "On the Welsh Triads," 536.

59. Preston-Matto, *Aislinge Meic Conglinne*, xi.

6. **An Banshenchas:** A collection of medieval poetry and texts that describe legendary women of Ireland. The name translates to "the women lore."[60] The material is provided in historical context, so Eve is also mentioned.

7. **Arthurian Legends:** The numerous tales of King Arthur may refer to a historical figure who lived in the second or fifth century CE, but more importantly, Arthurian characters also serve as archetypal figures of myth, some of whom appear to merge into Celtic mythology as goddesses.[61]

Literature associated with the Celtic goddesses will be mentioned in the category listing whenever possible. Due to the Roman occupation of the Celtic Britannia and other regions, occasionally the goddesses are influenced by the Romans and not attested in any of the above literary works.

## Celtic Goddesses

Celtic goddesses are among the most widely known in the world. In modern times, some Celtic deities are worshiped by modern-day Pagans and Neopagans who adapted Celtic knowledge into contemporary practices.

## Achall

**Keywords:** Healing, Love

**Category:** Ulster Cycle

The daughter of the King of Tara, Cairpre Nia Fer, and Fedelm Nochruthach, Achall died of a broken heart when her brother, Erc, perished in the *Ulster Cycle*.[62] She became immortalized as a namesake of a hill near Tara. Her devotion to her brother is revered as exemplifying the healing powers of love, and as such, she assists with healing broken hearts and lost causes.

## Achtland

**Keywords:** Fertility, Sky

**Category:** Mythological Cycle

---

60. Ní Bhrolcháin, "Manuscript Tradition of the Banshenchas," 109–35.

61. Matthews, Matthews, and Chandler, *Arthurian Magic*, 17.

62. Gwynn, *Poems from the Dindshenchas*, 46–53.

Some sources cite her as a mortal woman who could not find satisfaction with humans, so she married a member of the Tuatha Dé Danann and transformed into a supernatural being so they could be together. Achtland is wife of the giant Connla. She placed Connla's head against a stone in the west and his feet on a stone in the east while she combed his hair. The imagery of having his body stretched across the world is reminiscent of Egyptian goddess Nut who stretched her body across the earth as a representation of the night sky.[63]

## Áine

**Keyword:** Wealth

**Category:** Mythological Cycle

Summer goddess associated with midsummer who took revenge on a king. She is the consort of Gerald Fitzgerald and member of the Tuatha Dé Danann. She is a goddess of wealth and prosperity who often appears as a red mare and is considered the Great Fairy Queen who made her home in Knockainy in Limerick County, Ireland.[64]

## Airmed

**Keyword:** Healing

**Category:** Mythological Cycle

Airmed healed the injured in war during the Second Battle of Magh Tuiredh, a mythological set of two battles described in the Mythological Cycle that took place between the Tuatha Dé Danann and opposing forces. After her father killed her brother, she wept over his grave, and her tears gave rise to all the herbs in the world.[65]

## Anu

**Keywords:** Fertility, Mother Earth

**Category:** Mythological Cycle

---

63. Gray and Moore, *Mythology of All Races*, 150.

64. MacCullough, *Religion of the Ancient Celts*, 70–1.

65. MacCullough, *Religion of the Ancient Celts*, 77.

Mentioned briefly in literature, she was another member of the Tuatha Dé Danann, who could have been absorbed into the more well-known goddesses such as Danu as an Earth Mother.[66]

## Arianrhod

**Keyword:** Moon

**Category:** Mabinogi

Welsh star goddess and consort of trickster Gwydion, she is associated with the moon and called the Silver Wheel, which also refers to the passage of time and life, death, and reincarnation. In the Fourth Branch of the *Mabinogi*, Arianrhod jumps over her uncle Math's magical staff and gives birth to Lleu Llaw Gyffes, hero of Welsh mythology.

## Badb

**Keyword:** War

**Category:** Mythological Cycle

Badb is a warrior goddess and consort of Neit, the war god. She is a Mórrígan member along with her two sisters and is known to show favor to her chosen soldiers by making the opposing groups confused. She appears as a crow and can foresee events, including the death of prominent people. She is considered part of Tuatha Dé Danann.

## Banba

**Keyword:** Protection

**Categories:** Mythological Cycle, Tutelary, Personification

Patron goddess of Ireland, she is called the Spirit of Ireland, a protective territorial deity who is the personification of Ireland along with her sisters, Fódla and Ériu. Her consort is Etar, and she is part of the Tuatha Dé Danann.

## Bébinn

**Keyword:** Fertility

**Categories:** Ulster Cycle, Mythological Cycle

---

66. MacCullough, *Religion of the Ancient Celts*, 67.

A Tuatha Dé Danann member and consort of Áed Alainn,[67] she was called the Melodious Woman, a birth and fertility goddess. River goddess Boann who sometimes lives in the Otherworld in Welsh and Irish mythology was her sister.

## Be Chuille

**Keyword:** Magic

**Category:** Mythological Cycle

Cattle goddess Flidais's daughter, Be Chuille, is a good witch and member of Tuatha Dé Danann who helps defeat an evil sorceress named Carmen whose sons destroyed the food supply.[68] She enchanted trees and stones during a mythological battle. She helped creator god Lugh and became known as Lugh's Witch.

## Boann

**Keyword:** River

**Categories:** Ulster Cycle, Mythological Cycle

Personification of the River Boyne, she is a member of Tuatha Dé Danann. Her name means "white cow," and her consort is mentioned as either Elcmar, who has associations with horses, or Nechtan, who is associated with a well or spring of wisdom near the River Boyne.[69]

## Branwen

**Keywords:** Love, Beauty

**Category:** Mabinogi

As goddess of love and beauty in Wales, the second branch of the Welsh *Mabinogi* is named for Branwen. Her brother, the king of Britain, Bran the Blessed, arranged her marriage to Irish king Matholwch, who mistreated her and ultimately caused a war to break out. Upset about the war and destruction, Branwen died of a broken heart.

---

67. Monaghan, *Encyclopedia of Celtic Mythology and Folklore*, 4.

68. Monaghan, *Encyclopedia of Celtic Mythology and Folklore*, 75.

69. O hOgain, *Myth, Legend & Romance*, 326–7.

# Brigit

**Keywords:** Fertility, Healing

**Category:** Mythological Cycle

Goddess of spring, fertility, healing, poetry, passion, fire, home and hearth, and soldiers called brigands, Brigit was wife of Bres, king of Tuatha Dé Danann, and they had one son, Ruadán. Brigit was the daughter of the Dagda, a hooded Celtic god with ties to the Druids. Mentioned in *Cormac's Glossary*, written by Christian monks, she was later conflated with Saint Brigit. The Scottish Gaelic holiday Imbolc or Saint Brigit's Day is celebrated on February 1 to mark the halfway point between the winter solstice and spring equinox. She may be associated with the Norse goddess Bragi.[70]

# Brigantia

**Keyword:** Victory

**Category:** Tutelary

The Celtic equivalent to Nike or Victory in the Roman pantheon, Brigantia personified victory. Associated with water nymphs, she has several bodies of water in Britain named for her. Some scholars believe she and Brigit are one and the same; however, archeological evidence suggests otherwise. Brigantia is related to the Brigantes tribe, British Celts who lived in what is now northern Britain prior to the Roman occupation. Although unattested in literature, numerous inscriptions on stone monuments throughout Europe and Britain suggest she was widely revered.[71]

# Cailleach

**Keywords:** Hag, Ancestral

**Categories:** Aislinge Meic Conglinne, Ancestral

The Cailleach is a shape-shifting hag from the Gaelic Celt traditions of Scotland, Ireland, and Manx from Isle of Mann mentioned in the twelfth-century epic *Aislinge Meic Conglinne* as a white nun of Beare.[72] Known as Scotland's Win-

---

70. Stokes, *Sanas Chormaic*.

71. Green, *Celtic Goddesses*.

72. Kuno, *Aislinge Meic Conglinne*, 213–9.

ter Queen, or Beira, in Ireland, she is called Hag of Beira. She is an ancestor who shapes the hills and mountains with her hammer and creates humanity. She represents winter months between Samhain and Beltane and gathers firewood on Imbolc (February 1). If the weather is sunny, winter will last longer. If the weather is stormy, spring will come sooner. Crone deities often have no consort; however, Cailleach is associated with Bodach, a weathered old man.

## Ceridwen

**Keyword:** Knowledge

**Category:** Mabinogi

Ceridwen is a shape-shifting Celtic Welsh goddess known as the keeper of the cauldron of knowledge and inspirational poetry who often takes the form of a white witch. Wisdom, transformation, beauty, change, death, rebirth, transformation, and the Underworld are all attributes of this multifaceted deity. Her consort is Tegid Foel, tutelary deity for Llyn Tegid, a lake in Wales.

## Clíodhna

**Keywords:** Love, Beauty

**Category:** Mythological Cycle

**Also Known As:** Clídna, Clionadh, Clíodna, Clíona

In myth, she is Tuatha Dé Danann's Queen of the Banshees who wailed to either warn people of a coming death or to lament the passing of loved ones. In some myths, she is a tutelary deity for County Cork, where Cormac MacCarthy built the Blarney Castle in 1446. MacCarthy credited Clíodhna with helping him with a legal battle after following her instructions to kiss the castle stones. Since then, the ritual of kissing the Blarney Stone has helped many develop the winning gift of gab.[73]

## Danu

**Keywords:** Wisdom, Mother Goddess

**Categories:** Mythological Cycle, Primordial, Personification

---

73. Marsh, *Legends and Lands of Ireland*, 108.

All Tuatha Dé Danann mentioned in this chapter or elsewhere are mythological descendants of Danu. Tuatha DéDanann was the ancient tribe of Ireland that was banished from heaven. Danu is a primordial creation goddess who shaped her people and is associated with fertility. She also personified the wind.

## Epona

**Keyword:** Horse

**Category:** Personification

Epona was a Roman horse goddess adopted from Gaul. When the Romans conquered Gaul, they participated in honoring many of the local deities, including Epona, who represented horses and mules. Like many deities, the Romans affixed their names to local goddesses and attributed many of the qualities they admired about the deities to the local versions. Unlike many Celtic goddesses, Epona had a wide following and was mentioned by Christian and Roman writers.[74]

## Ériu

**Keyword:** Protection

**Categories:** Mythological Cycle, Banshenchas, Personification, Tutelary

A Tuatha DéDanann member, she and her sisters, Banba and Fódla, personified and protected Ireland. Cetar was her consort according to the *Banshenchas*. She is also associated with Tuatha Dé Danann member Mac Gréine.

## Ernmas

**Keywords:** Mother, Fertility

**Category:** Mythological Cycle

She and her consort, Delbáeth, are parents of many of the trios within the Tuatha Dé Danann, including Ériu, Banba, and Fódla, and the war goddess trinity the Mórrígan. She is a fertility goddess sometimes referred to as the she-farmer.

---

74. Cook, *Epona*.

# Étaíne

**Keyword:** Beauty

**Categories:** Ulster Cycle, Mythological Cycle

A gorgeous sun goddess who married Midir of the Tuatha DéDanann, she became the subject of the poem "Tochmarc Étaíne," which translates to "The Wooing of Étaíne," part of the Irish Mythological Cycle that tells the tale of how her husband pursued and wed her despite the fact he was married to another woman when they first met.

# Flidais

**Keyword:** Fertility

**Categories:** Ulster Cycle, Mythological Cycle

A fertility goddess who owned a magical herd of cattle that fed healing milk to soldiers. In the *Ulster Cycle*, she has an affair with Fergus mac Roich, whose name literally means "manliness," and leaves her husband, Adamair, High King of Ireland, with her cattle.[75]

# Fódla

**Keyword:** Protection

**Categories:** Mythological Cycle, An Banshenchas, Personification, Tutelary

A personification of Ireland, she is a giantess and protective territorial deity along with her sisters Ériu and Banba. In *An Banshenchas*, she is the wife of Detar, and in other sources, she's the wife of Mac Cecht of Tuatha Dé Danann, king of Ireland, making her queen of Ireland.

# Fúamnach

**Keyword:** Witch

**Category:** Mythological Cycle

Fúamnach is the scorned wife of Midir and a Tuatha Dé Danann witch who cursed and cast several spells on her former husband's new wife, Étaíne, the subject of the poem "The Wooing of Étaíne."

---

75. Leahy, *Heroic Romances of Ireland*.

## Henwen

**Keywords:** Harvest, Mother

**Category:** Welsh Triads

Depicted as a sow in mythology, King Arthur chased her. She is associated with prosperity, harvest, and peace. Others claim her as a goddess of motherhood.

## Macha

**Keyword:** Protection

**Categories:** Ulster Cycle, Mythological Cycle

Macha is part of both the Mórrígan, one of the trio of sisters in the three Morrígna with her sisters Mórrígan and Nemain, and Tuatha Dé Danann. She is a sovereignty deity associated with kingship, horses, and land. She is sometimes the wife of Nemed, leader of the early settlers of Ireland, or she is queen of Cimbaeth or a wife of Crunnchu.

## Medb

**Keyword:** War

**Categories:** Ulster Cycle, Personification

**Also Known As:** Maeve

Irish warrior queen and sovereignty goddess, Medb bewitched men with her beauty and attained power from her marriages, including her alliance with Ailill mac Máta, the legendary king of Connachta. She personified mead and gained great importance because of the popularity of mead at Irish kings' coronations. She instigated the dispute over a bull in Táin Bó Cúailnge, *The Cattle Raid of Cooley*, the national epic of Ireland included in the *Ulster Cycle*. She may be the inspiration for the poem "Queen Mab" by Percy Shelley and Shakespeare's *Romeo & Juliet*, during a scene where the character Mercurio refers to Queen Mab as a fairy midwife.[76]

---

76. Shakespeare, *Romeo & Juliet*, 19.

# Morgan Le Fay

**Keyword:** Healing

**Categories:** Mabinogi, Arthurian

**Also Known As:** Morgen

Featured in the tale *Vita Merlini* or *Life of Merlin*, written by Geoffrey of Monmouth around 1150, Morgen (the earliest spelling of her name, which means "of the sea") lives on the Fortunate Isle and is the eldest of nine sisters. Beautiful Morgan has exceptional healing talent, abilities to shape-shift into a bird, and she saves her half-brother King Arthur by tending his wounds.[77] She was Arthur's half-sister, daughter of Uther Pendragon. She may have originated in Welsh fairy tales as a shape-shifting fairy, or le fay. Her official consort was King Urien from Arthurian legends, but she has several other lovers, including Sir Accolon of Gaul.[78]

# (The) Mórrígan

**Keywords:** Great Queen

**Categories:** Ulster Cycle, Mythological Cycle

Known for prophecy, she can predict outcomes of battles and is personified by a crow or Badb. The Mórrígan is associated with fate, destiny, and encourages soldiers to act valiantly and with great bravery. A member of the Tuatha Dé Danann, Mórrígan and her two sisters Macha and Nemain are collectively called the three Morrígna. At times, Nemain is replaced by the goddess Anand.

# Nemain

**Keyword:** War

**Categories:** Ulster Cycle, Mythological Cycle

A Tuatha Dé Danann member, she is one of the trio of sisters in the three Morrígna with her sisters Mórrígan and Macha. She personifies the sacrifices and hazards of war. Neit, Celtic war god, is her consort. She personifies chaos in war.

---

77. Parry, *Vita Merlini*, 47–50.

78. Malory, *Le Morte d'Arthur*, 97, 104.

# Olwen

**Keyword:** Sun

**Categories:** Mabinogi, Arthurian

The term *Golden Wheel* refers to Olwen, whose name comes from *ol*, meaning "track," and *gwyn*, meaning "white." She personifies the sun and is known for her gentleness and light and is the sister of moon goddess Arianrhod.[79] Her father would die if she ever married, but she fell in love and married King Arthur's cousin Culhwch, thus causing her father's death. The story of Culhwch and Olwen dates to the eleventh century as one of the earliest examples of tales featuring King Arthur.[80]

# Rhiannon

**Keywords:** Great Queen

**Category:** Mabinogi

A Welsh goddess, Rhiannon is mentioned in the first and third branches of the *Mabinogi*. This great queen and horse goddess from the Otherworld has three birds that wake the dead and lull the living to sleep. She rides her horse slowly, but nobody can ever catch her, and she easily carries weary travelers on her back. She may be an iteration of Epona, goddess of Gaul. In one myth, she is falsely accused of killing her son and must pay restitution. Her husband, Pwyll Pen Annwn, Lord of Dyfed, remains loyal and defends her, and eventually everyone realizes the accusations were false.[81]

# Sequana

**Keyword:** River

**Category:** Personification

Personification of the Seine River in France, her name comes from *sawk*, the Celtic or Gaelic word for *holy*, and *onna*, meaning "water."[82] A 2,000-year-old bronze statue of Sequana sits in a museum in Dijon, France, and ruins of

---

79. Bromwich and Evans, *Culhwch and Olwen*, 117.

80. Guest, *Mabinogion*, 258–60.

81. John, *Mabinogion*, 25–6.

82. Sciolino, *Seine*, 25.

her once frequented temple are located at the source of the Seine, an hour from Dijon. Archaeologists uncovered massive amounts of votive offerings in the water left behind by early pilgrims who scientists believe arrived prior to the Roman occupation of Gaul.[83]

## Sheela Na Gig

**Keyword:** Fertility

**Category:** Tutelary

The naked female Sheela Na Gig statues featuring exaggerated female genitalia adorned churches around the British Isles and depict an early form of a Pagan fertility goddess.[84] Occasionally portrayed with wicked faces in protective amulets, they've also been likened to the Cailleach as an old hag.

## Summing Up

Reflections of the reverence for the natural world and communing in harmony with nature are all themes inherent in the ancient Celtic wisdom. Influences from the Celtic world are still present in the modern-day United Kingdom, proving that the whispers of our ancestral past still matter. The magical, mystical lands of Ireland, Wales, and Scotland and the stories and myths of the goddesses who dwelled there in early times still capture the hearts and imaginations of people from around the world in the present day.

## Recommended Reading

*Arthurian Magic* by John and Caitlin Matthews with Virginia Chandler

*The Book of Celtic Magic* by Kristoffer Hughes

*Magic of the Celtic Otherworld* by Steve Blamires

---

83. Sciolino, "In Dijon, Where Mustard Rules."

84. Freitag, *Sheela-Na-Gigs*, 1.

## Chapter Three
# Greek and Roman Goddesses

The influence of the Greek culture on Western civilization cannot be understated. The Romans adopted many of the Greek deities into their eclectic pantheon, and you will explore them both. Greek and Roman mythology permeates our popular culture. Of all their conquered territories, no civilization had more influence on Rome than the Greeks. Many of the best-known Roman goddesses are counterparts to Greek equivalents, and both pantheons are extensive. For that reason, I cannot list every single goddess here, but I will share some of those I found most interesting.

## Greek Cosmology

Greeks believed, as many early peoples did, that the universe and everything in it began in a swirl of chaos. Gaia, the embodiment of Earth, arose from the great abyss of Tartarus, the Underworld described in Plato's *Gorgias*. Gaia later merged with Uranus to form much of the natural world. Plato states that upon death, people would encounter a dualistic afterlife where just and kind souls ascend to the Islands of the Blessed, while the wicked descend to the hellish pit of Tartarus to receive an eternity of vengeance and punishment for their earthly deeds.[85]

Other than the works of poet Homer, much of what we know about Greek mythology is found in *Theogony* by the poet Hesiod. Greek goddesses will be categorized as the following supernatural beings from the Greek pantheon:

---

85. Jowett, *Gorgias by Plato*.

1. **Titans:** Primordial deities who were children of Gaia (Mother Earth) and Uranus (Father Sky or heaven), as well as their descendants. Hesiod's *Theogony* cites twelve original Titans—six males and six females.[86]

2. **Olympians:** Twelve major gods and goddesses who became the major deities in the Greek pantheon after defeating the Titans in a war. They are named after their home on Mount Olympus.[87]

3. **Graces/Charites:** Three daughters of Zeus and Eurynome who embodied the qualities of charm, grace, beauty, and creativity, attended festivals, and were mentioned by poet Hesiod.[88]

4. **Oceanids:** Three thousand, a number meant to imply they are beyond comprehension, sea nymphs who are the daughters of Titans Oceanus and Tethys.[89]

5. **Nereids:** Fifty sea nymph daughters of the Oceanid Doris and Nereus, the Old Man of the Sea.[90]

6. **Horae:** Daughters of Zeus and Themis, they are goddesses of seasons and the passage of time. They originally represented the hours in each day as well as seasons, but their most famous members became increasingly relevant to order and justice.[91]

7. **Moirai:** Greeks believed that destiny was fixed. These daughters of Zeus and Themis determined "Lots, or Destinies."[92] They are also known as Parcae or the Fates.

8. **Nymphs:** Minor deities; nature spirits who animate the natural world. Sometimes named, and other times too numerous and abundant to make into individual deities, they are nevertheless worshiped by the ancient Greeks.

86. Evelyn-White, *Theogony of Hesiod.*
87. Evelyn-White, *Theogony of Hesiod.*
88. Nosselt, *Mythology Greek and Roman*, 58.
89. Evelyn-White, *Theogony of Hesiod.*
90. Evelyn-White, *Theogony of Hesiod.*
91. Nosselt, *Mythology Greek and Roman*, 50.
92. Nosselt, *Mythology Greek and Roman*, 51.

9. **Muses:** Nine beautiful daughters of Jupiter and memory goddess Mnemosyne who presided over music and the arts.[93]

The list above represents a small percentage of one of, if not the, most abundant pantheons of the ancient world.

## Roman Cosmology

Romans believed the city of Rome stood at the center of the universe, and this belief seems to have prevailed from the earliest of times throughout the entire course of the Roman Empire. Terminus, god of boundaries, stood at the far reaches of the Roman cosmos to mark the territories of the Empire surrounding Rome. Human activities were viewed as part of the universal flow, as were other cities, rivers, and geographical locations, each seen as part of the wider cosmos that encompassed the gods and goddesses and humankind.[94]

Much of what we know about ancient Rome is thanks to Julius Caesar, who documented his conquests and the subjugated peoples who were absorbed into the Roman Empire and Republic. Not only did the Romans seize territories, they also became quite adept at absorbing the spiritual beliefs, gods, and goddesses of the peoples they conquered. They adapted the names of the gods and goddesses, converted them into Latin, and used the borrowed pantheons for their own best interests. Although Roman brutality is well known, officials allowed their subjugated citizenry to maintain their belief systems so long as people showed respect to the original Roman deities.[95]

Like the Greeks, Romans obsessively deified every minute aspect of society. Goddesses fall into many categories, including the following supernatural beings:

1. **Nixi:** Birth and childhood deities who were often depicted kneeling or squatting. In Rome, they were honored in Capitoline Minerva by three kneeling female statues to represent the pains suffered in childbirth.[96] They are regarded as goddesses and guardians who embody childbirth. They tended to every single aspect of birth and raising children and became deified in ancient

---

93. Nosselt, *Mythology Greek and Roman*, 53.

94. Graham, "Toward a Late Roman Cosmology of Space and Frontiers," 27–50.

95. Wells, *Barbarians Speak*, ix.

96. Grimal, *Penguin Dictionary of Classical Mythology*, 295.

Rome because of the importance given to successful births and family as a whole. Government considered family paramount to the overall success and vitality of Rome. Much of what we know of these birth and childhood deities who helped nurture the most vulnerable came from a book called *The City of God* by Saint Augustine.[97]

2. **Camenae:** A specific group of four nymphlike childbirth goddesses who were prophetic deities who presided over the wells and fountains where the Vestal Virgins found their water. In Ovid's classic poem *Metamorphosis*, he describes the Camenae as ancient nymphs.[98]

3. **Dii Consentes:** Roman counterparts to the twelve Greek Olympians, including six gods and six goddesses. Many of these deities may have been incorporated by both the Greeks and the Etruscans prior to Roman take-over of that region, which is between the Tiber and Argo Rivers in Italy.[99] We will explore the goddesses here.

4. **Nymphs:** Nature spirits who were primarily female, they were widely accepted in Greece and adopted by the Romans and discussed frequently in *Metamorphosis* by Ovid. Although they do not have goddess status, they are nevertheless important female deities who interacted with the Romans and animated the natural world.[100]

5. **Parcae:** Also known as the Fates, or Moirai in Greece, they were three female deities who personified destiny and controlled life and death for mortals. They assisted with the three major parts of life: birth, marriage, and death.[101]

6. **Flamines:** Flamines were priests who tended cults of deities. There were two kinds—Flamines maiores, who tended the wealthy, and twelve plebeian, or lower class, priests called Flamines minores.[102]

---

97. Dods, *Works of Aurelius Augustine.*

98. Ovid, *Metamorphoses,* chapter 14.

99. Lindsay, *Etruscan Inscriptions Analysed,* 252.

100. Ovid, *Metamorphoses.*

101. Daly and Rengel, *Greek & Roman Mythology A to Z,* 99.

102. Holstein, *Rites and Ritual Acts,* 24.

Like their Greek subjugates, the Romans believed in the deification of all aspects of life and therefore created one of the most extensive pantheons in the ancient world.

The above lists for both Greek and Roman deities represent some of the categories, but not all of them, so when applicable throughout the listings, I will share any other unusual goddess groupings.

## Greek and Roman Goddesses

The goddesses here should be viewed as a mere fraction of the thousands of sacred beings worshiped by the Greeks and Romans who deified every single aspect of their lives and the world around them. In both cultures, all aspects of daily life were deified—every little action or phenomenon was recognized as holding the divine spark and was considered worthy of worship.

## Abeona

**Keyword:** Protection

**Categories:** Roman, Nixi

In Saint Augustine's *City of God*, he described nervous mothers paying homage "to Abeona when going away."[103] This vague description has led scholars to understand Abeona as a protector of both children and travelers as they make their way out of the home. Modern writers have expanded her influence to include toddlers taking their first steps, although we have no proof of that attestation. The Latin word *abeo* means "going away from." Goddess Adeona is her counterpart.

## Abudantia

**Keyword:** Abundance

**Categories:** Roman, Personification

Associated with the cornucopia, she personified abundance and riches and helped people with prosperity. She helped create an influx of funding or protect savings and investments. Her image appeared on coinage, symbolizing the wealth brought to the empire, and helped individuals accumulate wealth and prosperity.[104]

---

103. Dods, *Works of Aurelius Augustine*, 159.

104. Sheard, *Llewellyn's Complete Book of Names*, 31.

## Acca Larentia

**Keyword:** Mother

**Category:** Roman

Originally an Etruscan agricultural goddess, she emerged after the Roman-Etruscan War of 264 BCE.[105] Her shepherd husband, Faustulus, discovered the twins who founded Rome, Romulus and Remus, and brought them home so she could care for them. Another story describes her as a consort to Hercules who won her during a game of dice, and another claims she was merely a sex worker. Regardless, every December 23, the Larentalia festival was held in her honor.

## Adeona

**Keyword:** Protection

**Categories:** Roman, Nixi

One translation for the Latin word *adeois* comes from Saint Augustine, who mentioned mothers enlisting help "to the goddess Adeona when coming."[106] Her counterpart, Abeona, is enlisted to help the child travel safely. Once the return trip is planned, Adeona ensures the child's safe passage home. She is but one of many examples of the Romans' deification of every minute detail of their lives.

## Aestas

**Keyword:** Summer

**Categories:** Roman, Personification

While some consider her a goddess, *Aestas* means "summer" in Latin. She personified the summer and was mentioned in the second book of *Metamorphoses* for her wheaten garland crown.[107] Initium Aestatis is a summer festival held in her honor on June 27 and June 30.[108]

---

105. Brice, *Warfare in the Roman Republic*, 66–8.

106. Dods, *Works of Aurelius Augustine*, 159.

107. Ovid, *Metamorphoses*, 38.

108. Franklin, *Magical Celebrations*, 188.

# Aequitas

**Keyword:** Equity

**Categories:** Roman, Personification

*Aequitas* is a Latin term to represent fairness, equity, and conformity. Because of the emperor's constant quest for power and attempts to position himself as the ultimate authority above Roman citizens, Aequitas became deified into a goddess. As a propaganda tool, she was featured on Roman coins and became Aequitas Augusti.[109] She represented and personified the ideal of fairness in trade and the conformity of bending to the will of the state that would be rewarded in society.

# Aglaea

**Keyword:** Beauty

**Categories:** Greek, Charites/Graces

**Also Known As:** Aglaia

Hesiod described her as "shining," and she is said to be the youngest of the Graces who embodies the ideal qualities of beauty, brilliancy, splendor, adornment, and glory. She married Hephaestus after his divorce from Aphrodite.[110]

# Alcyone

**Keyword:** Star

**Categories:** Greek, Nymph, Personification

The personification of one of the seven stars in the Pleiades star system, Alcyone was a nymph and daughter of Atlas and the Oceanid Pleione collectively called the Atlantides. Sea god Poseidon was her consort and they had several children together. Alcyone is also the name of a woman who received the wrath of Zeus after she and her husband began calling themselves Zeus and Hera. Zeus killed her husband and she drowned herself, and out of pity, Zeus turned her into a kingfisher bird.[111]

---

109. Fears, "Cult of Virtues and Roman Imperial Ideology," 827–948.

110. Nosselt, *Mythology Greek and Roman*, 58.

111. Sheard, *Llewellyn's Complete Book of Names*, 45.

# Alemona

**Keyword:** Fertility

**Categories:** Roman, Nixi

As one of the important goddesses of childbirth and fertility, Alemona provides nourishment for unborn babies in the womb and tends to all the aspects of childbirth and care.[112]

# Aletheia

**Keyword:** Truth

**Categories:** Greek, Personification

**Roman Equivalent:** Veritas

Greek philosopher Plato used the word *Aletheia* to denote truth as it relates to myth.[113] She is Zeus's daughter, but in *Aesop's Fables*, Prometheus crafted her. She personifies truth or disclosure. Her name translation refers to the state of not being concealed.

# Amphitrite

**Keyword:** Sea

**Categories:** Greek, Oceanids, Nereids

**Roman Equivalent:** Salacia

She is daughter of Nereus and Doris and the most gorgeous of all the Nereids. In some stories, she is among the three thousand ocean nymph daughters, and in others, she is among the fifty daughters of the Man in the Sea who fled into the Atlas Mountains when Poseidon wanted to marry her to protect her purity. Poseidon sent a dolphin to convince her to marry him, and when she agreed, the dolphin became the Delphinus constellation.[114]

---

112. Clarke, *Concise View of the Succession of Sacred Literature*, 138.

113. Various Authors, *Routledge Library Editions*, 100.

114. Nosselt, *Mythology Greek and Roman*, 63.

# Angerona

**Keyword:** Protection

**Category:** Roman

She helped people overcome pain and sorrow and kept the sacred name of the city so it would be protected from enemies. She presides over winter solstice and helps people bear the pain of the shortest and darkest day of the year. On December 21, a festival was held in her honor.[115]

# Anna Perenna

**Keyword:** Time

**Category:** Roman

Mentioned in *Fasti* by Ovid and in Virgil's *Aeneid*, Anna Perenna became an important and multifaceted goddess. Ovid described her as a nymph and an old woman who took food to protestors, which is why she became a favorite goddess for the plebeians, Roman citizens who comprised the middle class.[116] After the assassination of Julius Caesar on the Ides of March or March 15 in 44 BCE, her festival celebrated on March 15 marked the beginning of the Roman New Year. Mars is her consort.

# Annona

**Keywords:** Fertility, Agriculture

**Categories:** Roman, Personification

An agricultural and fertility goddess who personified the grain supply for the city of Rome and ensured the food supply was healthy. Those who worshiped her expected to receive an abundant and fresh food supply. She worked with grain goddess Ceres to ensure proper food distribution.[117]

# Antevorta

**Keyword:** Fertility

**Categories:** Roman, Camenae

---

115. Adkins and Adkins, *Handbook to Life in Ancient Rome*, 381.

116. McIntyre and McCallum, *Uncovering Anna Perenna*, 4–6.

117. Spaeth, *Roman Goddess Ceres*, 10.

Like all Camenae, she presided over childbirth and especially related to instances where the child emerged headfirst. She and all the Camenae are associated with the child's fate. She and her sister Postvorta were considered either companions of goddess Carmenta or divine aspects of her where Postvorta represented the past and Antevorta the future.[118]

## Apate

**Keyword:** Deceit

**Categories:** Greek, Personification

**Roman Equivalent:** Fraus

She personified the concept of deception.[119] Paying homage to her helped people guard against becoming victims of her mischievous ways. Her mother is Nyx the night goddess and her counterpart was Dolos, the trickster god.

## Aphrodite

**Keywords:** Love, Desire, Fertility

**Categories:** Greek, Olympian

**Roman Equivalent:** Venus

Uranus's son, the Titan Cronus, severed his father's genitals, and Aphrodite, whom Hesiod cites as golden and foam-born, sprang out of the ocean.[120] Aphrodite is goddess of passion and sensual pleasures, fertility, and procreation. She is symbolized by roses, doves, sparrows, swans, and myrtles. Aphrodite had an enthusiastic cult following. She became an unfaithful wife to her husband, Hephaestus, the god of fire and metalworking, by having an affair with war god Ares, among many others.

## Artemis

**Keyword:** Hunt

**Categories:** Greek, Olympian

**Roman Equivalent:** Diana

---

118. Auset, *Goddess Guide*, 259.

119. Auset, *Goddess Guide*.

120. Evelyn-White, *Theogony of Hesiod*.

A virgin goddess, Artemis embodied successful hunting and represented maidens, mothers, wild places, nature, animals, virginity, the moon, and the hunt. She is Apollo's twin sister, born on the island of Delos, and daughter of Leto and Zeus.[121]

## Asteria

**Keyword:** Star

**Categories:** Greek, Titaness

According to Greek poet Hesiod in his book *Theogony*, Asteria is Perses's wife and witchcraft goddess Hecate's mother. She and her sister Leto were daughters of first-generation Titans Coeus and Phoebe.[122] After Zeus impregnated Leto, he pursued Asteria, who had no interest in him. She escaped his clutches and turned herself into a bird and later into the island of Delos so that her sister could take refuge there and give birth to Artemis and Apollo.

## Athena

**Keywords:** War, Wisdom, Protection

**Categories:** Greek, Tutelary, Personification

**Roman Equivalent:** Minerva

Athena personifies Athens, the art of war, and craftwork. The Parthenon in Athens is dedicated in her honor, as well as many Greek festivals, including the Panathenaea, celebrated every four years in direct competition to the Olympic Games.[123] Several myths discuss the birth of Athena. One says Zeus gave birth to Athena himself after experiencing a horrible headache. After asking Prometheus to crack his head open, Athena emerged fully grown, armed and ready for battle. Hesiod said that Zeus had an affair with Athena's mother Metis and feared his wife's wrath, so Zeus took the baby from Metis and gave birth to Athena by himself. In retribution, Hera conceived blacksmith god Hephaestus by herself.[124] In one myth, Athena married Hephaestus but left the marital bed before consummation.

---

121. Evelyn-White, *Theogony of Hesiod*.

122. Evelyn-White, *Theogony of Hesiod*.

123. Kyle, *Athletics in Ancient Athens*, 24.

124. Evelyn-White, *Theogony of Hesiod*.

# Atropos

**Keywords:** Fate, Death

**Categories:** Greek, Moirai or Fates

As the oldest of the Moirai, she represented unalterable fate and chose how the person would die and she cut the thread of life. Hesiod described her as the daughter of Zeus and Themis in *Theogony*.[125]

# Aurora

**Keyword:** Dawn

**Categories:** Roman, Personification

**Greek Equivalent:** Eos

Aurora personifies the dawn and rides her chariot across the sky. She embodies the red light of morning as the sun reaches over the horizon.[126] Her brother is sun god Sol and her sister is Luna the moon. She has two versions of her consort: the god Astraeus or the mortal Tithonus, the prince of Troy.

# Bellona

**Keyword:** War

**Category:** Roman

**Greek Equivalent:** Enyo

Bellona is an ancient war goddess likely adapted from the Sabines.[127] Her cult met near the temple of Apollo near the area where the senate met to discuss victories. A consort of war god Mars, she is always shown wearing her military helmet. During her June 3 festival, priests offered her a blood sacrifice by wounding themselves.

# Bona Dea

**Keywords:** Fertility, Protection, Healing

**Category:** Roman

---

125. Evelyn-White, *Theogony of Hesiod*.

126. Charlton, *E. T. A. Hoffman's Musical Writings*, 183.

127. Dalyand Rengel, *Greek & Roman Mythology A to Z*.

Wife of Faunus, the god of the fields, Bona Dea is a prophecy and secrecy goddess who assists women with the virtue of chastity, healing, fertility, and protection. Known as the Good Goddess, she became a popular women's goddess who held secrets from the Roman men and allowed women to drink and do sacrifices. Men were not even allowed to know her name.[128]

# Britannia

**Keyword:** Protection

**Categories:** Roman, Personification, Tutelary

Featured on coinage, Britannia served as protector and personification of Britain within Roman Britain and tutelary deity of the area now known as Britain. An emblem during the Napoleonic Wars, she was associated with naval dominance.[129] Modern people still honor her to the present day. She is often seen or depicted wearing a helmet and holding a shield.

# Bubona

**Keyword:** Cows

**Categories:** Roman, Personification

A minor deity of cattle, Saint Augustine discussed her role in ensuring there were enough cattle.[130] She was also mentioned by Pliny the Elder, who discussed a festival honoring cattle.

# Calliope

**Keyword:** Poetry

**Categories:** Greek, Muses

Daughter of Zeus and Mnemosyne, she is the muse of epic poetry who appears holding a book and has tablets by her side.[131] She normally wears a golden crown and is consort of Apollo and mother of Orpheus and Linus.

---

128. Smith, *Dictionary of Greek and Roman Biography and Mythology*, 1:499.

129. Goulbourne, *Race and Ethnicity*, 62, 68.

130. Dods, *Works of Aurelius Augustine*.

131. Nosselt, *Mythology Greek and Roman*, 53.

# Callirrhoe

**Keyword:** Water

**Categories:** Greek, Oceanids, Naiad

In *Theogony*, poet Hesiod sites Callirrhoe as an Oceanid with several consorts. Hesiod mentions her union with Chrysaor, son of Poseidon and Medusa, and with him, she became mother of the monsters Echidna, a half-woman half-snake, and the giant Geryones.[132] In mythology, Callirrhoe was a Naiad water spirit who accompanied Persephone after Hades lured her into the Underworld.

# Candelifera

**Keyword:** Childbirth

**Categories:** Roman, Nixi

She is another of the many deities who help with birth. Known as the candle bearer, she supplies light to help the infant emerge from the womb, or for those born at night.[133] Philosopher Plutarch believed light symbolized birth and candles were magical tools worthy of veneration.

# Canens

**Keywords:** Singing and Songs

**Categories:** Roman, Nymph, Personification

Canens was a nymph who personified song.[134] A witch turned her husband, Picus, into a woodpecker, and Canens threw herself into the Tiber River in Rome when she couldn't find him.

# Cardea

**Keyword:** Protection

**Categories:** Roman, Nixi

Romans had three gods of doorways, including Forculus for double doors and Limentinus for thresholds. Cardea serves the dual role as a deity of doorways and

---

132. Evelyn-White, *Theogony of Hesiod*.

133. Auset, *Goddess Guide*, 22.

134. Adkins and Adkins, *Handbook to Life in Ancient Rome*, 285.

another of the many protective childhood goddesses who guards the hinges on the doors to protect children from bloodsucking evil winged creatures or witches known as striges who would suck children's blood and carry them away.[135]

## Carmenta

**Keyword:** Magic

**Categories:** Roman, Camenae, Flamines Minores

Carmenta was consort of Mercury and a chief nymph of the Camenae set of deities who presided over wells and springs and gave prophecies.[136] Legend states that she altered the Greek alphabet to invent the Latin alphabet. Her name is a derivative of the English word *charm* because of her prophetic abilities. The priest dedicated to tending her cult was named Flamen Carmentalis.

## Celaeno

**Keyword:** Star

**Categories:** Greek, Nymph

Called the dark one, she personified one of the stars in the Pleiades star system and was one of the daughters of Atlas and the Oceanid Pleione, collectively called the Atlantides.[137] Celaeno is also the name of a harpy, a half-human half-bird creature that personifies wind and storms mentioned in Homer's poems.

## Ceres

**Keywords:** Fertility, Agriculture

**Categories:** Roman, Aventine Triad, Dii Consentes, Flamines Minores

**Greek Equivalent:** Demeter

As an important grain goddess, her name was written on an urn dating from 600 BCE, making her the first known Roman goddess.[138] Ceres helped with the successful growing of food and plants and acted as Roman counterpart to the Greek Demeter. She is a cult goddess in the Aventine Triad—a group of three

---

135. Adkins and Adkins, *Handbook to Life in Ancient Rome*, 285.

136. Auset, *Goddess Guide*, 259.

137. Coulter and Turner, *Encyclopedia of Ancient Deities*, 117.

138. Spaeth, *Roman Goddess Ceres*, 1, 22.

deities including Ceres, Liber the god of wine and grapevine cultivation, and Libera, an early wine goddess. The Triad members were worshiped by the Plebeians or commoners with her priest Flamen Cerealis tending her cult.

## Cinxia

**Keyword:** Fertility

**Categories:** Roman, Nixi

In the consummation of marriage, she helped the groom by loosening the bride's girdle to signify the transition from virgin to married woman.[139] Husbands said prayers over their pregnant wives and tied a belt around them briefly to signify a successful carrying to term of any pregnancies.

## Clementia

**Keyword:** Mercy

**Categories:** Roman, Personification

She personified the virtue embodied within Julius Caesar himself. She also represented the virtues of forgiveness, penance, absolution, acquittal, and salvation exemplified by Julius Caesar toward his followers as a model to follow for the highest ideals of Rome. People worshiped her to protect themselves against overreach of power by government.[140]

## Clio

**Keywords:** History, Music

**Categories:** Greek, Muses

Clio is the Muse of history and daughter of Zeus and Mnemosyne. According to writer Apollodorus, she is the consort of Pierus of Magnes.[141] She is also the Muse for the lyre, a stringed instrument from antiquity, and carries a papyrus roll in her hand.[142]

---

139. Jordan, *Dictionary of Gods and Goddesses*, 66.

140. Jordan, *Dictionary of Gods and Goddesses*, 66.

141. Frazer, *Apollodorus*, 19.

142. Nosselt, *Mythology Greek and Roman*, 53.

# Cloacina

**Keyword:** Water

**Category:** Roman

Former Etruscan goddess assigned to the drains and sewers to ensure they remained flowing. She became conflated with Venus as Venus Cloacina, who represented peace between the Romans and the Sabines, the group of people who lived in southern Italy at that time whom the Romans engaged in numerous conflicts and battles. Altars were erected to her as a symbol of the newfound accord, and famed poet Lord Byron wrote a poem about her.[143]

# Clotho

**Keyword:** Fate

**Categories:** Greek, Moirai or Fates

As the youngest of the Moirai, she met with people at their birth and spun the thread of life. She could decide when you were born and who lived or died. Hesiod says that she and her two sisters, Atropos and Lachesis, give mortals evil or good.[144]

# Clymene

**Keyword:** Water

**Categories:** Greek, Oceanid, Nymph

Clymene is one of the three hundred Oceanid nymphs. Sun god Helios fell in love with her and together they had a son named Phaethon who personified planet Jupiter and died when he attempted to race his father's chariot across the sky. Clymene is also mother to the group of nymphs called the Heliades, "daughters of the sun," who were transformed into poplar trees after their brother's death. Called the goddess of infamy and fame, she is featured prominently in Ovid's *Metamorphoses*.[145]

# Concordia

**Keyword:** Harmony

**Categories:** Roman, Personification

---

143. Martin, *Tree-Kangaroos of Australia and New Guinea*, 102.

144. Evelyn-White, *Theogony of Hesiod*.

145. Ovid, *Metamorphoses*.

**Greek Equivalent:** Harmonia

Personification of the abstract concept of harmony and peace within marriage, Concordia is the counterpart of Discordia. Concordia had several temples in her honor, including one in the Roman Forum, and her feast was celebrated on April 30.[146] She also helped create harmonious relations between different factions of society.

## Cuba

**Keyword:** Childhood

**Categories:** Roman, Nixi

She helps children transition from their cradle to the bed. This childhood development represented a rite of passage that deserved spiritual energy and protection.[147]

## Cunina

**Keyword:** Protector

**Categories:** Roman, Nixi

She was a protective maternal goddess who shielded babies and children from maleficent magic.[148] Superstitions about dark energies were common for many reasons, including high infant and maternal mortality.

## Decima

**Keyword:** Destiny

**Categories:** Roman, Parcae

Female personification of destiny, she and her sisters, Morta and Nona, controlled life and death, similar to Greek Moirai. Decima measured the thread of life with her rod to determine lifespan. She also helped in childbirth to ensure the baby came to full term.[149]

---

146. Monaghan, *Encyclopedia of Goddesses and Heroines: Africa, Eastern Mediterranean, Asia*, 453.

147. Carroll, *Gods, Goddesses, and Saints*, 304.

148. Carroll, *Gods, Goddesses, and Saints*, 304.

149. Clarke, *Concise View of the Succession of Sacred Literature*, 138.

# Demeter

**Keywords:** Harvest, Fertility

**Categories:** Greek, Olympian

**Roman Equivalent:** Ceres

Golden-haired Demeter was an Olympian goddess of family, agriculture, and fertility and the daughter of Rhea and Cronos.[150] Related to agriculture, she assisted with the successful and abundant harvest of grain. Consort to Zeus, she became the center of the Eleusinian Mysteries. Developed in the plains of Eleusis, followers worshiped Demeter, her daughter Persephone, and her son Iacchus and performed rituals to honor the various stages of life, death, and rebirth. To the ancient Greeks, the natural world held many mysteries of the changing seasons—growth of crops and withering away of food sources in winter.

# Diana

**Keywords:** Hunt, Protection

**Categories:** Roman, Dii Consentes

**Greek Equivalent:** Artemis

Goddess of animals, the hunt, and champion of women, Diana protects domestic animals and was invoked to aid with protection during childbirth and conception. Diana also manifested as the triple goddess Diana Triformis—Diana, Luna, and Hecate—to embody the huntress, moon, and Underworld realms. People worshiped the triple goddess Diana as early as the sixth century BCE as Diana of Nemi.[151] According to poet Virgil, Diana crossed thresholds between this world and the next as a guardian to prevent evil from entering the world.

# Dike

**Keyword:** Justice

**Categories:** Greek, Horae

**Roman Equivalent:** Justitia

---

150. Evelyn-White, *Theogony of Hesiod*.
151. Green, *Roman Religion and the Cult of Diana at Aricia*.

She is the personification of justice and sister of Eunomia and Eirene.[152] Horae were initially used to mark the passage of time but evolved to include a structured social order, which is what Dike represented. Daughter of Zeus and Themis, she embodies moral order, social rules, and enforced justice.

## Dione

**Keywords:** Mother, Water

**Categories:** Greek, Titaness, Oceanid, Hyades, Nereid

Dione has several versions of her creation myth. Sometimes considered an alternate name for Aphrodite, in other accounts, she is Aphrodite's mother, consort of Zeus, and the daughter of Oceanus and Tethys.[153] In another legend, she is one of the many Hyades, a rain-making nymph, and another reference makes her daughter of the Oceanid Doris and a member of the Nereids.

## Disciplina

**Keywords:** Discipline, Order

**Categories:** Roman, Personification

She personified the ideal of discipline in the realms of education, self-control, persistence, and orderly conduct.[154] Roman soldiers followed her as a model of discipline. Cilurnum Fort located along Hadrian's Wall had an established Cult of Disciplina discovered during excavations. Hadrian himself apparently encouraged her worship. Frugality, sternness, and faithfulness were among her many virtues.

## Discordia

**Keyword:** Discord

**Categories:** Roman, Personification

**Greek Equivalent:** Eris

---

152. Dalyand Rengel, *Greek & Roman Mythology A to Z*.

153. Coulter and Turner, *Encyclopedia of Ancient Deities*, 152.

154. Coulter and Turner, *Encyclopedia of Ancient Deities*, 153.

Daughter of Nyx and consort of war god Mars, Discordia is the personification of the night and personal strife.[155] Her Greek counterpart, Eris, played an important role in starting the Trojan War by placing an apple that read "for the most beautiful" in front of the gathering at the wedding of Peleus and Thetis. When Hera, Athena, and Aphrodite fought over the apple, Zeus allowed Paris to decide the most beautiful, and when he chose Aphrodite, she helped him win the affections of Helen of Troy, thus beginning the war.

## Doris

**Keywords:** Mother, Water

**Categories:** Greek, Oceanid

Doris is an Oceanid and mother of the fifty ocean nymphs called Nereids with her consort Nereus, the eldest son of Earth Mother Gaia and the sea god Pontus.[156] Doris and all the Oceanids are mentioned in Homer's *Iliad*, and she is prominently featured in Hesiod's *Theogony*. Her name may be attributed to the Dorians, an ethnic group of ancient Greece.[157]

## Echidna

**Keyword:** Snake

**Categories:** Greek, Chthonic

In *Theogony*, Hesiod described her as beautiful, deadly, and immortal, a half-nymph who lives in a cave far away from mortal men with fair cheeks and the lower half of a huge snake with awful speckled skin. She never ages and she never dies. She and her partner, Typhaon, whom Hesiod describes as terrible, became parents of many feared monsters in Greek mythology, including the fifty-headed hound of Hades and the evil-minded Hydra.[158]

---

155. Coulter and Turner, *Encyclopedia of Ancient Deities*, 66.

156. Butler, *Iliad of Homer*, Book XVIII.

157. Frazer, *Apollodorus*, 57.

158. Evelyn-White, *Theogony of Hesiod*.

# Egeria

**Keywords:** Spring, Water

**Categories:** Roman, Camenae

According to legend, she lamented the death of her lover and consort, Numa Pompilius, the second king of Rome, and goddess Diana took pity on her and turned her into a spring. She had a gift of prophecy and positively influenced the Roman legal system through her relationship with Pompilius by establishing societal law and order and modeling the perfection and order found in nature for societal norms.[159]

# Eileithyia

**Keyword:** Childbirth

**Category:** Greek

Daughter of Zeus and Hera, during the annual birth of the divine child ceremony, people paid homage to her. She is associated with midwifery. Ares and Hebe are her siblings.[160]

# Eirene

**Keyword:** Peace

**Categories:** Greek, Horae, Personification

**Roman Equivalent:** Pax

Daughter of Zeus and Themis, she embodied peace and became very popular in Athens when citizens began a cult for peace after a major naval victory.[161] Citizens erected statues to her and made numerous offerings to that end. Another deity with the same name is the daughter of Poseidon, Olympian and god of the sea.

# Electra

**Keyword:** Star

**Categories:** Greek, Nymph

---

159. Daly and Rengel, *Greek & Roman Mythology A to Z*, 49.
160. Evelyn-White, *Theogony of Hesiod*.
161. Evelyn-White, *Theogony of Hesiod*.

Electra personified one of the stars in the Pleiades star system. She was a consort of Zeus and a daughter of Atlas and the Oceanid Pleione, collectively called the Atlantides. Sea god Thaumus was her consort.[162] The name *Electra* also refers to the character in Greek tragedy, as well as to one of the many Oceanids (one of the Danaids in Ovid's *Metamorphoses*), as well as to the assistant to Helen of Troy.

# Empanda

**Keyword:** Charity

**Categories:** Roman, Charity

Goddess of the rustics, she helped the hungry. People in need would go to the gates of her temple to receive food. She admits anyone who needs help. She may be an aspect of Juno.

# Enyo

**Keyword:** War

**Categories:** Greek, Olympian

**Roman Equivalent:** Bellona

She destroys cities and assisted her consort, war god Ares, in battle. She was instrumental in destruction of Troy and represents strife and destruction. In *Theogony*, she is described as saffron-robed.[163]

# Eos

**Keyword:** Dawn

**Categories:** Greek, Personification

**Roman Equivalent:** Aurora

She personified the rising sun and dawn and lived in Oceanis. She rose each morning. She is mother to the winds and stars.[164] She had several consorts, including Orion, Astraeus, and Ares, among others.

---

162. Evelyn-White, *Theogony of Hesiod.*
163. Evelyn-White, *Theogony of Hesiod.*
164. Evelyn-White, *Theogony of Hesiod.*

# Erato

**Keywords:** Erotic and Lyrical Poetry

**Categories:** Greek, Muses

Daughter of Zeus and Mnemosyne, she is the muse of erotic poetry and mimicking.[165] She is charming to look at and often holds roses and wears a myrtle wreath. Malus, namesake of a cape and peninsula in Greece, is her consort.

# Eucleia

**Keywords:** Grace, Purity, Fertility

**Categories:** Greek, Charites/Graces

Virgin daughter of Aglaea and Hephaestus, she embodies glory in battle and good repute or reputation. Brides and grooms venerated her by making sacrifices to her before their weddings to ensure marital harmony and success.

# Eunomia

**Keywords:** Order, Time

**Categories:** Greek, Horae

Daughter of Zeus and Themis, as a Horae, she is one of the goddesses who relates to the season and passage of time. Eunomia embodies good order and justice and helped maintain society in the major population centers such as Athens.[166] She also represented green pastures in springtime.

# Eupheme

**Keyword:** Acclaim

**Categories:** Greek, Charites/Graces

Daughter of Aglaea and Hephaestus, she embodies praise and positive words and applause or honor and maintaining a stellar reputation.[167]

---

165. Evelyn-White, *Theogony of Hesiod*.

166. Evelyn-White, *Theogony of Hesiod*.

167. Borza, *Shadow of Olympus*, 192.

# Euphrosyne

**Keyword:** Joy

**Categories:** Greek, Charites/Graces

A daughter of Zeus, she was one of the graces who embodied joy and cheer.[168] She and her sisters attended to the needs of the goddess Aphrodite.

# Eurynome

**Keyword:** Water

**Categories:** Greek, Oceanid

She is visualized as a mermaid. As Zeus's third wife, she is mother of the Charites or Graces, Aglaea, Euphrosyne, and Thalia. Titan Oceanus is her father.[169]

# Euterpe

**Keywords:** Delight, Poetry

**Categories:** Greek, Muses

Daughter of Zeus and Mnemosyne, she is muse of music and lyric poetry. Ancient poets called her a giver of light. She is associated with flutes, music, and rejoicing and is typically depicted carrying two flutes in her hands.[170] She is consort of the Olympian Apollo or Strymon, son of Oceanus and Tethys.

# Euthenia

**Keyword:** Prosperity

**Categories:** Greek, Charites/Graces

Daughter of Aglaea and Hephaestus, she embodies the quality of prosperity and abundance. Nilus is her consort. In art, she is depicted wearing a wreath of corn and she holds a cord in her right hand and a sceptre in her left.[171]

---

168. Nosselt, *Mythology Greek and Roman*, 58.

169. Nosselt, *Mythology Greek and Roman*, 58.

170. Nosselt, *Mythology Greek and Roman*, 53.

171. Poole, *Catalogue of the Coins of Alexandria*, lxxix.

## Febris

**Keywords:** Fever, Protection

**Categories:** Roman, Personification

The personification of fevers, Febris protected people from fever and malaria.[172] Februus, the Etruscan purification god, was her counterpart. Because illness was of such concern to people, several temples were erected in her honor to help appease her, protect people, and cure the ill. She also caused fevers for enemies of the state. *Apocolocyntosis*, by Seneca the Younger, mentioned her.

## Felicitas

**Keywords:** Good Fortune

**Categories:** Roman, Personification

A fruitful, blessed, lucky woman's goddess for prosperity, Felicitas helped people improve all areas of life and embodied an abundant state of being. She differed from goddess Fortuna.[173] She had coinage created as one of the several Roman luck and fertility deities.

## Feronia

**Keywords:** Freedom, Abundance

**Category:** Roman

As the goddess of civil rights, she helped grant freedom to Roman slaves and embodied the virtues of equality and civil rights. Originally she was a goddess of fertility and abundance in agriculture who lived in the forest, but as food security was a constant concern for the lower class, she evolved into a champion of the plebeians, or commoners, of Rome. She may have originated as an Etruscan goddess adopted by the Romans.[174]

## Fides

**Keywords:** Trust and Faith

**Categories:** Roman, Personification

172. Monaghan, *Encyclopedia of Goddesses and Heroines: Africa, Eastern Mediterranean, Asia*, 454.

173. Monaghan, *Encyclopedia of Goddesses and Heroines: Africa, Eastern Mediterranean, Asia*, 447.

174. Monaghan, *Encyclopedia of Goddesses and Heroines: Africa, Eastern Mediterranean, Asia*, 454.

Honesty is yet another quality that became a goddess and a source of the word *fidelity*. She helped maintain honesty and good will in relationships.[175] The term *bona fide*, meaning "genuine or real," comes from her.

## Flora

**Keyword:** Flowers

**Categories:** Roman, Flamines Minores

A fertility goddess who became associated with springtime and youth, Flora had a temple near Circus Maximus tended by her priest, Flamen Floralis. Favonius, the god of light wind and breezes or the west wind, was her consort. She was opposite of Ceres, who promoted married love, while Flora was celebrated by sex workers.[176]

## Fornax

**Keywords:** Fertility, Agriculture

**Categories:** Roman, Personification

Associated with Vesta, goddess of the hearth, she personified the oven and oversaw the proper baking of bread.[177] As such, she is a form of grain, agriculture, and fertility goddess due to the importance of food.

## Fortuna

**Keywords:** Fortune, Chance, Luck

**Categories:** Roman, Personification

**Greek Equivalent:** Tyche

Fortuna personified luck, chance, and good fortune. Her consort was Bonus Eventus—Good Outcome. She served as the goddess of chance or lot and often appeared blindfolded to symbolize the whims of fate with good or bad luck. Represented by the Wheel of Fortune, Fortuna never held scales of justice because fortune is not given equally. She had links to astrology and the aspects of your sun, moon, and rising sign to determine your fortunes in life. She brought fortune

---

175. Monaghan, *Encyclopedia of Goddesses and Heroines: Africa, Eastern Mediterranean, Asia*, 454.

176. Monaghan, *Encyclopedia of Goddesses and Heroines: Africa, Eastern Mediterranean, Asia*, 452.

177. Monaghan, *Encyclopedia of Goddesses and Heroines: Africa, Eastern Mediterranean, Asia*.

to various aspects of daily life, such as luck in marriage. As Fortuna Virilis, she made women enticing to men.[178]

## Fulgora

**Keyword:** Lightning

**Categories:** Roman, Personification

Fulgora personified the natural phenomenon of lighting.[179] Sand that is struck by lightning is called Fulgerite. Worshiping her helped protect people from lightning strikes.

## Furrina

**Keywords:** Spring, Water

**Categories:** Roman, Personification, Flamines Minores

An incredibly early goddess within Roman history, Furrina became obscure by the first century BCE. Her status among the Flamines Minores through the work of her priest Flamen Furrinalis kept her energy alive, and she had a sacred shrine on the Tiber River.[180]

## Gaia

**Keyword:** Earth

**Categories:** Greek, Titaness, Primordial

**Roman Equivalent:** Tellus Mater

Rising out of the depths of chaos and the great abyss of Tartarus, Mother Gaia is the Supreme Primordial Being, the embodiment of Earth who represents the minerals, soil, and soul of Earth itself. She gave birth to Uranus and all other phenomena in the world. Uranus later became her consort and together they created other natural phenomena. She is mother of all the Titans.[181]

---

178. Monaghan, *Encyclopedia of Goddesses and Heroines: Africa, Eastern Mediterranean, Asia*, 455.

179. Monaghan, *Encyclopedia of Goddesses and Heroines: Africa, Eastern Mediterranean, Asia*, 447.

180. Monaghan, *Encyclopedia of Goddesses and Heroines: Africa, Eastern Mediterranean, Asia*, 455.

181. Evelyn-White, *Theogony of Hesiod*.

# Harmonia

**Keyword:** Harmony

**Categories:** Greek, Personification

**Roman Equivalent:** Concordia

Daughter of war god Ares and Cytherea, Harmonia's name can be deceiving.[182] Although she represented harmony and agreement, she received a cursed necklace during her wedding to Cadmus that caused discord for everyone who received it after her. The necklace was a gift from her husband, and later, she and Cadmus were turned into serpents.

# Hebe

**Keyword:** Youth

**Categories:** Greek, Personification

**Roman Equivalent:** Juventas

Daughter of Zeus and Hera, Hebe represents everlasting youth and beauty. She is typically depicted as a young girl. As goddess of immortality, she became quite revered for her assistance to warriors and statesmen. Her opposite is Geras, the god of old age who is a shriveled old man and son of Nyx. She embodies those who are in their prime of life and served as a cupbearer who poured ambrosia and nectar to the Olympians. Hercules was her consort.[183]

# Hecate

**Keywords:** Witchcraft, Magic, Protection

**Category:** Greek

**Roman Equivalents:** Trivia, Diana

Zeus honored Hecate above all other deities, and those who wanted favor, according to Hesiod, called upon her.[184] Egyptians worshiped Hecate during the Ptolemaic period in Alexandria. Three-headed Hecate had once been venerated as a mother goddess and evolved to include magic and sorcery. She is symbolized

---

182. Evelyn-White, *Theogony of Hesiod.*

183. Nosselt, *Mythology Greek and Roman,* 58.

184. Evelyn-White, *Theogony of Hesiod.*

by a spinning wheel. In her role as a Diana Triformis goddess, she guards the crossroads between the earthly realm and the Underworld. After Persephone's kidnapping and decent into the Underworld, Hecate guided her back to the world of the living. Hecate images placed at crossroads protected cities, and Hecate amulets were kept within individual homes. She is a virgin but is sometimes associated with Apollo.

# Hemera

**Keyword:** Day

**Categories:** Greek, Personification

**Roman Equivalent:** Dies

Daughter of Nyx and Erebus, she personified the transition from dawn, the goddess Eos, mentioned in Hesiod's *Theogony*, to midday, and later she gave way to Hesperide, goddess of dusk and sunset. Sky god Aether was her brother.[185]

# Hera

**Keyword:** Marriage

**Categories:** Greek, Olympian

**Roman Equivalent:** Juno

Queen of the gods and consort of Zeus, Hera rules over Mount Olympus and symbolizes happiness and success in marriage or partnership. She is immortalized in myth for her jealous rants over Zeus's many lovers and illegitimate offspring, including Artemis and Apollo. Their mother, Leto, was cursed by Hera and had to give birth to the divine twins on the remote island of Delos.[186]

# Hersilia

**Keyword:** Courage

**Categories:** Roman, Tutelary

Hersilia was likely a Sabine goddess and became consort of Romulus, one of the founders of Rome. Because of that association, she became instrumental in the development of the Roman civilization and is credited with helping end

---

185. Monaghan, *Encyclopedia of Goddesses and Heroines: Africa, Eastern Mediterranean, Asia*, 427.
186. UNESCO World Heritage, "Delos."

the war with the Sabines. The Roman founders, including Hersilia, were partly mythical. When Romulus was deified as the god Quirinus, Hersilia became a mythical queen as well as a goddess.[187]

# Hestia

**Keyword:** Hearth

**Categories:** Greek, Olympian

**Greek Equivalent:** Vesta

Hestia is the widely venerated virgin goddess of family and state, domesticity, home, and hearth. She embodies the ideal qualities of caring for the home and hearth, enjoying the company of loving family connections and good health. Greeks and Romans believed they must keep her flame lit to ensure the overall health and well-being of the family unit. Hesiod lists her as the daughter of Cronos and Rhea.[188]

# Juno

**Keywords:** Love, Marriage

**Categories:** Roman, Dii Consentes

**Greek Equivalent:** Hera

Goddess of love, marital love, and happy marriage, she is the wife of sky god Jupiter, daughter of Saturn, and a protector with warrior aspects. She, Jupiter, and wisdom goddess Minerva became known as the Capitoline Triad. Juno became jealous when Jupiter birthed Minerva from his head, so she received a helpful herb from Flora to help her give birth to Mars. During the week before a birth, she received offerings.[189]

# Justitia

**Keyword:** Justice

**Categories:** Roman, Personification

**Greek Equivalent:** Dike

---

187. Fraser, *Golden Bough*, 193.

188. Evelyn-White, *Theogony of Hesiod*.

189. Clarke, *Concise View of the Succession of Sacred Literature*, 138.

Another personification of Justice, she is often depicted as a blindfolded woman carrying the scales of justice and a sword to demonstrate the swiftness of justice, the blind applications of justice, and the weighing of sides.[190]

## Juturna

**Keyword:** Water

**Categories:** Roman, Naiad

Originally a water spirit or nymph, Jupiter bewitched her into having an affair with him and deified her as compensation. Juturna became one of the more prominent of the many Roman water nymphs. Most nymphs watched over only one body of water, but Juturna presided over several locations, including a well in Latium and another near Forum Romanum. She conceived Fontus, the god of wells and springs, by her consort, Janus, the god of doorways, fate, and time.[191]

## Juventas

**Keyword:** Youth

**Categories:** Roman, Personification

**Greek Equivalent:** Hebe

She personified youthfulness and rejuvenation and helped young men who were transitioning into manhood.[192] Worshipers invoked her name to assist the youth with an upcoming battle, but when battles didn't go well, she eventually took the blame and became downgraded.

## Ker

**Keyword:** Death

**Categories:** Greek, Chthonic

Keres, the plural of Ker, were female spirits similar to the Norse Valkyries who tended the wounded on the battlefield and related to a person's destiny. They

---

190. Coulter and Turner, *Encyclopedia of Ancient Deities*, 254.

191. Coulter and Turner, *Encyclopedia of Ancient Deities*, 254.

192. Daly and Rengel, *Greek & Roman Mythology A to Z*, 75.

are not named as individuals, but Greeks believed everyone was assigned their own Ker, who stayed with them as a companion.[193]

## Lachesis

**Keyword:** Fate

**Categories:** Greek, Moirai or Fates

As a member of the Moirai, she showed up within three days of a baby's birth with her measuring stick, measured the thread of life, and drew lots to determine lifespan. She is another of the three daughters of Zeus and Themis who controlled destiny.[194]

## Laetitia

**Keywords:** Abundance, Fertility, Prosperity

**Categories:** Roman, Personification

She represents all that is joyful, luxurious, prosperous, lush, and abounding. She is associated with agriculture and plentiful harvests and, as such, is often shown in green with floral wreaths and garlands. She is also a personification of happiness and having a glad demeanor.[195]

## Laverna

**Keyword:** Gain

**Categories:** Roman, Chthonic

As an Underworld deity and protector of thieves, she makes sure thieves don't get caught and can pretend to be honest.[196] She likes alcohol poured with the left hand.

## Leto

**Keyword:** Motherhood

**Categories:** Greek, Titaness

---

193. Daly and Rengel, *Greek & Roman Mythology A to Z.*

194. Evelyn-White, *Theogony of Hesiod.*

195. Monaghan, *New Book of Goddesses & Heroines*, 347.

196. Monaghan, *New Book of Goddesses & Heroines*, 347.

Daughter of Phoebe and Coeus, she is mother of Apollo and Artemis with Zeus.[197] She represents caring for children. Leto punishes mortals for their false perception of self-importance.

## Libera

**Keyword:** Winter

**Category:** Roman

The daughter of Ceres who is sometimes associated with Proserpina, her temple was on Aventine Hill, which is why she is among the Aventine Triad with her mother and her consort, Liber, god of freedom and wine.[198]

## Libitina

**Keyword:** Funerals

**Categories:** Roman, Personification

Romans personified the burial ritual through goddess Libitina, the embodiment of funerary practices. Ancient undertakers were called libitina-rii.[199] She became associated with Venus because a temple dedicated to Venus was on a hill in the grove of Libitina, where Roman officials collected a death tax.

## Luna

**Keyword:** Moon

**Categories:** Roman, Personification

**Greek Equivalent:** Selene

Luna is the moon goddess who rides a two-yoke chariot pulled by horses or oxen. Sometimes she is with her counterpart, the sun god Sol, and they drive a four-yoke chariot together. Luna, Diana, and Hecate were part of the Diana Triformis as triple goddess figures. Luna had no cult centers, so she may have solely been an aspect of Diana.[200]

---

197. Evelyn-White, *Theogony of Hesiod*.

198. Spaeth, *Roman Goddess Ceres*, 1, 22.

199. Daly and Rengel, *Greek & Roman Mythology A to Z*.

200. Monaghan, *Encyclopedia of Goddesses and Heroines: Africa, Eastern Mediterranean, Asia*, 457.

# Maia

**Keyword:** Star

**Categories:** Greek, Nymph, Personification

She was a nymph who personified one of the stars in the Pleiades star system. A daughter of Atlas and the Oceanid Pleione (collectively called the Atlantides). She became Hermes's mother with Zeus.[201]

# Melia

**Keyword:** Tree

**Categories:** Greek, Oceanid, Nymph

The Oceanid Melia became a well-known cult figure at Thebes as consort of Apollo and Inachus. She was mother to Theban prophet Tenerus, known as the seer who tended the temple in Thebes. In some sources, Melia was consort to Inachus. In some accounts, she is one of the Meliae, spirits of ash trees whom Hesiod said were nymphs in *Theogony*.[202]

# Mellona

**Keyword:** Honey

**Categories:** Roman, Personification

The personification of honey whom Saint Augustine said helps with successful honey production and the proper flavor and sweetness of honey.[203] *Mel* is the Latin word for honey.

# Melpomene

**Keyword:** Tragedy

**Categories:** Greek, Muses

Daughter of Zeus and Mnemosyne, she is known as the muse for tragic actors and is seen holding the mask of Dionysus, a symbol for the theater. She wears a veil over her head and holds a dagger in one hand and the tragic mask in the other.[204]

---

201. Evelyn-White, *Theogony of Hesiod*.
202. Evelyn-White, *Theogony of Hesiod*.
203. Dods, *Works of Aurelius Augustine*.
204. Nosselt, *Mythology Greek and Roman*, 53.

# Merope

**Keyword:** Star

**Categories:** Greek, Nymph, Personification

She personified one of the stars in the Pleiades star system as a daughter of Atlas and Pleione (collectively called the Atlantides).[205] She became the only one of the seven sisters to marry a mortal Sisyphus, which, according to the myth, explains why she is the faintest star in the cluster.

# Metis

**Keyword:** Wisdom

**Categories:** Greek, Oceanid

Metis refers to wisdom, skill, or craft and cunning. In mythology, she gave Zeus a potion to help him retrieve his brothers and sisters from Cronus's belly. She became Zeus's first wife, and once Zeus heard a prophecy that Metis would have a son who would be stronger than him, he swallowed Metis during her pregnancy with goddess Athena, who eventually emerged from his head wielding a shield and sword and became goddess of wisdom and war.[206]

# Minerva

**Keyword:** Wisdom

**Categories:** Roman, Dii Consentes

**Greek Equivalent:** Athena

Minerva is the virginal goddess of handicraft, professions, arts, war, and competition in business. She is symbolized by the owl, which represents wisdom. Sky god Jupiter birthed her from his head, and she became part of the Capitoline Triad with Jupiter and Juno, a patrician cult center for the Roman ruling class.[207] She competed with Neptune to name Athens and created the olive tree. She turned Medusa into a monster who turned people to stone after Minerva caught her kissing Neptune in her sacred temple. She also turned Arachne into a spider after she challenged Minerva in the art of weaving.

---

205. Blacket, *Researches into the Lost Histories of America*, 215.

206. Evelyn-White, *Theogony of Hesiod*.

207. Spaeth, *Roman Goddess Ceres*, 7.

# Mnemosyne

**Keyword:** Memory

**Categories:** Greek, Titaness

With her consort Zeus, she is the mother of the nine muses who personifies memories and remembrance. Her parents are goddess Gaia and sky god Uranus. She is related to the streams of Lethe and Mnemosyne that helped people who drank their waters forget the past.[208]

# Morta

**Keywords:** Death, Fate

**Categories:** Roman, Parcae

She was one of the three Parcae who controlled destiny with her sisters, Decima and Nona.[209] She controlled life and death, similar to Greek Moirai, and Morta decided how people would die and cut the thread of life. She also presided over infant deaths.

# Necessitas

**Keyword:** Destiny

**Categories:** Roman, Personification, Primordial

**Greek Equivalent:** Ananke

Necessitas is the personification of inevitability and necessity. Considered an important primordial deity because of her powers, Necessitas could dictate fate and destiny and influence the course of a person's life.[210]

# Nemesis

**Keyword:** Retribution

**Categories:** Greek, Personification

She personifies the idea of revenge and paybacks. Hesiod described her as a goddess. She retaliates against human arrogance or hubris and is the daughter

---

208. Nosselt, *Mythology Greek and Roman*, 53.

209. Clarke, *Concise View of the Succession of Sacred Literature*, 138.

210. Daly and Rengel, *Greek & Roman Mythology A to Z*.

of Nyx and Erebus, and Helen of Troy's mother. She was one of the consorts of Zeus and Tartarus.[211]

# Nerio

**Keyword:** War

**Categories:** Roman, Personification

War goddess and consort of Mars, she personified the virtue of valor and bravery on the battlefield.[212] She could be an aspect of Bellona or Minerva.

# Nike

**Keyword:** Victory

**Categories:** Greek, Personification

**Roman Equivalent:** Victoria

Mentioned by Hesiod in *Theogony*, Nike served as guardian for the senate. People carried her amulet in their hands as a protective device. A daughter of Styx and Pallas the giant, she could sometimes be conflated with Athena. She is the personification for all kinds of victories in wars, politics, sports, or life in general.[213]

# Nona

**Keyword:** Fate

**Categories:** Roman, Parcae

Nona is one of the fates of destiny who, along with sisters Decima and Morta, controlled life and death, similar to Greek Moirai. Nona spun the thread of life and helped babies come to full term in the womb.[214]

# Nyx

**Keyword:** Night

**Categories:** Greek, Primordial

---

211. Hornum, *Nemesis*, 6.
212. Adkins and Adkins, *Handbook to Life in Ancient Rome*, 299.
213. Evelyn-White, *Theogony of Hesiod*.
214. Clarke, *Concise View of the Succession of Sacred Literature*, 138.

Born of chaos as one of the first beings in existence, Nyx is the primordial manifestation of the night and mother of several deities, including Hypnos and Nemesis. Erebus, the personification of darkness, was her consort.[215] Nyx had polarizing qualities of bringing rest and sleep or bringing death.[216]

# Ops

**Keyword:** Fertility

**Categories:** Roman, Personification

She is the personification of Earth's fertility, riches, goods, abundance, gifts, and the idea of having plenty, or more than enough.[217] Saturn is her consort.

# Palatua

**Keyword:** Protection

**Categories:** Roman, Flamines Minores

As the patron deity of the center of the Roman Empire on Palatine Hill, Palatua had her own priest, Flamen Palatualis, through the Flamines Minores.[218] She was a guardian and protective deity.

# Pax

**Keyword:** Peace

**Categories:** Roman, Personification

**Greek Equivalent:** Eirene

Pax personified peace and was often pictured holding an olive branch.[219] Emperor Augustus brought Pax into the forefront by using her to help bring stability to Rome as a symbol of law, order, and civil peace. By worshiping peace, he hoped to bring that influence to all Roman citizens.

---

215. Evelyn-White, *Theogony of Hesiod.*

216. Daly and Rengel, *Greek & Roman Mythology A to Z*, 102.

217. Dalyand Rengel, *Greek & Roman Mythology A to Z*, 106.

218. Adkins and Adkins, *Handbook to Life in Ancient Rome*, 300.

219. Adkins and Adkins, *Handbook to Life in Ancient Rome.*

# Persephone

**Keyword:** Underworld

**Category:** Greek

**Roman Equivalent:** Proserpina

Daughter of Zeus and Demeter, Persephone represented the hidden aspects of life and the shadow self that remains hidden within the subconscious. As goddess of resurrection and rebirth, Underworld god Hades fell in love with her and kidnapped her.[220] She left the Underworld half of the year, which explains the seasons. Demeter caused the crops to die during fall and winter months when her daughter lived in the Underworld. Eleusinian Mysteries followers worshiped Persephone and celebrated her resurrection from the Underworld through secret rites and initiations.

# Peitho

**Keyword:** Persuasion

**Categories:** Greek, Oceanid

**Roman Equivalent:** Suada

Considered both a goddess and a personification of certain kinds of persuasive sexual seduction, she also embodied political persuasion and rhetoric. Some accounts say she is the wife of the messenger to the gods, Hermes, and others say she is married to Phoroneus, King of Argos. Hesiod says she is the Titan daughter of Tethys and Oceanus, making her an Oceanid. Other accounts say she is Aphrodite's daughter.[221]

# Pheme

**Keyword:** Fame

**Categories:** Roman, Personification

She personified fame. Virgil wrote about her in the *Aeneid* and she was also in Ovid's *Metamorphoses*. As fame, she could embody the energy of popularity or

---

220. Evelyn-White, *Theogony of Hesiod.*
221. Evelyn-White, *Theogony of Hesiod.*

the opposite—that of scandal, and she could mix truth and lies with her multiple eyes, ears, and tongues.[222]

## Philophrosyne

**Keyword:** Kindness

**Categories:** Greek, Charites/Graces

Daughter of Aglaea, the youngest of the Graces, and Hephaestus, she embodies friendliness, kindness, and a welcoming attitude.[223]

## Philotes

**Keyword:** Affection

**Category:** Greek

Flirtatious daughter of Nyx, she is known for friendship, sex, and physical affection. She is one of the daimons, a lesser spirit who animates or guides. She is a friend to all.[224]

## Phoebe

**Keyword:** Prophecy

**Categories:** Greek, Titaness

Phoebe is one of the original Titans, a daughter of Gaia and Uranus. A Moon goddess, her name describes her as "shining." Hesiod describes her as "gold-crowned." As the original owner of the oracle of Delphi, she serves as a goddess of prophecy. Titan Coeus is her consort, and Apollo, Artemis, and Hecate are her grandchildren.[225]

## Pleione

**Keywords:** Mother, Star

**Categories:** Greek, Oceanid

222. Jackson, *Those Who Write for Immortality*.

223. Evelyn-White, *Theogony of Hesiod*.

224. Barcellos, *Friendship and Its Paradoxes*, 122.

225. Evelyn-White, *Theogony of Hesiod*.

Orion followed Pleione through the night sky and fell in love with her. In order to escape him, Zeus turned her daughters into stars. Her consort is Atlas. The mother of the star system Pleiades—Alcyone, Celaeno, Electra, Maia, Merope, Sterope, and Taygete—she was also Hermes's grandmother.

## Polyhymnia

**Keyword:** Hymns

**Categories:** Greek, Muses

Daughter of Zeus and Mnemosyne, she is the muse of hymns, myths, and sacred songs and poetry. She is depicted carrying a scroll and has her index finger over her lips.[226] Cheimarrhoos, son of war god Ares, was her consort.

## Pomona

**Keywords:** Harvest, Fruit

**Categories:** Roman, Personification, Flamines Minores

A temple dedicated in her honor was tended by her priest, Flamen Pomonalis. Pomona personified trees, orchards, and fruit.[227] She helped with success in apple harvests and helped ensure the sweet ideal flavor of the apples. She married seasonal god Vertumnus after he tricked her by disguising himself as a woman.

## Postvorta

**Keywords:** Fertility, Childbirth

**Categories:** Roman, Camenae

She represented the past and helped with childbirth during a breech birth when the babies were born feetfirst. She and all the Camenae are associated with the child's fate.[228] She and her sister, Antevorta, were considered either companions of goddess Carmenta or divine aspects of her where Postvorta represented the past and Antevorta the future.

---

226. Nosselt, *Mythology Greek and Roman*, 53.

227. Monaghan, *Encyclopedia of Goddesses and Heroines: Africa, Eastern Mediterranean, Asia*, xlv.

228. Auset, *Goddess Guide*, 259.

# Proserpina

**Keyword:** Underworld

**Categories:** Roman, Chthonic

**Greek Equivalent:** Persephone

Initially an agricultural goddess associated with wine and fertility, she is Ceres's daughter whose cult originated in southern Italy. She shares a similar mythological story to Greek Persephone. Roman god of the Underworld Rex Infurnus falls in love with her and abducts her, carrying her to the Underworld. Her mother, Ceres, restores her to the upper world for half the year.[229] Proserpina must spend the other half of the year in the Underworld, which gave rise to the seasons and created winter.

# Rhea

**Keyword:** Mother

**Categories:** Greek, Titaness

Rhea is the mother of several important deities, including Zeus, Hestia, Demeter, Hera, and Hades.[230] She is the consort and sister of Cronus, also a Titan, who is not to be confused with Chronos, the personification of time.

# Rhodos

**Keyword:** Rhodes

**Categories:** Greek, Personification

Rhodos is a nymph daughter of Aphrodite and wife of sun god Apollo who told Zeus he wanted an island rising up from the sea. Apollo claimed Rhodos and had seven sons with her and remained with her until Aphrodite cursed him to fall in love with the mortal Babylonian princess, Leucothoe. She is the personification of the Greek Island of Rhodes mentioned in Ovid's *Metamorphosis*, and is symbolized by the rose.[231]

---

229. Spaeth, *Roman Goddess Ceres*, 12.

230. Evelyn-White, *Theogony of Hesiod*.

231. Ovid, *Metamorphosis*, book 4, 204–5; Monaghan, *Encyclopedia of Goddesses and Heroines*, 262.

# Roma

**Keyword:** Rome

**Categories:** Roman, Personification

She personified the power of both the city and state of Rome and served as a tutelary protective goddess for the city. Her divinity also became equated with the divine rule of Rome and the authority of the government to rule over the people. Equated with the rise of the Roman Empire, Emperor Hadrian built a temple in her honor.[232] The image of Roma emblazoned on coins commanded the people to hold her in high esteem and indirectly suggested punishments for any who dare disobey, and as such, she became a piece of propaganda for the government at large.

# Salacia

**Keyword:** Sea

**Categories:** Roman, Personification

**Greek Equivalent:** Amphitrite

She personified the ocean and salt water. In both her Roman and Greek myths, she hid from her soon-to-be-husband, Roman sea god Neptune, before they married to protect her virginity, and he sent a dolphin to find her.[233]

# Salus

**Keywords:** Protection, Healing

**Categories:** Roman, Personification

**Greek Equivalent:** Hygieia

Her name refers to salvation and safety and she is charged with the well-being and physical health of both the state and of individuals. Roman coins featured her image along with the snake of Asclepius, the Greek and Roman god of medicine, who inspired the caduceus.[234] Because of that, some scholars believe

---

232. Monaghan, *Encyclopedia of Goddesses and Heroines: Africa, Eastern Mediterranean, Asia*, 462.

233. Monaghan, *Encyclopedia of Goddesses and Heroines: Africa, Eastern Mediterranean, Asia*, 277.

234. Bispham and Miano, *Gods and Goddesses of Ancient Italy*, 139.

Asclepius is her consort. Each year on August 5, Romans held a ceremony in her honor to encourage the health of the Roman state.

# Securitas

**Keyword:** Security

**Categories:** Roman, Personification

Featured on coins, she personified personal security and safety of the entirety of the Roman Empire.[235] Personifying the Empire meant the Empire itself was worshiped, which would translate into loyal and obedient actions on the part of the citizenry.

# Selene

**Keyword:** Moon

**Categories:** Greek, Personification

**Roman Equivalent:** Luna

Daughter of Theia and Hyperion, Selene is the personification of the moon. Her name refers to the light and brightness of the moon.[236] She is seen driving her chariot across heaven during the night. The mortal shepherd Endymion is her consort.

# Spes

**Keywords:** Hope, Fertility, Abundance

**Categories:** Roman, Personification

**Greek Equivalent:** Elpis

Featured on coins and in temples, Spes personified hope and assisted with the emperor's ability to ensure blessed conditions.[237] Several temples were erected in her honor to hope for favorable outcomes. She embodied hope for the Roman Republic and also appeared in the imperial cult dedicated to family members of the emperor. Spes Augusta had a specific tie to the well-being and favor of Emperor Augustus.

---

235. Adkins and Adkins, *Handbook to Life in Ancient Rome.*

236. Evelyn-White, *Theogony of Hesiod.*

237. Adkins and Adkins, *Handbook to Life in Ancient Rome.*

## Sterope

**Keyword:** Star

**Categories:** Greek, Nymph, Personification

She was another nymph and one of the personifications of one of the stars in the Pleiades star system and daughter of Atlas and the Oceanid Pleione (collectively called the Atlantides).[238] Her consorts are Ares and King Oenomaus.

## Strenua

**Keywords:** Strength, New Year, Time

**Category:** Roman

Strenua was likely a Sabine goddess adopted by the Romans to commemorate the New Year. She became the embodiment of purification, physical and mental strength, and well-being. Beginning in 153 BCE, Romans celebrated Strenua through a festival in her honor.[239]

## Suada

**Keywords:** Fertility, Marriage

**Categories:** Roman, Personification

**Greek Equivalent:** Peitho

She personified persuasion, especially in the realm of sexual influence and seduction, and for that reason, she was associated with Venus. Plutarch said she was one of the five deities needed to ensure a successful marriage, along with Hera, Artemis, Aphrodite, and Zeus.[240]

## Taygete

**Keyword:** Star

**Categories:** Greek, Nymph, Personification

---

238. Blacket, *Researches into the Lost Histories of America*, 215.

239. Fowler, *Roman Festivals of the Period of the Republic*.

240. Cole Babbitt, *Greek Questions of Plutarch*, 8–9.

Another personification of the stars in the Pleiades star system, Taygete was daughter of Atlas and the Oceanid Pleione (collectively called the Atlantides).[241] When Zeus pursued her, she asked Artemis to intervene, so she turned Taygete into a doe with golden horns. Taygete became the personification of that deer called a Ceryneian Hind, a mythological creature pursued by Hercules.

## Tellus Mater

**Keywords:** Earth Mother

**Category:** Roman

**Greek Equivalent:** Gaia

The Roman counterpart to Gaia, Tellus (also known as Terra) is the consort of Caelus and the embodiment and personification of the earth and fertility. She is a primordial deity considered among the most important goddesses in the Roman pantheon collectively known as Di Selecti. She is agricultural in nature and assists Ceres with crops and harvests.[242]

## Terpsichore

**Keyword:** Dance

**Categories:** Greek, Muses

Daughter of Zeus and Mnemosyne, she is the muse of dancing and chorus who carried a lyre.[243] She is a mother of some of the sirens. She had several consorts, including Apollo, Achelous, and Ares.

## Tethys

**Keyword:** Rivers

**Categories:** Greek, Titaness

Divine Mother of the rivers and streams, Tethys is mother of the three thousand Oceanids.[244] In Homer's *Iliad*, he suggests that Tethys was the mother of all instead of Gaia. Oceanus was her consort and the father of the Oceanids.

---

241. Blacket, *Researches into the Lost Histories of America*, 215.

242. Spaeth, *Roman Goddess Ceres*, 34, 118.

243. Nosselt, *Mythology Greek and Roman*, 53.

244. Evelyn-White, *Theogony of Hesiod*.

# Thalia

**Keywords:** Abundance, Comedy

**Categories:** Greek, Charites/Graces, Muses, Nerid, Nymph

There are several goddesses named Thalia in the Greek pantheon, including one of the Charites/Graces. Thalia was a consort of Apollo who embodied festivities and abundant banquets. She was also a muse and a daughter of Zeus and Mnemosyne who inspired pastoral poetry and comedy and carried a tambourine in one hand, a shepherd hook in the other, and had a comic mask at her feet.[245] In some sources, Thalia is a Nereid, one of the daughters of Nereus and Doris, and finally, she is a nymph daughter of Hephaestus—a vegetation goddess.

# Theia

**Keyword:** Sun

**Categories:** Greek, Titaness

She is a Titaness, consort of Hyperion, and mother of the sun Helios, moon Selene, and dawn Eos.[246] There is also an Oceanid by the same name who became mother of the Ceracopes, mischievous forest creatures who once stole Hercules's weapons.

# Themis

**Keyword:** Justice

**Categories:** Greek, Titaness, Personification

A consort of Zeus, she personifies law and order, customs, and traditions. She embodies fairness in justice. According to Hesiod, she is mother of the Horae, Fates, and several other deities, including Eunomia, Dike, and Erine.[247]

# Thyone

**Keywords:** Earth Mother

**Categories:** Greek, Olympian

**Also Known As:** Semele

---

245. Nosselt, *Mythology Greek and Roman*, 53.

246. Evelyn-White, *Theogony of Hesiod*.

247. Evelyn-White, *Theogony of Hesiod*.

The mortal Semele served as a priestess of Zeus, who seduced her and became her consort. Jealous Hera befriended her and told Semele that Zeus was a god, but she didn't believe Hera and made Zeus reveal himself. Since no mortal could look at a god, Semele burst into flames and died after giving birth to Dionysus, god of wine and libation.[248] Dionysus rescued his mother from Hades and she became the goddess Thyone, and from then on resided on Mount Olympus.

## Trivia

**Keywords:** Harvest, Fertility, Protection

**Category:** Roman

**Greek Equivalent:** Hecate

Trivia is likely an early form of goddess Diana who guarded the crossroads.[249] She was an agricultural deity mentioned by the poet Virgil. She could also be used in later times as a descriptive term used for the Diana that refers to her multiple forms as guardian of gateways and thresholds, including the Underworld and crossroads.

## Tyche

**Keyword:** Fortune

**Categories:** Greek, Oceanid

**Roman Equivalent:** Fortuna

Daughter of Tethys and Oceanus, she brought positive messages to people and helped with things that were out of one's control and assisted with the overall prosperity of a city.[250]

## Urania

**Keyword:** Heavens

**Categories:** Greek, Muses

Daughter of Zeus and Mnemosyne, she is the muse of astronomy who holds a globe in her left hand and a staff in her right hand, which she uses to point

248. Evelyn-White, *Theogony of Hesiod*.
249. Monaghan, *Encyclopedia of Goddesses and Heroines: Africa, Eastern Mediterranean, Asia*, 270.
250. Evelyn-White, *Theogony of Hesiod*.

to the stars.[251] Her name means "Heavenly" and Hesiod described her as divine in form.[252] Later she became associated with Christian writings. She had several consorts, including Apollo, Hermes, and Amphimarus.

## Venus

**Keyword:** Love

**Categories:** Roman, Dii Consentes, Ancestral

**Greek Equivalent:** Aphrodite

As goddess of love and desire associated with prosperity, victory, sexuality, and fertility, Venus became among the most widely revered goddesses in Rome. Julius Caesar considered Venus the ancestor of the Julian Dynasty and emblazoned her face on coins.[253] Several versions of Venus were adopted to help Romans with various aspects of love, victory, and success. She also represented physical sexuality and the lure of worldly possessions and materialism. She is related to Cupid, who some say is her son by Mars, while Ovid states the Cupids are twins who represent both the kind and cruel aspects of love. Venus became jealous of the beautiful princess Psyche and wanted Cupid to punish her.[254]

## Veritas

**Keyword:** Truth

**Categories:** Roman, Personification

**Greek Equivalent:** Aletheia

She is truth personified. Daughter of Saturn, she is considered virginal but also appears naked, holding a mirror to represent total truth in transparency. Romans valued truth as a prized virtue.

---

251. Nosselt, *Mythology Greek and Roman*, 53.

252. Evelyn-White, *Theogony of Hesiod*.

253. Art Institute of Chicago, "Denarius (Coin) Depicting Goddess Venus."

254. Monaghan, *Encyclopedia of Goddesses and Heroines: Africa, Eastern Mediterranean, Asia*, 276.

## Vesta

**Keyword:** Hearth

**Categories:** Roman, Dii Consentes

**Greek Equivalent:** Hestia

Virgin goddess of home and hearth, Vesta took a thirty-nine-year vow of chastity giving rise to the priestesses called Vestal Virgins, who observed thirty years of celibacy. Vesta protected the home and kept the hearth fires burning. The Roman holiday Vestalia celebrating Vesta occurred between June 7and 15. In the home, she is personified as the fire in the hearth.[255] Members of the Roman household had to take great care to never let the hearth fire go out. To do so would be an ill omen as the fire represented the health and well-being of the entire family.

## Victoria

**Keyword:** Victory

**Categories:** Roman, Personification

**Greek Equivalent:** Nike

Like her Greek counterpart, Nike, Victoria personified the essence of victory. Romans had several temples in her honor, and she became widely honored by generals returning from successful military campaigns. In *City of God*, Saint Augustine described her assistance with foreign injustice and bringing wars to a successful ending.[256]

## Volumna

**Keywords:** Childhood, Protection

**Categories:** Roman, Nixi

In *City of God*, Saint Augustine mentioned her and her counterpart, Volumnus. A deity who protected the nursery and helped children behave, she also

---

255. Adkins and Adkins, *Handbook to Life in Ancient Rome*, 273.
256. Dods, *Works of Aurelius Augustine*.

helped people receive what Augustine called "good things," which may be an expansion into more areas of existence beyond children.[257]

## Voluptas

**Keywords:** Pleasure and Delight

**Category:** Roman

The daughter of Cupid and Psyche, Voluptas took charge of human sensual pleasure to help drive away unhappiness in life.[258] She is associated with consorts Mars or Vulcan.

## Summing Up

Like many early cultures, Greeks and Romans didn't use the term *religion*. Daily life involved interacting with the gods and recognizing the divinity in all things. This philosophy meant the Roman and Greek pantheons included deities who represented every single thing in both the known and the unseen worlds. Groups of deities were named as the personal embodiments of physical phenomena, and often their names were sprinkled around with other groupings, making the Greek/Roman pantheon a complex and enthralling study.

With so many colorful characters and the profound influence the Greeks and Romans had on Western civilization, it's no wonder these goddesses continue to mesmerize us to the present day.

## Recommended Reading

*Practicing Greek Polytheism Today* by Tony Mierzwicki

*Roman Gods & Goddesses* by William White

*Encyclopedia of Greek and Roman Mythology* by Luke and Monica Roman

---

257. Dods, *Works of Aurelius Augustine.*
258. Coulter and Turner, *Encyclopedia of Ancient Deities*, 501.

*Chapter Four*

# Mesoamerican and Inca Goddesses

*Mesoamerica* is a term used by archaeologists to describe several cultures within the region of Central America with shared societal functions, including religious beliefs and heritage.[259] The Olmec culture is believed to be the earliest Mesoamerican civilization, dating from 1200 to 300 BCE.[260] The early Olmec people left ten stone carvings of masculine godlike figures who appear to be clearly male or early forms of the common jaguars or feathered serpent deities who would come to eventually dominate the later cultures in that region. Unfortunately, they left behind no written records of their practices, so scholars are left to wonder and speculate, and because their deities are masculine and we know so little about them, we will explore some of the later people who inhabited this region who worshiped the divine feminine and goddesses.

## Mesoamerican Cosmology

After the Olmecs vanished, the later ancient Indigenous people who lived in Mexico and Central and South America included the Zapotec, Maya, Aztecs, and Inca.

259. Witschey and Brown, *Historical Dictionary of Mesoamerica*, ix.
260. Bernal, *Olmec World*, 127.

## *Zapotec 500 BCE–900 CE*

The Zapotec civilization, known as Cloud People, became the first in Mesoamerica to develop a calendar and created an advanced civilization at Monte Albán in the modern state of Oaxaca, Mexico. Like the Olmec, the Zapotec people worshiped deities, and their pantheon included a few goddesses whose names we know because of the testimony given in an Inquisition called the Balsalobre Trials, which took place in the Sola Township between 1653 and 1657. At that time, the church wanted to put a stop to idolatry and completely wipe out the religious expressions of the local people.[261] Friar Diego Luis was tried in 1635 for performing divination relating to maize, childbirth, and funeral rituals. Later in 1653, Luis came under scrutiny again for continuing practices of idolatry. During his later trial, he gave damning testimony against everyone he helped with various offerings to the gods and goddesses. The Church also demanded that Friar Luis provide the names of the gods and goddesses worshiped at that time.

## *Maya Period 250 CE–950 CE*

According to the important Maya manuscript of myths and legends called *Popol Vuh*, the world began in darkness with the only light surrounding three serpent gods covered in feathers. When these serpents met with the group known as the Heart of Heaven, the six of them created the world through sound when two of the serpent gods shouted the name Earth. Waters receded, revealing rolling mountains. Lush green jungles filled with trees. They created Spirits of the animals, including jaguars, serpents, and deer, before finally attempting to make human beings. All life, including plants, animals, and insects, came before humans, who were the final creation that arose from corn.[262]

Creating people wasn't easy. They first tried forming humans from mud, but found that they melted away. Next, they tried wood, but felt these new beings lacked souls, so they became the monkeys. Finally, they molded humans from corn and succeeded making the corn people, ancestors of the Maya.

The Hero Twins, an important part of Maya cosmology, represent many of the dual forces of nature, including the sun and moon. In many twin mythologies, the twins are male and female; however, in Maya cosmology, these twins were

---

261. Tavarez, *Invisible War*, 121.
262. Spence, *Popol Vuh*.

both males. That is not surprising considering most deities in the Maya pantheon are males.

Another bad actor, Friar Diego de Landa, purposefully burned twenty-seven sacred Maya books and destroyed some five thousand idols. Because of his destruction and lack of respect, the Maya were needlessly deprived of their cultural heritage and left with very little to go on concerning the Maya history and myth. Friar de Landa wrote a book describing the Yucatan during this time as a way of apology; however, the wrong cannot be righted when any sacred object is destroyed.[263] Today, only four codices remain:

1. **Dresden Codex:** Severely water damaged during World War II, the codex is seventy-eight pages of colored drawings that were discovered in Dresden, Germany, and are now housed in the Saxon Museum.

2. **Madrid Codex:** Now housed in Madrid, Spain, at the Museum of the Americas. Also called the Codice Trocortesiano.

3. **Paris Codex:** France acquired this twenty-two-page document in 1832, which is now housed in the national library in Paris.

4. **Grolier Codex:** Many scholars consider Grolier a fake, so it is rarely referenced. The document is currently housed in a private club called The Grolier Club in New York City.

The codices provide scholars with much of what is known about the Maya deities, although, sadly, many of the documents are in poor condition.

### Aztec Civilization 1345 CE–1521 CE

Before discussing the Aztecs, I must briefly mention their predecessors, the Toltecs. The Toltec civilization only lasted from 900 CE until 1150 CE, and the Aztecs held them in such high regard, they adopted many of their deities and customs, beginning with the mighty feathered serpent god Quetzalcoatl, among others. Many Aztec deities likely originated in the earlier period. Documents of Toltec deities are rare but overlap the Aztec.

The nomadic Aztecs, who called themselves the Mexica, descended from the Nahua people, a classification that includes all early people who spoke the Nahua

---

263. Gates, *Friar Diego de Landa's Yucatan.*

language. *Azteca* means "crane people." Legend says they migrated into Mexico from a place called Aztlan in the thirteenth century. Nobody knows if this place was real or not, so Aztlan remains a myth. In 1325 CE, the wandering Aztecs followed their war god Huitzilopochtli to an island on Lake Texcoco where they saw an eagle perched atop a cactus eating a snake. Interpreting this as a good omen, they founded Tenochtitlan, now known as modern-day Mexico City, on that exact spot. The key to their success had to do with the complex irrigation systems they built around the city by creating manmade islands.

The Aztecs became known for human sacrifice and bloodletting at their incredible Templo Mayor complex in what is now located in the center of Mexico City. When Cortés arrived in 1519 to try to seize gold and power, he eventually succeeded in founding what became the modern Mexico City by 1521.[264] One of his main motivators for doing so had to do with putting an end to what he perceived as the barbaric practices of human sacrifice he witnessed there and establishing the Catholic religion.

Much of what we know about Aztec goddesses and mythology came from information found in several codices:

1. **Codex Borbonicus:** Created after the Spanish conquest by the Aztec priests.

2. **Codex Borgia:** Named after Italian cardinal Stefano Borgia, who owned the manuscript before the Vatican Library acquired the documents after his death.

3. **Codex Fejérváry-Mayer:** Rare Aztec manuscript that survived the Spanish conquest.

4. **Codex Florentine:** Compilation of twelve books by Franciscan friar Bernardino de Sahagun.

5. **Codex Rios:** Italian translation of the Codex Telleriano-Remensis features a divinatory calendar and history of the Aztecs.

The Aztec civilization came to a final end in 1521 when Tenochtitlan fell to Hernán Cortés. The mighty empire eventually succumbed to Cortés's army due to the Spaniards' advanced military technology and the introduction of smallpox,

---

264. Townsend, *Fifth Sun*, 27, 43, 131.

which wiped out thousands of Indigenous people who could not fend off European diseases.

## Inca 1400 CE–1533 CE

The mighty Inca civilization began very late in the timeline of Andean culture, which dates back to 20,000 BCE during a period of hunter-gatherers and evolved over time into the Inca state and empire, which thrived in Peru until 1533 CE when the Spaniards conquered the region.[265] To date, their vast empire remains the largest ever within the Americas and is filled with a rich and fascinating cultural history that enthralls spiritual seekers. Like many early cultures, gods and goddesses were developed to explain the natural world and help people overcome challenges with everything from food to harvests and weather.

## Mesoamerican and Inca Goddesses

Without archeological discovery, very little would be known about any civilization, and that is especially true with the Mesoamerican and Inca deities. The codices discovered in both cultures proved invaluable. One bit of information learned by studying these texts is that the Maya had a special prefix to designate males and females. The words *Ix*, *Xku*, and *Ku* are common designators for goddess names.[266]

## Ah Uaynih

**Keyword:** Sleep

**Category:** Maya

A goddess who was both male and female, Ah Uaynih assisted the god of death in putting people to sleep. The male form of this deity brought eternal slumber to women, while the female aspect assisted men in death.[267]

---

265. Rostworowski de Diez Canseco and Iceland, *History of the Inca Realm*, 3–5; Jones, *Complete Illustrated History of the Inca Empire*.

266. Thompson, *Maya History and Religion*, xxxii.

267. Thompson, *Maya History and Religion*, 326.

## Ah-Wink-Ir-Masa

**Keyword:** Nature

**Category:** Maya

She protected wild animals and had a particular affinity to deer and ensuring hunters took only what was needed to sustain life in a spirit of honoring the animal for their sacrifice.[268]

## Akhushtal

**Keyword:** Childbirth

**Category:** Maya

She is a fertility goddess, which can refer either to crops and food or to children. *Akna* meant "our mother," so for that reason, she seems more closely linked to childbirth and assists with everything from conception through helping midwives with the birth.[269]

## Atlatonan

**Keyword:** Earth, Water

**Category:** Aztec

**Also Known As:** Atlatonin

She was an earth, fertility, and water goddess whose name means "she who shines the water." She is associated with corn god Centeōtl.[270] Combining these three critical elements into her supernatural abilities suggests she was primarily concerned with agriculture and the successful harvests of food.

## Axomamma

**Keywords:** Harvest, Fertility, Potatoes

**Category:** Inca

One of the daughters of the primary goddess Pachamama, Axomamma was a fertility goddess whose name meant "potato mother." She personified and became

---

268. Holland, *Holland's Grimoire of Magical Correspondence*, 24, 193.

269. Auset, *Goddess Guide*, 3, 95.

270. Bancroft, *Native Races of the Pacific States of North America*, 423.

a sort of protective tutelary deity for the potato. Potatoes were a vital source of food for the Inca, so of course they prayed for good harvests by worshiping the goddess and the potato itself.[271] Axomamma helped Inca cultivate crops rather than simply relying on potatoes grown out in the wild. Deformed potatoes were often worshiped as the embodiment of Axomamma.

## Cavillaca

**Keyword:** Sea

**Category:** Inca

The moon god Coniraya wanted to mate with this beautiful virgin goddess, but she turned him down, so he transformed himself into a bird and injected semen into a fruit. Cavillaca unwittingly ate the fruit, became pregnant, and gave birth to a son.[272] She demanded her baby's father show himself, and when he did, she felt so ashamed that she took the baby to the coast and jumped into the sea, transforming them both into stone.

## Chalchiuhtlicue

**Keywords:** Protection, Mother, Fertility, Water

**Categories:** Aztec, Codex Borbonicus

**Also Known As:** Acuecueyotl, Acuecueyotlcihuatl

Aztec creation myths described five suns, and Chalchiuhtlicue reigned during the period of the fourth sun. Tlaloc the rain god was her consort. She swallowed the sun and moon and served as a protective force for women and children. Chalchiuhtlicue was mentioned in relation to midwifery and blessing ceremonies for children.[273] Water was seen as a giver of life, and she personified bodies of water, including rivers, oceans, and streams and the eastern direction.

## Chantico

**Keywords:** Hearth, Fire, Fertility

**Categories:** Aztec, Codex Rios

---

271. Cock-Starkey, *Lore of the Wild*, 49.

272. Urton, *Inca Myths*, 64–5.

273. Bancroft, *Native Races of the Pacific States of North America*, 119, 120.

**Also Known As:** Quaxoloti, Cantico, Chiconaui, Chicunaui Itzcuintli, Papaloxaual

She ruled over fires and the hearth and was called "she who dwells in the house." She is associated with fertility, is patroness of stonecutters, and is said to be the creator of jewelry.[274] In Aztec myth, Chantico broke a religious fast by eating fish with paprika and became cursed and turned into a dog known as Nine Dogs. Montezuma used a Chantico idol to curse Hernán Cortés. She is known for associations with gold and is at times called yellow woman.

## Chaska

**Keywords:** Dawn, Twilight, Dusk, Venus

**Categories:** Inca, Personification

Gorgeous virginal goddess of dawn, twilight, and dusk, she personified the planet Venus as the morning star, one of the brightest in the night sky.[275]

## Chen

**Keyword:** Homosexuality

**Category:** Maya

Chen is sometimes depicted as male and sometimes as female. A counselor of royalty who encouraged homosexual partnerships for the emperor's descendants, she also dealt with magic, maize, and personal power. Drawings in Naj Tunich Cave in Guatemala depict males engaged in sexual conduct, which convinced some scholars that prehistoric Maya embraced homosexuality. The cave drawings depict males and other figures dressed as females who lack breasts, which may also suggest that they depict men dressed as women for ritual purposes.[276]

## Chicomecoatl

**Keywords:** Fertility, Harvest

**Categories:** Aztec, Codex Borgia

**Also Known As:** Chalchiuhcihuatl, Chicomeccatl, Xilonen

---

274. Kroger and Granziera, *Aztec Goddesses and Christian Madonnas*, 33.

275. Rowe, *Inca Culture at the Time of the Spanish Conquest*, 295.

276. Stone, *Images from the Underworld*, 5.

Consort of Centeōtl the corn god, she personified the life-giving corn or maize and helped with agriculture by creating an abundant and plentiful harvest, and if crops were poor or lacking, she took responsibility.[277] Symbolized by an ear of corn and mentioned in the Codex Borgia, she carries flowers or a sunflower shield and holds a dual function as both the patroness who brings food as well as the wicked force who denies the people by creating poor harvests. Priests engaged in human sacrifice every September to appease her.

# Chimalman

**Keyword:** Mother

**Category:** Aztec

One of the deities worshiped by the Toltecs along with Quetzalcoatl and Huitzilopochtli, she is Quetzalcoatl's mother. Chimalman's name translated to "shield hand" and comes from a legend about her consort Mixcoatl. After rejecting him initially, he shot five arrows at her, which she caught with her bare hands.[278] She is also said to have come from the ancient Aztec homeland Aztlan.

# Chirakan-Ixmucane

**Keyword:** Creation

**Categories:** Maya, Primordial

She served as one of the thirteen deities who created humans according to the Popol Vul. When four gods who created the world split into more deities, she was created.[279]

# Cihuacōātl

**Keywords:** Fertility, Childbirth

**Category:** Aztec

**Also Known As:** Ciuacoatl, Quilaztli

---

277. Aguilar-Moreno, *Handbook to Life in the Aztec World*, 197.

278. Carrasco and Sessions, *Cave, City, and Eagle's Nest*, 175, 381.

279. Coulter and Turner, *Encyclopedia of Ancient Deities*.

Fertility and midwifery goddess called Our Mother and Princess is associated with sweat baths given to pregnant women.[280] Her consort was Quilaztli and she was Mixcoatl's mother. She created human beings by mixing their bones with the blood of Quetzalcoatl. The term *Cihuacōātl* also refers to an official in the government who advised the Aztec emperor. She ensured the victory and success of the state.

## Citlālicue

**Keyword:** Stars

**Category:** Aztec

She was a primordial creation goddess. Known as Star Skirt, she and her consort, Citlalatonac, meaning "where the stars shine," created all the stars in the night sky, including the Milky Way.[281]

## Coatlicue

**Keywords:** Mother, Fertility

**Categories:** Aztec, Codex Florentine, and Codex Rios

Coatlicue is an agricultural fertility goddess who feeds on corpses and is known for wearing a snake skirt. She is depicted with sagging breasts to suggest the feeding and nourishing of her hundreds of children. She is consort of Mixcoatl, god of the Milky Way. She is mother of war god Huitzilopochtli and his sister, Coyolxāuhqui, as well as four hundred star gods. She became pregnant when a ball of feathers fell on her, causing her to give birth to Huitzilopochtli.[282]

## Colel Cab

**Keyword:** Bees

**Category:** Maya

Colel Cab, Mistress of the Earth as she was known, protected bees and their hives and ensured abundant honey production. The word *colel* means "our lady

---

280. Thompson, *Maya History and Religion*, 117.

281. Milbrath, *Star Gods of the Maya*, 275.

282. Read and Gonzales, *Mesoamerican Mythology*, 150.

the moon goddess," and *cab* denotes "the beehive."[283] She also enhanced the sweetness of the honey. Even in modern times, beekeepers invoke her to help keep hives safe and productive.

## Copacati

**Keyword:** Protection

**Categories:** Inca, Personification

She acted as tutelary guardian and personification of the sacred Lake Titicaca believed to be the origin of the universe. According to some accounts, a carved stone Copacati idol, a fierce figure surrounded by snakes, sat atop a hill near the lake for protection.[284]

## Coyolxāuhqui

**Keywords:** Moon, War, Sacrifice

**Category:** Aztec

She is the moon goddess. She is Coatlicue's daughter and became so incensed when her mother became impregnated with war god Huitzilopochtli by a ball of feathers, she murdered Coatlicue and cut off her head. In retaliation, Huitzilopochtli burst forth from Coatlicue's womb, cut off Coyolxāuhqui's head, and hurled it into the sky, where it became the moon. Because of her violent history, she is associated with sacrifices and war.[285]

## Goddess "I"

**Keyword:** Water

**Categories:** Maya, Dresden, Madrid Codex

Goddess I has a youthful appearance and is pictured in the Dresden Codex with a serpent on her head. Scholar Paul Schelhas named her in 1904 using the letter system and called her a water goddess, a description that has remained to this day.[286] She cares for bodies of water such as springs, wells, and oceans.

---

283. Macriand Vail, *New Catalog of Maya Hieroglyphs*, 97.

284. Besom, *Of Summits and Sacrifice*, 77.

285. Read and Gonzales, *Mesoamerican Mythology*, 150, 154, 156.

286. Tremain, "Patterns in the Dresden Codex," 6–12.

Like the numbered gods of the Olmec, her name is unknown. She is old and has claws for feet. She has the crossbones of a death god and stands near water, which means she may deal with floods and may be related astronomically to the waxing and full moons.[287]

## Goddess "O"

**Keywords:** Old Woman

**Categories:** Maya, Madrid Manuscript

She is the second goddess identified by a letter in the Schellhas-Zimmerman-Taube classification of Maya gods. She is only mentioned once in the Madrid Manuscript and is described as an old lady because of the drawings around her eyes, which suggest advanced age. She may also be an aged healer and practitioner of divination.[288]

## Huixtocihuatl

**Keywords:** Purification, Salt

**Category:** Aztec

Patron deity for the victims of ritual sacrifice, she is associated with salt and water cleansing rituals and purification rites performed before sacrificial ceremonies. She was the banished elder sister of the rain gods, and salt makers worshiped her.[289]

## Ītzpāpālōtl

**Keyword:** Mother

**Category:** Aztec

Mixcoatl's mother and ruler of the heavenly paradise realm called Tamoanchan, she guarded those who succumbed to infant mortality and was known as the Obsidian Butterfly because she would appear as a clawed butterfly or bat.[290] Women who underwent childbirth were viewed as courageous and equivalent to men going into battle, so when mothers or babies died, they received a special

---

287. Milbrath, *Star Gods of the Maya*, 295.

288. Taube, *Major Gods of Ancient Yucatan*, 68, 103.

289. Kroger and Granziera, *Aztec Goddesses and Christian Madonnas*, 52.

290. Carrasco and Sessions, *Cave, City, and Eagle's Nest*, 12.

seat in heaven. In addition to her helpful qualities, Ītzpāpālōtl was known as a *cihuateteo*, a malicious spirit of a woman who died in childbirth who could also shape-shift into a doe to seduce men.

## Ixazalvoh

**Keywords:** Divine Mother

**Category:** Maya

She invented weaving and presided over childbirth, fertility, healing powers, divination, and oracles and gave sacred messages to people as the goddess of female sexuality.[291]

## Ixchel

**Keywords:** Moon, Mother, Fertility

**Categories:** Maya, Dresden Codex

**Also Known As:** Ix Chebel Yax, Ix Chel

This jaguar goddess may be the same deity as Goddess "O" mentioned in the Schellhas-Zimmerman-Taube classification of codical deities and the Dresden Codex. She is a fertility goddess who had several consorts including Voltan, the earth and drum god, Itzamna, and Chac. She assists with fertility, pregnancy, and marriage and served as a protector of children, midwifery, medicine, and helping women become pregnant. Conflated with Virgin Mary, she is referred to as grandmother. She is also a rain goddess shown as a youthful beauty or an old plump woman. Isla de Mujeres (Island of Women) near Cozumel had many Ixchel statues. De Landa described her as the goddess of making children. In some depictions in pottery and art, she is seen as a powerful old woman and is sometimes interpreted as an aging lunar deity.[292]

## Ix Tab

**Keyword:** Suicide

**Categories:** Maya, Dresden Codex

---

291. Coulter and Turner, *Encyclopedia of Ancient Deities*, 245.
292. Read and Gonzales, *Mesoamerican Mythology*, 199, 209.

Suicide goddess pictured in the Dresden Codex as a female hanging from a rope in the sky.[293] She accompanied people who hanged themselves on their journey into the afterlife. The Maya believed self-inflicted death by suicide was honorable and doing so helped you gain immediate passage to the afterlife. Upon such death, these divine souls would be greeted by Ix Tab, who would take them into paradise to live in eternity with other special souls, including those who died in childbirth, individuals slain in battle, victims of sacrifice, or those who perished on the ball court.

## Iztaccihuatl

**Keyword:** Mountain

**Category:** Aztec

Iztaccihuatl was the personification of a dormant volcano with snowcapped peaks. According to legends about the volcano, Princess Iztaccihuatl fell in love with a warrior named Popocatépetl. When someone falsely told her he had been killed in battle, she died of a broken heart. When he returned and learned of her passing, he also died of grief. They were both covered in snow and transformed into the beautiful volcanic mountains that stand together for eternity to this day. The peaks are in the Iztaccíhuatl-Popocatépetl National Park in Mexico.[294]

## Malinalxochitl

**Keyword:** Snakes, Scorpions, Insects

**Category:** Aztec

A sorcery goddess, she is sister of Huitzilopochtli and goddess of scorpions and insects that inhabit the desert. She helped repel the insects for her loyal followers, but could turn the deadly creatures against her enemies if provoked. Huitzilopochtli cast a spell to strand her and her followers on a hill so she could no longer disturb the people. She then established a town called Malinalco where even today the people are said to be well versed in spells.[295]

---

293. Sharerand Traxler, *Ancient Maya*, 744.

294. Aldana, *Mexico's Famous Archaeological Relics*.

295. Aguilar-Moreno, *Handbook to Life in the Aztec World*, 33.

# Mama Allpa

**Keyword:** Fertility

**Category:** Inca

The Great Nourisher, she is a fertility goddess associated with a successful harvest and agriculture. She is also linked to childcare and as such is always shown with multiple breasts to embody the idea of feeding many and caring for the people.[296]

# Mama Cocha

**Keywords:** Sea, Rain, Water, Mother

**Category:** Inca

The consort and sister of creator god Viracocha, she was a sea goddess who helped protect sailors and fisherman. She is a water and rain goddess associated with the sacred Lake Titicaca.[297]

# Mama Coca

**Keywords:** Coca Leaves

**Categories:** Inca, Personification

As a sacred plant to the Inca, *Mama Coca* is a term used to describe the plant itself, which was worshiped as a goddess. Inca ruler Mayta Capac called his wife Mama Coca, which was considered a high distinction and honor.[298] In myth, she had multiple lovers who tore her into pieces. One of her parts would emerge as a coca leaf plant. The Inca believed the coca leaves helped improve their health and happiness, and the plant is still widely used today.

# Mama Ocllo

**Keywords:** Mother, Fertility

**Categories:** Inca, Primordial

**Also Known As:** Mama Occlo

---

296. Coulter and Turner, *Encyclopedia of Ancient Deities*, 303.

297. Coulter and Turner, *Encyclopedia of Ancient Deities*, 304.

298. Mortimer, *Peru*, 152.

As the first woman, she is a fertility and domestic goddess, sun god Inti's daughter who assisted women with the home and hearth, domestic bliss, marriage, and spinning and weaving. She and her consort and brother, Manco Capac, were primordial deities who created the world beginning in Cuzco, Peru.[299]

## Mama Quilla

**Keywords:** Mother Moon

**Category:** Inca

Daughter of the god Viracocha, Mama Quilla became consort and counterpart of her brother, sun god Inti. She presided over all aspects of fertility, including successful marriage, regulating menstrual cycles, and childbirth.[300] Numerous festivals were held in her honor.

## Mama Quinoa

**Keywords:** Harvest, Grain, Fertility

**Categories:** Inca, Personification

She personified quinoa and the Inca worshiped her to ensure bountiful harvests of their precious grain. People made figures and dressed them in women's clothing as ritual objects to pay homage to the crops. To this day, quinoa remains an important part of the diet for people living in the Andes.[301]

## Mama Wayra

**Keywords:** Mother, Air

**Categories:** Inca, Personification

The word *wayra* denotes different kinds of winds—some fierce and dangerous, and others mild. One example is *uraña* wind, a cold and malevolent force said to cause illness.[302] Mama Wayra is the personified wind and air who protected people and birds from the destructive aspects of the wind and purified the world.

---

299. Coulter and Turner, *Encyclopedia of Ancient Deities*, 304.

300. Coulter and Turner, *Encyclopedia of Ancient Deities*, 304.

301. Small, *Top 100 Food Plants*, 438.

302. Bolin, *Rituals of Respect*, 20, 234.

# Mayahuel

**Keywords:** Maguey, Fertility

**Categories:** Aztec, Codex Borgia, Codex Borbonicus

Mentioned in Codex Borgia and Codex Borbonicus, she is the personification of the maguey plant used to produce pulque, the alcoholic beverage.[303] She and her husband, fertility god Patecatl, assisted in healing with the native plants.

# Mictēcacihuātl

**Keyword:** Protection

**Categories:** Aztec, Chthonic

Known as Lady of the Dead, she watches over the bones of the dead and leads festivals in honor of the deceased. These festivities eventually evolved into Dia de las Muertos (Day of the Dead). Mictlan is the lowest level of the Underworld that she and her consort, Mictlāntēcutli, king of Mictlan, rule over. Legend says she was sacrificed shortly after her birth. She is associated with Santa Muerte, the dressed skeleton figures people display during the festivals.[304]

# Nohuichana

**Keywords:** Fertility and Harvest

**Category:** Zapotec

In the written testimony during the Balsalobre trials, Friar Luis stated that locals made offerings to Nohuichana for a bountiful and successful fishing trip. A fertility goddess, she also presided over the rivers and water sources, protected children, and served as an agricultural deity who presided over maize. Her counterpart was the primary god Pichanagobeche.[305]

# Oxomoco

**Keyword:** Mother

**Categories:** Aztec, Popol Vuh, Florentine Codex, Primordial

---

303. Kroger and Granziera, *Aztec Goddesses and Christian Madonnas*, 12.

304. Rollin, *Santa Muerte*, 27.

305. Herzfeld and Lenhart, *Semiotics 1980*, 100–1.

A primordial being who emerged from the void as half of the first human couple. Oxomoco and her consort, Cipactonal, are equated to the Aztec version of Adam and Eve. Created by the first four gods, Huitzilopochtli, Quetzalcoatl, Tezcatlipoca, and Camaxtli, some scholars consider Oxomoco to be the male half of this couple, but more evidence suggests Oxomoco is female.[306] The couple is associated with the calendar and astrology as well as the night.

## Pachamama

**Keywords:** Lady Earth, Fertility

**Categories:** Inca, Personification

**Also Known As:** Mama Pacha

Pachamama is the personification and protector of Earth or Mother Nature. She is also responsible for harvests and ensuring abundance from the fields.[307] She personifies the earth in elemental form. As the most important Inca goddess and Divine Mother, she is still worshiped to this day. Most Pachamama ceremonies happen in August, but some occur once a month. Rituals involve drinking matéor burning items to ward off unwanted influences. She can take the form of a dragon and cause earthquakes. Pacha Kamaq, the creator of the world, was her consort.

## Sachamama

**Keywords:** Mother Tree, Snake

**Category:** Inca

She is a forest goddess who is the embodiment of the Mother Tree, or the tree of life. She physically manifests herself by appearing as a snake or boa constrictor with two heads and lives in the jungle as a guardian of the Amazon Rainforest.[308]

## Temazcalteci

**Keyword:** Purification

**Category:** Aztec

---

306. Coulter and Turner, *Encyclopedia of Ancient Deities*, 368; Seler, *Tolamatl of the Aubin Collection*, 39.

307. MacDonald, *Pachamama Tales*, 12.

308. Bane, *Encyclopedia of Spirits and Ghosts in World Mythology*, 107.

Doctors worshiped her. She assisted with everything from childbirth to diagnosing and divining illnesses as an aspect of Toci, an aged deity with black circles around the eyes who also helps with steam baths. She is the eater of filth and presides over purification rites associated with medicine, protection, steam baths, and bathing, all with health as the end goal.[309]

## Tlazōlteōtl

**Keywords:** Temptation, Sensuality

**Category:** Aztec

She is the goddess of temptation and sensuality who enjoys tempting people to sin and then cleansing them from sin. She is the patroness of adulterers.[310] Aztecs believed such sins could be forgiven if they were confessed and if the offender participated in a ritual purification. Such cleansing ceremonies would be conducted on a specific auspicious date selected by the Aztec priests.

## Toci

**Keywords:** Mother, Tobacco

**Category:** Maya

A Great Mother goddess associated with tobacco. Women wore tobacco in her honor at festivals. Female medical and midwifery practitioners wore gourds filled with tobacco in ceremonies.[311]

## Tonantzin

**Keyword:** Mother

**Category:** Aztec

She is known as the Divine Mother, a name that suggests her collective maternal energies—Great Mother goddess, Honored Mother, and Beloved Mother and caregiver. She was a beloved goddess comparable to Mother Mary.[312]

---

309. Bancroft, *Native Races of the Pacific States of North America*, 353.

310. Bancroft, *Native Races of the Pacific States of North America*, 380, 506.

311. Thompson, *Maya History and Religion*, 119.

312. Burkhart, *Before Guadalupe*, 6, 11.

# Urpay Huachac

**Keywords:** Wildlife, Hunting, Fish

**Category:** Inca

According to Inca myth, she created, guarded, and protected fish in ponds. When creator god Viracocha attempted to seduce her two daughters, after succeeding with her first daughter, her second daughter turned into a dove and flew away. Viracocha became angry and scattered fish into the sea and rivers, which is why they are there to this present day.[313]

# Xochiquétzal

**Keywords:** Fertility, Love, Flowers

**Category:** Aztec

Called Precious Feather Flower, she is a fertility goddess who presided over pleasure, beauty, love, luxury, and excess. She is linked to rain god Tlaloc and other consorts. Aside from her romantic exploits, she protects young mothers during childbirth and assists with embroidery and weaving, cotton and flowers, and the moon.[314] In the Maya pantheon, Goddess "I" is her counterpart.

# Xochitlicue

**Keyword:** Fertility

**Categories:** Aztec, Codex Florentine

She is another fertility goddess who oversees life, death, and rebirth and is named as Huitzilopochtli's mother in the Codex Florentine. She is known for her skirt of flowers. Chimalman and Coatlicue are her sisters.[315]

# Xonatzi Huilia

**Keyword:** Protector

**Category:** Zapotec

313. Urton, *Inca Myths*, 65.

314. Herzfeld and Lenhart, *Semiotics 1980*, 100.

315. Nicholson, *Topiltzin Quetzalcoatl*, 63.

Consort of Underworld god Leera Huilia, she was an illness and death goddess who protected people.[316]

## Xquiq

**Keyword:** Moon

**Category:** Maya

She personifies the waning moon. According to mythology, the Maya death gods, the Lords of Xibalba, had sacrificed Hun Hunahpu, and when Xquiq saw his head on a calabash tree, Hun Hunahpu's skull spit on her, and she became pregnant with the Hero Twins.[317]

## Xumucane

**Keywords:** Mother of All

**Category:** Maya

Called Divine Midwife, she is part of the Maya creation myth and helped create the first humans out of cornmeal along with her consort, Xpiayoc, after other means failed. She personifies the waxing moon and Venus. Considered the grandmother of the Hero Twins and great-grandmother of all humans, she helps with all births, while Xpiayoc helps with all marriages. They are the very first Daykeepers, or shamans.[318]

## Zara Mama

**Keywords:** Fertility, Harvest

**Category:** Inca

Known as Grain or Maize Mother, she personifies the harvest of corn and certain grains that grew in multiples. The people created figures of her wearing a shawl and stood her up in cornfields to bless and encourage crops.[319] People sometimes turned her into smaller doll forms that were worshiped to ensure

---

316. Tavarez, *Invisible War*, 203.

317. Brinton, *Essays of an Americanist*, 124.

318. Read and Gonzales, *Mesoamerican Mythology*, 85, 89.

319. Small, *Top 100 Food Plants*, 438.

proper food supplies, or they hung her image on willow trees as an offering for a good crop.

## Summing Up

The Mesoamerican and Inca legacy left behind through the fantastic architectural wonders and pyramids we still have access to in modern times is a true gift to humanity.

Among spiritual seekers, fascination with the Maya civilization remains constant and makes this an incredibly popular topic, perhaps due to the great mystery that still surrounds their disappearance from the world. Sites in Crystal River, Florida, and the 1,100-year-old site uncovered near Blairsville, Georgia, appear to be ancient Maya cities now covered by overgrowth, proving that the Maya may not have vanished into thin air, but instead skillfully escaped drought conditions to thrive in a new environment.[320]

Aztecs left behind a rich legacy through the ruins they borrowed from their predecessors in Teotihuacan and the Templo Mayor site in downtown Mexico City that was destroyed by Spanish conquerors in 1521.

Like the Maya, the Inca civilization is another favorite for many modern seekers who take trips to Peru. Thanks to the widespread archaeological excavations in this area, scholars will hopefully continue to understand more over time about this incredible group of people. With cultures such as the Zapotec and Olmec, we know very little and may never know fully about these fascinating peoples, but the wonders of the Inca and each of the Mesoamerican groups make these pantheons worth further exploration.

Today, the decedents of all these mighty civilizations continue to live in the areas of Mexico and Central and South America. New DNA research proves the vast diversity of the population living in those areas as descendants of Aztecs, Maya, and others, and such studies will bring scholars closer to understanding the true timeline of migration into those areas.[321]

---

320. Florida State Parks, "Crystal River Archaeological Park"; Archaeology World Team, "Massive 1,100-Year-Old Maya Site Discovered in Georgia's Mountains?"

321. Gómez et al., "Y Chromosome Diversity in *Aztlan* Descendants," 102487.

## Recommended Reading

*The Complete Illustrated History of the Inca Empire* by David M. Jones

*Historical Dictionary of Mesoamerica* by Walter R. T. Witschey and Clifford T. Brown

*The Invisible War* by David Tavarez

*Fifth Sun* by Camilla Townsend

*Chapter Five*

# Norse Goddesses

Goddesses of Norse mythology were worshiped in early Scandinavian countries, including Sweden, Denmark, Norway, and Iceland, as a collection of folktales and myths of early Germanic tribes.[322] The teachings that remain survived and passed down through the centuries via written poems and prose. Norse mythology and the tales of gods and goddesses originated from the Codex Regius, a bound brown book of ancient tales. Discovered by Icelandic bishop Brynjolf Sveinsson, he presented the priceless manuscript to the Danish king Frederick III in 1662. Another document called manuscript R was written around 1270 by a writer who attempted to duplicate the items contained within the original Codex Regius. Six other poems survive in a manuscript called AM 748 4, which was later named A. The literature is said to date back to the thirteenth century, but it may have been created prior to the Scandinavian conversion to Christianity in the late tenth century.

From these earliest sources, the body of Norse mythology emerged. What we know of the goddesses comes from two collections. *Poetic Edda*, Icelandic literature dating from 1000 to 1300 CE, relayed myths told through oral tradition about the gods and goddesses and the creation of the world derived from the manuscripts mentioned above. The other main source is called *Prose Edda*, known also as the younger Edda, written around 1200 CE by Snorri Sturluson, an Icelandic aristocrat and politician turned poet. Both texts are the best sources

---

322. Sawyer, *Oxford Illustrated History of the Vikings.*

of scholarship for people who want to explore the complexities of the Norse pantheon. The word *Edda* is ambiguous as scholars are still uncertain of the exact meaning for the term, although most agree *Edda* is Icelandic and refers to poetry. Snorri used the term to describe the collection of documents found in the earlier codices, and when Bishop Sveinsson discovered them, he attached the term *Edda* to all the early Icelandic literature. These documents remained in Copenhagen for centuries and were returned to their rightful home in Iceland back in 1970.[323]

## Norse Cosmology

Aside from the literature mentioned above, Norse cosmology offers no religious scriptures to follow, and it wasn't a revealed religion from the gods to any specific person. The tales did reveal a creation myth from which all the gods, goddesses, and other natural phenomena originated.

According to Norse mythology, the world began from nothing and emerged through a yawning void called Ginnungagap, which gave rise to create the icy primordial realm of Niflheim, which ultimately collided with a fiery realm of the giants called Muspelheim. After the collision of ice and fire in the beginning of the world, a primordial cow Auðumbla emerged, along with Ymir, ancestor of all the Jötunn. Ymir sucked the utter of Auðumbla, and the sacred cow freed the Æsir ancestor Búri from the rime stones. Búri supernaturally gave birth to Borr, Odin's father. Odin and his two brothers, Vili and Vé, eventually created all known things in the world, including the first people by tearing Ymir into pieces and turning his flesh into the earth, his skull into the sky, his blood into the ocean, and his bones into mountains.[324]

After undergoing many fascinating challenges and triumphs, gods and goddesses collide at the end of the world called Ragnarök each day at sunset, only to arise again and start all over. The final battle is a bloody and colorful end to daylight as darkness consumes humanity and all is lost. Hope springs eternal through the dawning of a new day.

The Norse deities are divided into many groupings of supernatural beings who also fall under the goddess category. In this chapter, you will explore the following:

---

323. Larrington, *Poetic Edda*, x–xii.

324. Lindow, *Norse Mythology*.

1. **Æsir:** The main gods in the Norse pantheon associated with war including the All-Father, one-eyed high god Odin, who traded one of his eyes for wisdom, and Odin's son, the hammer-wielding thunder god Thor, among many others.

2. **Ásynjur:** Goddesses of the Æsir.

3. **Vanir:** Fertility deities associated with prophecy and wisdom who engaged in a war with the Æsir and eventually merged with them through marriage.

4. **Jötunn:** Mythical beings who started the earth. They are the giants of Norse mythology, and there are many female giants who feature prominently in the pantheon. The most well-known of the Jötunn is Loki, the trickster god and blood brother of Odin who stirs up mischief and plots against the Æsir in several tales.

5. **Valkyrie:** Supernatural beings who guide the souls of dead soldiers to one of two afterlife destinations: Valhalla, the Great Hall where half of the noble dead who died in battle live through eternity with Odin, or the goddess Freyja's Fólkvangr, a field where the other half who died in battle go after death. During the final days, these slain warriors will rise and engage in the final battle of Ragnarök.

6. **Norns:** Three female deities who spin the fate of humans and are comparable to the Fates or Moirai in Greek and Roman mythology.

This rich pantheon of colorful characters makes an interesting exploration.

## Norse Goddesses

While there are numerous gods and goddesses within the Norse pantheon, details about the goddesses are quite vague as many of those stories have not survived. Women typically play secondary roles to the men in these stories but are still important figures within the mythology.

## Angrboða

**Keyword:** Sorrow

**Category:** Jötunn

Trickster god Loki took the jötunn, or giant, Angrboða as his lover. She became mother of Loki's gigantic children Jormungundr the Midgard Serpent,

Hel the goddess of the Underworld, and Fenrir, a massive wolf. In Norse myth, Loki's brother Odin had a prophetic dream about the dangers posed by these offspring, so he and Loki traveled to the land of the giants to collect them. Later, as Odin predicted, they played an important role during the end of days in Ragnarök.

## Bestla

**Keywords:** Union, Wife

**Category:** Jötunn

Bestla was the daughter of a giant named Bolthorn. She married Bor, the son of Buri, ancestor of the gods. She gave birth to the primary god Odin and his two brothers, Vili and Vé. Together, the brothers eventually created all known things in the world.

## Beyla

**Keywords:** Fertility, Earth, Bees

**Category:** None

Very little is known of Beyla other than the fact that she and her husband, Byggvir, were servants to the god Frey and goddess Freyja. Beyla is mentioned in the introduction to the *Poetic Edda* poem "Lokasenna," where she attempts to warn trickster Loki of Thor's arrival, and he shouts at her and calls her filthy, which may be why she is associated with manure, fertilizer, and the earth. She is often cited as a bee goddess because scholars believe her name refers to bee, cow, or bean.

## Bil

**Keywords:** Waning Moon

**Category:** Ásynjur

Mentioned solely in *Prose Edda*, Snorri Sturluson described Bil and her brother, Hjúki, being taken up from the earth and carried into the sky where they now follow moon god Mani across the sky, which implies they are the personifications of waxing and waning moons. Snorri states Bil is part of the Ásynjur.

Some speculate Bil is associated with bilwis, a creature mentioned widely in Germanic literature that rolls across the cornfields to destroy crops.[325]

## Eir

**Keywords:** Help, Mercy, Healing

**Category:** Valkyrie

She represents help, assistance, and mercy. She is a patron for anyone who works in medicine and is familiar with various treatments and specializes in the use of herbs. She lives on a healing mountain called Lygjaberg, and if women climbed the mountain, she healed them of illness. She could also bring the dead back to life. She is mentioned in the *Poetic Edda*.

## Embla

**Keywords:** First Woman

**Categories:** Primordial, Personification

With the help of the gods, the first female, Embla, arose from a sacred elm tree. Her counterpart, the first man named Ask, was formed from a sacred ash tree. They are only mentioned once in "Völuspá," a poem within the *Poetic Edda*, as having little ability until Odin gave them breath, Hœnir gave them voice, and Lóðurr imbued them with blood.

## Freyja

**Keywords:** Fertility, War, Magic

**Category:** Vanir

**Also Known As:** Freya

The most beautiful Norse goddess, Freyr's sister and consort of Óðr, beloved Freyja rode on a chariot pulled by cats or traveled on a golden boar. She is the goddess of love, battles, and death who is associated with fertility, beauty, and magic. In *Poetic Edda*, the king of the Jötunn steals Thor's hammer and won't return it unless Freyja marries him. She lends her magical Brísingamen necklace to Thor, who dresses up as Freyja to fool the thief and get his hammer back. In *Prose Edda*, trickster Loki steals the Brísingamen, which is eventually returned.

---

325. Bechstein, *Beutsches Sagenbuch*.

Among her many talents, Freyja is known for seiðr, a kind of magic foretelling and shaping of future mostly practiced by female seers in ancient times.

## Frigg

**Keywords:** Love, Marriage, Fertility, Motherhood

**Category:** Ásynjur

She is Odin's wife and mother of the most beautiful of all gods, Baldr. She has the gift of foresight and the ability to determine the course of fate through access to prophecies. In one myth, Baldr's death was foretold, so she attempted to intercede by making all beings and natural forces vow not to injure him. She is often depicted with a spinning wheel and spindle, which symbolizes the idea of weaving time. Frigg eventually merged with Freyja in the late Viking Age because their traits were similar. Friday is named for her, and she is related to Venus.

## Fulla

**Keywords:** Fertility, Healing

**Category:** Ásynjur

A confidant of Frigg in *Poetic Edda*, Fulla works as an assistant to goddess Frigg, and in return, Frigg shares her secrets. Fulla is mentioned in the Second Merseburg Incantation, a medieval spell from the tenth century where she healed a wounded foal.

## Gefjon

**Keywords:** Fertility, Harvest

**Category:** Ásynjur

Plowing and harvest goddess, Gefjon is known as the giving one and is mentioned in *Prose Edda* and other works. She plowed the area that became the island of Zealand, Denmark. As a virgin herself, anyone who died a virgin would automatically become her attendant. She married Skjöldr. She may also be mentioned in the epic *Beowulf* as the word *geofon*. The Gefion Fountain in the port of Copenhagen, Denmark, features a gorgeous statue of Gefjon and her oxen children pulling a plow.

# Gerðr

**Keyword:** Fertility

**Category:** Jötunn

**Also Known As:** Gerd

Fertility god of the Vanir Freyr saw the stunningly beautiful giantess Gerðr and fell in love with her at first sight. He sent his elf servant Skirnir to ask her to be his bride. Skirnir agreed to help, but asked Freyr for his sword for protection on the trip. Gerðr initially refused the marriage proposal, but eventually married him. They had a son, Fjölnir, who became king after his father's death. Freyr's loss of his sword cost him his life in the final battle in Ragnarök.

# Gná

**Keywords:** Protection, Home, Hearth

**Category:** Ásynjur

In *Prose Edda*, she rides a magical flying and seafaring horse named Hófvarpnir to do errands for Frigg. Her name means "she who projects," and she is known as a goddess of fullness, perhaps because her errands help complete Frigg's household.

# Gullveig

**Keyword:** Crone

**Category:** Vanir

Known as the East Wind Hag, in *Poetic Edda*, she went to the hall of Odin and the Æsir speared her three times. She resurrected from the dead three times. After her third rebirth, she became a prophetess or *seiðr*. She figured prominently in the war between the Æsir and Vanir, a battle that occurred before the two separate groups of gods eventually merged through marriage. Gullveig is also associated with gold.

# Gunnlǫð

**Keyword:** Guardian

**Category:** Jötunn

In *Prose Edda*, at the end of the Æsir-Vanir war, the two groups spit into a vat. Freyr and his sister, Freyja, lived among the Æsir from then on and decided to make something of the combined spittle. Kvasir, the wisest of all beings, emerged from the spit and was murdered in a plot to steal his wisdom. His blood turned into special mead that would make a genius of anyone who partook. The Mead of Poets eventually fell into the hands of Suttungr, who entrusted his daughter, the giantess Gunnlǫð, to guard the brew in a cave hidden in a mountain. Odin shape-shifted into a snake and seduced Gunnlǫð to gain access to the magical drink and return it to the gods.

# Hel

**Keyword:** Underworld

**Categories:** Jötunn, Chthonic

Daughter of Loki and the giantess Angrboða, her name means "Hidden One" in Old Norse. After Odin and Loki went to fetch her from her mother, she was assigned by the gods to preside over the Underworld called Niflheim. She watched over the dead who did not die bravely in battle. Hel is located beneath one of the roots of the World Tree, Yggdrasil. Her face is divided in two—half flesh and half blue to imply her connection with death. She is featured in many Norse tales from the thirteenth century. To this day, the name is so controversial, it's actually against the law to name your child Hel in Iceland.[326]

# Hlín

**Keywords:** Protection, Refuge

**Category:** Ásynjur

She works with Frigg as a guard and acts as a protective detail for anyone who Frigg tells her to keep safe. She is best known for her prophetic abilities and for foretelling Odin's death, according to the *Prose Edda*. Some scholars believe Hlín is another name for Frigg.

---

326. Specktor, "Sorry, but Your Name Is Probably Illegal in Iceland."

# Hnoss

**Keyword:** Treasure

**Category:** Ásynjur

**Also Known As:** Gersemi

She is mentioned in *Prose Edda* as a beautiful daughter of Freyja. *Hnossir* became a term used to describe anything of beauty or value, such as a treasure or precious object. Some sources refer to her sister Gersemi, but as Gersemi is also known as a treasure, they are most likely one and the same.

# Iðunn

**Keyword:** Immortality

**Category:** Ásynjur

**Also Known As:** Idun

Goddess of spring, youth, and immortality, she carries a basket of fruits that grant immortality to the Norse gods who must eat them to maintain their immortal status. The connection between new birth and renewal that happens every spring is tied to Iðunn's energy. She is Bragi's (god of poetry) wife, fitting because springtime often inspires artists and poets. She is mentioned in *Poetic Edda* when Loki the trickster accuses her of sleeping with her brother's murderer. In *Prose Edda*, she is mentioned as Bragi's wife. Another myth describes the giant Thiazi kidnapping Iðunn to steal her apples. In her absence, the gods begin to age, and they intervene to rescue her and regain their youthfulness after partaking in the apples once again.

# Járnsaxa

**Keyword:** Warrior

**Category:** Jötunn

Her name means "iron hammer" and she is known to be armed with an iron sword, which is appropriate since she is Thor's lover. With Thor, she became mother to Magni. She and her sisters were collectively the Nine Mothers of the god Heimdallr, who guarded against invaders by overlooking the Bifröst, the rainbow bridge of fire that connected the land of the living or Earth/Midgard with Asgard, the realm of the gods.

# Jörð

**Keyword:** Earth

**Categories:** Jötunn, Personification

Mentioned in *Poetic Edda* as Thor's mother and *Prose Edda* as a personification of Earth, she is Thor's mother with Odin. She is considered a personification of the earth itself and the daughter of Nótt, the personification of night.

# Laufey

**Keyword:** Leaves

**Category:** Jötunn

**Also Known As:** Nál

She is the mother of Loki the trickster god with her consort Fárbauti, a Jötunn giant whose name means "anger striker." He personified lightning that struck the foliage or leaves to create Loki. Laufey is sometimes referred to as Nál, meaning "needle." That may describe her thin frame, or some believe it refers to the needles on pine trees and foliage that may have caught fire from her husband's lightning strikes.

# Lofn

**Keywords:** Love, Comfort

**Category:** Ásynjur

Mentioned in *Prose Edda*, she arranges marriages during times of difficulty or if the match is forbidden. She is kind and gentle and provides comfort to those she brings together. Her actions were blessed by Frigg.

# Nanna

**Keywords:** Motherhood, Devotion

**Category:** Ásynjur

Mother of the Brave and goddess of peace, justice, and joy, she is called the daring one. Nanna is the wife of Odin's son Baldr, the most beautiful and beloved of all the gods. Forseti, the god of justice, is her son. After Baldr's death, she dies of grief, and the two are placed together on a funeral pyre. She and Baldr reunite in Hel. She is mentioned in both the *Prose Edda* and *Poetic Edda*.

# Njörun

**Keywords:** Sea, Earth

**Category:** Ásynjur

She is attested in the poem "Lokasenna" within *Prose Edda* as sister-wife of the Vanir god of the sea, Njörðr, and therefore she is the mother of the twins Freyja and Freyr. She may also be an earth or fertility goddess. In *Prose Edda*, she is listed as one of the Ásynjur.

# Nótt

**Keyword:** Night

**Categories:** Jötunn, Personification

A personification of the night, she is described as black. She is mentioned in *Poetic Edda* when Odin talks about her horse, Hrímfaxi, whom she rides across the sky at night. Her three marriages are mentioned in *Prose Edda*, including her first to Naglfari, which produced her son Auðr; her second union with Annar, resulting in her daughter, Jörð; and the third to Dellingr, which produced her son Dagr, the personification of day.

# Rán

**Keyword:** Sea

**Categories:** Jötunn, Personification

Rán is the personification of the sea and the counterpart to Ægir, who is the male god of the sea. The pair have nine daughters who are waves personified. Rán is mentioned in *Poetic Edda* and an Icelandic poem about a grieving father whose son is lost at sea. Lamenting his loss, the boy's father wishes Rán and Ægir could take his son's place. As such, Rán is a goddess for those who die at sea. She also has a helpful net that she once loaned to trickster Loki.

# Rindr

**Keyword:** Revenge

**Category:** Ásynjur

**Also Known As:** Rind, Rinda

Rindr is a giantess mentioned in both the *Poetic Edda* and *Prose Edda*. After the death of his son, the beautiful god Baldr, Odin wanted revenge. He visited a kingdom and encountered the beautiful giantess Rindr. She turned down his advances twice, so he cast a spell on her, resulting in the birth of Váli, who grew to full adulthood immediately after his birth and murdered Baldr's killer.

## Sága

**Keywords:** Seer, Prophecy

**Category:** Ásynjur

*Poetic Edda* reports that Odin and Sága drank together in Sökkvabekkr, a sunken bank. She is attested on her own, but stories of her and Odin imbibing together caused some scholars to believe she is another aspect of Frigg. They may be enjoying the waters of immortality together, and some illustrations show her taking notes for Odin, which might suggest that she is also linked to poetry and the creative arts.

## Sif

**Keywords:** Fertility, Harvest

**Category:** Ásynjur

*Sif* means "wife" in Old Norse, which is appropriate since she is Thor's wife whose golden hair represents wheat, harvest, and the land. In the *Prose Edda*, Thor became infuriated when Loki shaved off Sif's hair. He ordered Loki to restore her hair, so Loki enlisted the help of a group of dwarves who made her a golden headpiece. Her hair may represent wheat crops and fertility, making her an earth goddess. Plants and earth make her the perfect match to the god of storms and rain—they both help crops grow.

## Sigyn

**Keywords:** Victory, Loyalty

**Category:** Ásynjur

Sigyn's name means "Friend of Victory." She is the wife of trickster Loki and mother of two sons, Narfi and Váli. In one myth, Loki's evil deception results in the death of Odin's son Baldr. As a result, the gods demanded retribution. They trap Loki in a cave, and turn his son Váli into a wolf. After Váli kills his brother

Narfi, the gods bind Loki to the floor of the cave using Narfi's intestines and leave a venomous snake above him to drip poison onto his face. Sigyn remains loyal to Loki during his imprisonment by collecting the venom in a bowl to spare him agonizing pain. When the bowl fills, however, she has to leave to go and dump it out, and during those times, Loki shakes in pain, and his agony results in tremors that cause earthquakes.

## Sjöfn

**Keyword:** Love

**Category:** Ásynjur

As a goddess of relationships and marriage, she helps women and men in love, according to the *Prose Edda*. Her name is used as a figure of speech, or *kenning*, by poets. Some scholars also believe she may be another iteration of Frigg.

## Skaði

**Keyword:** Hunt

**Category:** Jötunn

Skaði is the daughter of the Jötunn Thiazi who kidnapped Iðunn and stole her immortality apples, resulting in his death. To compensate Skaði for the loss of her father, the gods agree she can marry one of their number. She chose Freyja's father, the sea god Njörðr. They live apart because she did not want to be near the light, warmth, and noise of the sea. Mentioned in both the *Poetic Edda* and *Prose Edda*, she wears skis to help her hunt in the ice-covered mountains and helps ensure a good hunt in winter by helping people get through tough times. Her name is linked to the term *Scandinavia*.

## Skuld

**Keywords:** Fate, Future

**Categories:** Norn, Valkyrie

Skuld is one of the three sisters who watered the roots of Yggdrasil, the World Tree, and determined one's fate. Skuld is the youngest of the Norns and represents the future. Her name relates to the words *should* or *possible happening*. She is attested as a Valkyrie in the *Prose Edda* and is often pictured carrying a shield.

# Snotra

**Keyword:** Wisdom

**Category:** Ásynjur

Known as the clever one, Snotra is goddess of wisdom, mentioned in the *Prose Edda* as wise and courteous. She is also listed in *Prose Edda* as a member of the Ásynjur. She is said to be an ancestor of the Goths. Her name is also used in *Beowulf* to denote the quality of wisdom.

# Sól

**Keyword:** Sun

**Categories:** Ásynjur, Personification

**Also Known As:** Sunna

As the personification of the sun, Sól drives the sun's horses across the sky. She is consort of Glenr and the sister of Mani the moon according to the *Poetic Edda* and *Prose Edda*. During Ragnarök, Sól is killed by a wolf, but not before she has a daughter who continues her procession across the sky.

# Thrúd

**Keywords:** Strength, Power

**Categories:** Valkyrie, Ásynjur

**Also Known As:** Þrúðr

She is mentioned in *Poetic Edda* and *Prose Edda* very vaguely as Thor and Sif's daughter who is engaged to a dwarf. Another being with the same name is mentioned as a Valkyrie who serves ale to the dead in Valhalla, the great hall in Asgard presided over by Odin. They may be one and the same, although this is not clear.

# Urðr

**Keyword:** Fate, Past

**Category:** Norn

**Also Known As:** Urd

Urðr is one of three sisters who tended and watered Yggdrasil, the World Tree. She and the other Norns determined fate. They spun the thread of life and cut the cords between the body and the physical world. Urðr represented the past.

## Vár

**Keywords:** Marriage, Fertility

**Category:** Ásynjur

She is the goddess of blessings, agreements, vows, and oaths mentioned in the *Poetic Edda* and *Prose Edda*. In the myth, thunder god Thor's hammer was stolen by the Jötunn king Thrym who will only return it if Freyja marries him. Thor dressed as a bride and Vár blessed the phony marriage between Thrym and Thor before Thor revealed his true identity and took his hammer back.

## Verdandi

**Keywords:** Fate, Present

**Category:** Norn

**Also Known As:** Verthandi

One of three sisters who watered the roots of Yggdrasil, the World Tree, and determined fate. Her name refers to becoming. She represented the present.

## Vör

**Keywords:** Protection, Wisdom

**Category:** Ásynjur

Known as the careful one, she is a protective wisdom goddess mentioned in the *Prose Edda* as one of the Ásynjur. People cannot hide anything from her because of her wisdom. She is considered protective for that reason, helping people discern truth.

## Summing Up

Stories of the Norse gods and goddesses have become more commonly accessible thanks to shows like *Game of Thrones* and the Marvel film franchise. The epic sagas capture our imaginations and allow us to venture into times long gone where magic infused every aspect of daily life. The retelling of mythological stories from hundreds of years ago brings new life and insight into some of the fascinating people who lived in early times through the retelling of tales told by the campfires of old. I hope you've enjoyed learning more about the rich history of these early people and the goddesses they loved and adored.

## Recommended Reading

*Norse Mythology* by Neil Gaiman

*Goddess Alive!* by Michelle Skye

*Norse Goddess Magic* by Alice Karlsdóttir

*The Poetic Edda* translated by Carolyne Larrington

*Part Two*

Living Goddesses

## Part Two

Within many modern world religions, goddess worship is alive and well. With any religious belief, only those who adhere to that religion can truly understand the complexities of meaning inherent within their faith. Out of my deepest respect to these cultural beliefs, I hope to share a brief look into the belief systems of some of the beautiful people we share our planet with and the goddesses they worship in hope of expanding understanding and unity.

*Chapter Six*

# African Goddesses

Africa is one of the most geographically diverse locales, and the mythology and spiritual traditions relayed through African mythology provide some of the richest, most diverse stories, legends, and morality tales of any place on Earth. While it would be next to impossible to fully cover such a region, you will explore some of the overarching themes of the mythology still beloved by different groups of people throughout Africa today and look at the goddesses and women from various African-born myths.

One of the challenges to this study is the fact that African mythos were passed down generation after generation through the oral tradition and through bards—gifted storytellers who share the tales and are often accompanied by singers and dancers. The myths we do have more information about often came from people who heard one of these incredible performances and recorded it, translated it, and then preserved it for future posterity. Anytime you have a performance of a tale, each storyteller infuses their own energy into the telling, so there are variations with each and every version. That said, those who become these important carriers of the traditional beliefs and customs are often selected at a very young age for their natural ability to remember minute details. Elders work with these children to ensure that every aspect of a story is preserved in the highest form so it may be accurately passed down through the generations.

# African Cosmology

African creation stories are wide and varied among the incredibly diverse cultures; however, there are some overall themes that recur repeatedly within various traditions:

**Separation from the Divine:** The presence of a single creator god who gives rise to all things and who then abandons humanity and returns to the heavenly realm to separate himself (or in some cases *herself*) from the people is a common theme in African myths. This is often due to a punishment for not following simple directions. Those divine instructions may be as simple as not planting their own food but relying on the creator to provide or eating specific forbidden foods, like Adam and Eve within Christianity. And like Adam and Eve, people are punished for eternity to suffer the pains of death and hunger and then strive to return to the creator.[327] Some theorists suggest Biblical stories could have originated in Africa and were later shared by Christian missionaries, or vice versa, but either way, there is a commonality among them.

**Clay Forming Creation:** Several African myths follow the idea of creators forming humans from clay. One of many examples occurs within the cosmology of the Dogon people of Mali who believe the creator god Amma created the earth by flinging clay into space. He became lonely and created the first woman and then a couple who lacked souls, so he created the Nummo, twin gods who finished the work of creation.[328]

**Androgynous Deities:** Before creation emerged into physical form, many mythological figures, gods, and goddesses in African tales are described as both male and female. Within the pure potentiality of consciousness, many people, such as the BaKongo, recognize that within that unmanifested state, the essence of both genders exists. I include several of these deities within our goddess list because there is an interchange of referring to them as both male and female.[329]

---

327. Ford, *Hero with an African Face*, 164.

328. Ford, *Hero with an African Face*, 182–3.

329. Ford, *Hero with an African Face*, 197.

**Harmony and Equality with Animals and Nature:** Deep respect for animal life is also present within African myth. Animals are portrayed as helpful and humans are often reminded that they are no better than anyone else and are certainly not superior at all to animals, which is a refreshing way to view life. Sometimes animals are brothers and sisters of people. Other times they provide immense help to the hero, such as in the story of Kimanaueze, the hero of the Ambundu people of Angola who wants to send a message to a goddess in heaven and tries to enlist several animals to help. Eventually a frog assists, which embodies the theme that animals help us rise above our limitations and become one with the creator.[330]

This list represents but a few of the higher ideals expressed within African myths found across the continent.

I will explore feminine divine within several categories defined by the diverse ethnic groups in this vast continent:

**Akan:** An ethnicity group who live mostly in the region of the Ivory Coast or Ghana and encompass several groups of people, including the Bono and Asante, as well as the Abron people from the kingdom of Cote d' Lvoire. Traditional beliefs recognize one supreme god and a belief in Ananse, the trickster spider prevalent in many African myths. In modern times, the traditional religion is integrated into Christianity.

**Baga:** *Baga* refers to a predominantly Muslim West African ethnic group from Guinea-Conakry. In the nineteenth and twentieth centuries, the people were subjected to a demolition of their traditional beliefs. Their sacred masks and other art were unethically dispersed throughout Europe in an attempt to wipe out their culture. Despite these horrific hardships, the people have prevailed, and traditional beliefs have been preserved for future generations.[331]

**Baganda:** The people of Uganda worship Gulu the sky god and other gods who aid them with every part of life, including securing abundant food supplies, achieving success in battles, and assisting the departed on their

---

330. Ford, *Hero with an African Face*, 62–3.
331. Abrams, *African Goddess Initiation*, 352.

journey into the afterlife. They had a legendary mortal king named Kintu who is considered the Baganda ancestor of the royal family of Uganda.[332]

**BaKongo:** The spiritual tradition of KiKongo-speaking people who revere a pantheon of deities mixed with ancestral veneration and animism.[333] They have a wonderful morality myth and flood story about an old woman who goes to a town and knocks on every door to seek help and shelter. Everyone slams the door in her face. Finally, the last door she knocks on opens and the people let her in and give her food, shelter, and nurse her back to health. Soon thereafter, creator god Nzambi floods the town and only the charitable family is saved.[334] This is one of many flood stories throughout history and shows the prevalence of this kind of tale in teaching morality and human kindness through helping others.

**Bambara:** Segu was a Bambara kingdom founded in the seventeenth century that withstood wars and tensions. The people had a rich history of *morikes*, men who divine the future, and *Djeli*, bardic storytellers who relayed stories through song and dance passed down through oral tradition. The most famous of these tales is the epic of Bakaridjan Kone about a young man who lived a moral and good life, and because of his goodness, he received poor treatment from the historical middle-aged King Da Monzon because he felt threatened by him.[335] Bambara believed the world began with the sound *yo*, which would be comparable to *om* in other religious systems.[336]

**Dinka:** The people who live near South Sudan believe in the Supreme Being Nhialic, creator of the world Jok, and rain god Deng. Nhialic created the first man and first woman out of clay and put them in a pot. When he let them out, they were fully grown. As in many African myths, in Dinka cosmology, at one time, Earth and heaven were close to each other, connected by a rope. Nhialic was offended and severed the rope between

---

332. Ford, *Hero with an African Face*, 60.

333. Ford, *Hero with an African Face*, 201.

334. Lynch, *African Mythology A to Z*, 45.

335. Courlander and Sako, *Heart of the Ngoni*.

336. Lynch, *African Mythology A to Z*, xv.

heaven and Earth, forcing people to experience hunger, sickness, and death.[337]

**Dogon:** The Indigenous people of Mali in West Africa whose cosmology centers around the star Sirius and the nearby dwarf star they call the deep beginning. Elaborate masks celebrate the connection the people have to the stars. Deified ancestors are those who lived before heaven and Earth were separated, and they were venerated because they never experienced death.[338]

**Efik:** The Indigenous people of Nigeria and Cameroon worship Abassi, a Supreme Creator God acknowledged as both the above and below, and also honor ancestral and guardian spirits.[339] Abassi created the first man and woman and tells them that so long as they only eat food he provides and do not bear children, they can come back to the sky. The husband loves his wife's cooking so much, he eats the food, and that leads to love-making and children, so they are banished from heaven and must fend for themselves and experience difficulties.

**Fon:** The people living in the Republic of Benin (formerly Dahomey from 1975 to 1990) in western Africa believe in Aido-Hwedo, the Cosmic Serpent who created the universe. Wido-Hwedo excreted the mountains, and the spinning heavens are caused from his coiled movements. The Fon follow a tradition of belief in the Vodun that was carried around the world by enslaved people and brought to areas such as Haiti, Cuba, and parts of the United States, where these traditions are still followed in modern times.[340]

**Hausa:** People of Nigeria who believe in Bori, a spiritual force within all creation.[341] We will explore their heroic legend about Bayajidda, the legendary founder and ancestor of the Hausas who is thought to be the son

---

337. Scheub, *Dictionary of African Mythology.*

338. Lynch, *African Mythology A to Z*, 10, 36.

339. Lynch, *African Mythology A to Z*, 1.

340. Lynch, *African Mythology A to Z*, xi.

341. Palmer, "52. 'Bori' Among the Hausas," 113–7.

of the king of Baghdad. Epics and myths are told in the traditional ways with dancing, instruments, and gifted storytellers.

**Ijo:** People who live in the southwestern part of Nigeria have a female creation deity named Woyengi who is the center of their cosmology. She embraces free will and allows humans to choose much of their fate and destiny.

**Kabyle:** Indigenous Berbers from Algeria are known as the Kabyle people. They represent 40 percent of the Algerian population as the largest Berber-speaking group within that region. The people have fought for equality and rights against foreign oppression.[342] They believe in spirits residing in all things and that humanity emerged from the earth. The first man and woman emerged from underground and had fifty boys and fifty girls who populated the earth.

**Lozi:** Refers to the mythology of the Lozi people who live in Zambia. Nyambe the Supreme Being is the origin of all things and determines human fate. Lozi worship ancestors and acknowledge spirits as divine aspects within traditional beliefs. In one creation myth, Nyambe tasks Kamunu, the first human, with naming other creations, including his siblings, the animals. When Kamunu begins killing the animals for food, Nyambe punished him by taking away his possessions until he finally took Kamunu's son, bringing death to the world.[343] The tale reflects the profound respect people hold toward animals by regarding them as equal rather than inferior.

**Nyanga:** The Bantu-speaking people living in the Walikale territory in the eastern part of Democratic Republic of Congo have a beautiful epic heroic tale about Mwindo. Like many African myths, the epic was relayed through the oral tradition and recorded by Daniel Biebuyck and published in 1969, which is why we know of it. The story takes place in Tubondo in Ihimbi. The evil chief named Shemwindo takes seven wives and insists they all give birth to girls. Any boys will be killed. Six wives have girls, but his seventh wife has an extraordinarily long pregnancy.

---

342. Myers, "Algeria's Amazigh Problem."
343. Lynch, *African Mythology A to Z*, 93.

Her unborn child, Mwindo, performs helpful chores before his birth and emerges from his mother's middle finger. When his father threatens his life, he leaves and takes refuge in another village with his aunt, who assists him in eventually prevailing and establishing a corulership with his father. Several prominent women mentioned in the myth will be discussed.[344]

**Soninke:** The people of the Sahel region of Africa, which includes Senegal, Mali, and Mauritania, whose culture thrived around 500 BCE. The Soninke created an important epic tale called the *Dausi* about a legendary empire called Wagadu. Bardic storytellers spread the epic widely between 300 and 1200 CE through oral tradition, until foreign invasions and the influence of Islam over traditional African cultural beliefs caused much of the text to be lost to the ages.[345]

**Yoruba:** Religion of the people of Nigeria, which likely came to that area from the Middle East and centered around the city of Oyo, which dated from 1200 to 1800 CE. The teachings blend real facts with myths and revolve around a Supreme God Olorun, Lord of Heaven, who does not associate with humanity other than through the Orishas or spirit inter- mediaries. Another key figure is thunder god Shango, a royal ancestor and fourth King of the Yorubas deified after death who transformed into a thunder and lightning god and wielded a two-headed axe.[346]

**Zulu:** People from South Africa who are among the many who speak the Bantu language. In their creation myth, humans emerged from reeds in a primordial swamp called Uthlanga. They also venerate and invoke helpful ancestors called Amadlozi.[347]

The mythological women portrayed within African myths help people through demonstrating their actions, which are relayed through the oral tradi- tion of storytelling combined with bardic performances and dance that bring these tales to life and allow listeners to consider their own lives in terms of what choices to make regarding the wider issues of discerning right from wrong, where

---

344. Biebuyck and Mateene, *Mwindo Epic*, 1.

345. Ford, *Hero with an African Face*, 118.

346. Johnson, *History of the Yorubas*.

347. Lynch, *African Mythology A to Z*, 7.

we humans fit into the universe as a whole, and themes about humanity's equality with animals and all other living creatures. The tales of deities are passed down and are only now beginning to be put in writing, so we understand more about the vast complexity of beliefs throughout Africa.

## African Goddesses

The feminine divine figures in African myth do not necessarily receive the title of *goddess* as many of them would be deified ancestors or mythological legendary women who embody the ideals for success in living or dealing with the environment within the wider world.

## a-Bol-Nimba

**Keywords:** Fertility, Prosperity

**Categories:** Baga, Ancestral

A-Bol is the primary creation deity worshiped by the Baga and carrier of the ancestral lineage. *Nimba* refers to her sacred mask, which is imbued with spiritual energy. Nimba masks are incredible pieces of art featuring a large-breasted curvaceous woman to signify successful harvest and abundance.[348]

## Abuk

**Keyword:** Fertility

**Category:** Dinka

**Also Known As:** Buk, Acol

Mother of the sky god, she is the goddess for all women who is symbolized by a snake. Known as the first woman, she married Garang in some myths and Deng the rain god in others. She is a fertility goddess who is venerated for gardening and water. She is sometimes symbolized by the moon, snakes, or sheep. She is river goddess for the Dinka and fertility goddess for the Nuer people. In Dinka myth, the creator god Nhialic offers to give her and her consort food but warns the couple not to take more than what they absolutely need. Abuk disobeys, so the creator cuts the rope between heaven and Earth and leaves human beings to fend for themselves.

---

348. Abrams, *African Goddess Initiation*, 352.

# Ahia-Njoku

**Keyword:** Harvest

**Category:** Igbo

She is goddess of yams for the people of Igboland. Men are responsible for harvesting the yams and pay homage to her.

# Ala

**Keyword:** Fertility

**Categories:** Igbo, Ancestral

As consort of Chukwu the creator god, she is the fertility and agriculture goddess for Odinala, the spiritual belief system of the Igbo people. She holds deceased ancestors in her womb. She is the mother of every single living thing, a guardian and protector for all who has control over life and death.

# Aminata

**Keywords:** Love, Fertility

**Category:** Bambara

In the tale of the epic hero Bakaridjan Kone, he and two other men fall in love with the beautiful mythical heroine Aminata. She allows all three of them to court her, which becomes problematic for the men who eventually must battle for her. Bakaridjan is disgraced by walking away from the fight and will eventually be redeemed. In the end, another suitor named Bamana Diase becomes her husband.

# Amma

**Keywords:** Creation, Mother

**Category:** Dogon

Amma is listed as a female creator in some places, while in others Amma is male. Like several creator deities within African myth, Amma emerged from the void in the form of a cosmic egg. The full potentiality of the universe was contained within her. She attempted creation and failed at first, so she planted a seed within herself that became two placentas with twins that divided into four parts to represent the cardinal directions. All the ingredients to create the universe ultimately emerged through her placenta, which divided periodically to give rise to certain aspects of the world.[349]

# Atai

**Keyword:** Creator

**Categories:** Efik, Primordial

With her partner, the sky god Abassi, she is a primordial creation deity responsible for life and death. Abassi did not want the first humans to live on Earth because he did not want them to be better than him. Atai convinced him to allow them to do so. Humans broke their promise by eating their own food and having children, so Atai punished them and brought death to the world.[350]

# Ayana

**Keyword:** Crone

**Category:** Hausa

In the legend of Bayajidda, he arrives in Daura and goes to the home of Ayana, an old woman, to ask for water. She directs him to the well where a deadly snake only allows people to drink on Fridays. Once Bayajidda kills the snake and makes water available to all, he is a hero.

# Bagwariya

**Keyword:** Mistress

**Category:** Hausa

In the legend of Bayajidda, once he asks Queen Magajiya Daruama to marry him, she must go through rituals before that union can be consummated, so Magajiya gives Bayajidda a mistress, Bagwariya, to keep him company in the interim and Bagwariya gives birth to a son called Karap da Gari, meaning "he who snatched the town."

---

349. Scheub, *Dictionary of African Mythology.*
350. Lynch, *African Mythology A to Z, 1.*

# Inkosazana

**Keyword:** Fertility

**Category:** Zulu

Inkosazana is a fertility goddess for agriculture who helps ensure plentiful crops. She lives in water and is sometimes depicted as a mermaid.

# Iyangura

**Keyword:** Protector

**Category:** Nyanga

Aunt of the epic hero Mwindo, she is Nyamwindo's sister who takes in her nephew to save his life and helps Mwindo achieve success. She is the ritual wife of Mukiti, a water serpent. Her status gives her a more equal status to him, which enabled her to make the decision to take Mwindo in and help him.

# Kahindo

**Keywords:** Luck, Fortune

**Categories:** Nyanga, Chthonic

She is the daughter of Muisa, god of the dead, who greets the deceased in the Underworld. Despite her connection with the departed, she is considered a good luck and fortune goddess. She helped Mwindo during his journey into the Underworld by helping him overcome her father's many tests. In return, Mwindo helped her heal her medical condition. In the end, Muisa is won over by Mwindo, and he offers him Kahindo's hand in marriage, which Mwindo refuses.

# Magajiya Daurama

**Keyword:** Queen

**Category:** Hausa

In the legend of Bayajidda, he takes his wife and goes into exile from his home in Borno and travels to a town called Dauro where a snake guards a well and makes drinking difficult. He dispatches the snake with his knife and captures the attention of the local queen Magajiya Daurama, who rewards Bayajidda by becoming his second wife. Before their marriage is consummated, Bayajidda has a child with Bagwariya called Snatcher of the Town. This upsets the queen who wants to ensure the town stays with her, so when she and Bayajidda have a son, the queen names him Bawo, meaning "give it back."[351]

## Magaram

**Keyword:** Mother

**Category:** Hausa

**Also Known As:** Magira

Magaram is the first wife of the legendary warrior prince Bayajidda who came to Nigeria after he was exiled from Baghdad. When he arrived in his new home, he realized the local king's forces were not as powerful as his, so he planned to kill him and take over. The king heard about the plot against him, and offered his daughter Magaram's hand in marriage to keep the peace. They had a child named Biram.

## Mame Cantaye

**Keyword:** Water

**Categories:** Senegal, Tutelary

This goddess is associated with the Langue de Barbarie, a peninsula in Western Senegal along the Atlantic coast that is located south of the city of Saint Louis. Her sister, Mame Coumba Bang, serves as the protective river goddess for the area.

## Mame Coumba Bang

**Keyword:** Water

**Categories:** Senegal, Tutelary

She is the primary goddess and protective deity who lives along the Senegal River and the city of Saint Louis. The term *Bang* in her name refers to a bench where she sits every morning until the sun comes up, and then she returns to the water. Worshipers provide her offerings such as sugared milk or anything white because white brings good luck. Offerings to the goddess help ensure protection and overall stability, and these are especially made after the rainy season before

---

351. Lange, *Hausa History*, 289–94.

the river opens up for summer swimmers. She helps with childbirth and receives offerings at birth, again at three months, and at baptism.[352]

# Mamlambo

**Keyword:** River

**Category:** Zulu

Mamlambo is a river goddess for the Zulu.[353] Unfortunately, very little is known of her other than she may be a snake or snakelike creature.

# Mawu

**Keyword:** Moon

**Category:** Fon

Mawu is the feminine half of the two-part Mawu-Lisa creation deity of the Fon. In the beginning, Aido-Hwedo, the cosmic serpent, carried Mawu-Lisa in his mouth while he created the universe. Her Mawu aspect represents the feminine lunar moon and presided over the night, while her counterpart Lisa is the day, represented by the masculine sun.[354] Together, Mawu-Lisa is an androgynous creation deity. Mawu-Lisa created the world in four days. On day one, Mawu-Lisa created humans. On day two, Earth became inhabitable. On the third day, people were given the ability to see, talk, and have consciousness, and on day four, Mawu-Lisa taught humanity how to survive.

# Mbaba-Mwanna-Waresa

**Keyword:** Fertility

**Categories:** Zulu, Personification

Zulu fertility and harvest goddess associated and personified by the rainbow. She is also goddess of beer and taught the people how to brew beer, so she is loved deeply for giving such a wonderful gift to humanity.

---

352. Margoles, *Mame Coumba Bang.*

353. Lynch, *African Mythology A to Z*, 138.

354. Lynch, *African Mythology A to Z*, 39.

# Mbokomu

**Keywords:** First Woman

**Categories:** Ngombe, Primordial, Ancestral

According to the Bantu's Ngombe mythology, Mbokomu is the ancestral goddess, first woman, and ancestor to everyone. The creator god Akongo lowered Mbokomu and her children to Earth and they began populating the planet.

# Mbuyu

**Keywords:** Fertility, Warrior

**Categories:** Lozi, Ancestral

She is the daughter of Mwambwa and consort of Nyambe, the Supreme Creator God. She became the second chief of the Luyi people after her mother and is considered an ancestor of the Lozi royal family, who are considered her direct descendants.[355]

# Moremi

**Keyword:** Queen

**Category:** Yoruba

Legendary queen Moremi Ajasoro was the wife of Oranmiyan and helped the Yoruba defeat their enemies by allowing herself to be taken by a warring tribe. She married the enemy king and stole secrets that helped the Yoruba people win their freedom. Because of her dedication and bravery, she was deified and revered in festivals. Her statue in Nigeria is the largest in that country and among the largest in all of Africa.

# Musoka

**Keywords:** Serpent, Water

**Category:** Nyanga

She is the sister of Mukiti, the water serpent, and sister-in-law of Iyangura, the aunt of the epic hero Mwindo. During Mwindo's escape from his father, Musoka attempts to block Mwindo from safely reaching his aunt.

---

355. Lynch, *African Mythology A to Z*, 93.

# Mwambwa

**Keyword:** Chief

**Category:** Lozi

She is the daughter and consort of Nyambe, the creator god and founder of the Luyi nation. She became the first chief of the Luyi people. Her name means "one who is talked about."

# Naete

**Keyword:** Sea

**Category:** Fon

Daughter of creator god Mawu-Lisa, she is the twin and wife of Agbe, the god of the sea. Mawu-Lisa put the two of them in charge of the water and the oceans.

# Nambi

**Keyword:** Sky

**Category:** Baganda

Nambi was the daughter of the Baganda sky god Gulu. She falls in love with Kintu, a mortal, and her father tests Kintu before allowing them to marry. Nambi, Kintu's cow, and a bee all helped him pass Gulu's tests and they married. Kintu eventually became the first Baganda king.

# Nana Buluku

**Keyword:** Creation

**Categories:** Fon, Primordial

She is the Supreme Being and creator goddess who gave birth to Mawu the moon and Lisa the sun. The sun and moon merged into the composite Mawu-Lisa, who handled the remainder of creation. Like Mawu-Lisa, her gender is ambiguous and may be more androgynous rather than female or male.

# Nasilele

**Keywords:** Creation, Moon, Fertility

**Category:** Lozi

Nasilele is the original consort and wife of Lozi Supreme Being Nyambe who created all people and everything on Earth. They once lived on Earth but ascended to the heavens on a spider's web. Once the couple arrived in the heavens, Nyambe became the sun and Nasilele became the moon.

## Ngula

**Keywords:** Mother, Fertility

**Category:** Lozi

Ngula is the mother of Lozi creator god Nyambe. Although she is his mother, he created her along with everyone and everything else on Earth. Her name means "she who is pregnant."

## Nimba

**Keywords:** Fertility, Harvest

**Category:** Baga

She is known for agriculture and creating healthy crops as well as for typical fertility and pregnancy. She is sometimes fused into one deity called a-Bol-Nimba or mentioned on her own. Nimba is also the ceremonial gigantic mask of the female form with a robust figure that symbolizes abundance, pregnancy, and harvest.

## Ninki-Nanka

**Keyword:** Water

**Categories:** Senegal, Tutelary

Ninki-Nanka is a terrorizing gigantic reptile creature said to be over a hundred feet long that is part of the folklore of people in West Africa. She is a protective deity who lives along the Sengal River at the river's source in Guinea. Along with Mame Coumba Bang, these goddesses serve as helpers for the community and receive periodic offerings.

## Nomkhubulwane

**Keywords:** Shape-Shifter

**Categories:** Zulu, Ancestral

She is an important ancestral deity and shape-shifter who is the same goddess as Mbaba-Mwanna-Waresa when she is in an animal form. She is a hunting and fertility goddess. Her name means "she who chooses the state of an animal."

## Nyame

**Keyword:** Creator

**Category:** Akan

Known as the goddess without beginning or end with associations to the fire that ignites and gives rise to all creation. Nyame is one of several Supreme Beings from African myth who has ambiguous gender. Some say Nyame is male and the Ashanti believe Nyame is androgynous. Her association with the moon suggests she is both sun and moon, engaging both the masculine solar and feminine lunar energies.[356]

## Nyamwindo

**Keyword:** Mother

**Category:** Nyanga

Mother of the epic hero Mwindo, she is one of seven wives of the evil Chief Shemwindo. She gave birth to her son through her middle finger. She was unable to protect him from her husband, so Mwindo left to live elsewhere.

## Nzambi

**Keywords:** Earth, Creation

**Category:** BaKongo

Nzambi is a Supreme Creator deity for the Kongo people who has an ambiguous or possibly androgynous gender.[357] Under the name of *Nzambi a Mpungu*, the creator is male; however, *Nzambi* as a singular refers to a goddess sent to Earth by Nzambi Mpungu. The Supreme Being is one of many who left humanity to return to the heavens.

---

356. Ford, *Hero with an African Face*, 116.
357. Ford, *Hero with an African Face*, 116.

# Oba

**Keyword:** River

**Category:** Yoruba

She is an Orisha, river goddess, personification of the Oba River, senior wife of storm god Shango who migrated to Cuba.[358] She is often conflated with Saint Catherine.

# Obosom

**Keyword:** Creation

**Category:** Akan

Obosom is an androgynous creator deity who is sometimes male, sometimes female.

# Oddudua

**Keywords:** Mother, Love

**Category:** Yoruba

Oddudua is an androgynous deity from the Yoruba pantheon who is sometimes male, sometimes female. In her feminine form, she is a goddess of love and wife of Obatawa and considered the primary creation goddess.

# Ogboinba

**Keyword:** Magic

**Category:** Ijo

When Ijo creator goddess Woyengi created humans, she decided to allow them to choose which gender they wanted to be. Ogboinba chose to be a female and wanted a good husband, so she asked the creator for special magical powers. According to legend, the one thing she forgot to ask for was a child. She became very wise and powerful and had a wonderful husband, but she wasn't happy and confronted the creator, which led to her downfall.[359]

---

358. Monaghan, *Encyclopedia of Goddesses & Heroines*, 24.
359. Lynch, *African Mythology A to Z*, 97, 98.

# Olókun

**Keyword:** Water

**Category:** Yoruba

She is the Orisha of great wealth and blesses people with abundance, health, and water. Some say this deity is male, others say she is either a female or androgynous. As a goddess, her consort is Emperor Oduduwa when Oduduwa is in masculine form. Olorun ruled the sky, and Olókun ruled the primordial waters.

# Osun

**Keywords:** Love, Beauty, Creativity

**Category:** Yoruba

**Also Known As:** Oshun

She is a consort of creator god Shango and presides over love, intimacy, beauty, wealth, and diplomacy. She is patron saint of Osun River in Nigeria. She is seen holding a mirror to admire her beauty. The divine creator Olodumare sent her as the sole female to help create the world. She represents sweet waters, fertility, and creativity.

# Otin

**Keyword:** Yoruba

**Category:** River

Otin is the personification of Otin River. People worshiped her after she came to help and protect the town of Inisa in Nigeria from hostile invaders even though she was from Otin. She is revered and honored for her bravery.

# Oya

**Keywords:** Protection, Wind

**Category:** Yoruba

Oya is the Orisha of winds and storms and a consort of storm god Shango. She personifies the Niger River and represents lightning and fire. Oya is a protector and was once human before being deified. In another version of her myth, she is associated with a buffalo as Red Buffalo Woman. Hunting god Ogun pursued and hunted her until she married him.[360]

## Thamuatz

**Keywords:** Hunting, Harvest, Creation

**Categories:** Kabyle, Primordial, Chthonic

Thamuatz and her consort, Itherther, are primordial beings who came from the Underworld called Tlam. The couple and their son, Achimi, were buffalo who helped spread hunting and meat to the people. Itherther created the mountains from his semen whenever he thought of Thamuatz.

## Wagadu

**Keyword:** Empire

**Categories:** Soninke, Personification

Wagadu is the personification of the legendary empire of the Soninke people mentioned in the myth *Gassire's Lute*, a story of a prince obsessed with immortality who becomes a storyteller. In the tale, which is part of the epic poem the *Dausi*, Wagadu is revered as a goddess. The epic describes the downfall of Wagadu, who disappeared four times due to vanity, falsehood, greed, and dissension. She embodies an ideal state of mind and a shining example of a utopian society that will rise again in all her glory at some future time.

## Woyengi

**Keywords:** Creation, Earth Mother

**Category:** Ijo

She is a female creator who came to Earth from heaven through a jolt of lighting and thunder. She arrived in a field and sat on a chair with her feet on a sacred stone and began to craft human beings from the earth. She held them and breathed life into each one of them. Initially they were not male or female because she allowed each being to choose their sex. Like many other African creators, she remained living in the void.[361]

---

360. Lynch, *African Mythology A to Z*, 112, 119.

361. Ford, *Hero with an African Face*, 123.

## Yasigi

**Keyword:** Beer

**Category:** Dogon

She is the goddess of festivals, celebrations, and beer. Born from the cosmic egg Amma, Yasigi helps people let go of seriousness and open themselves up to experience greater joy and fun in life. She is often depicted dancing with a beer ladle.

## Yemoja

**Keyword:** Mother

**Category:** Yoruba

Consort of Obatala, she is the Divine Mother of all the Orishas, the living embodiment of the ocean and all life because life started in the sea. When her waters broke, she gave birth to humanity and is therefore motherly and protective, particularly to women. She helps with all aspects of a woman's life, from fertility and childbirth to healing and the creation of wealth. She can be depicted as the moon or a mermaid.

## Summing Up

Throughout the continent of Africa, the secular is merged with the spiritual. Sacred activities are integrated into daily life. Each culture connects with mythology that speaks to their individuality and simultaneously connects them with the other members of their specific communities in a beautiful way.

With the spread of Christianity and Islam throughout Africa, traditional religions became interwoven into modern religious practices to ensure the continuity of their spiritual beliefs. While much of this may have been voluntary, there is also evidence that the people were forced into such practices, so they have had to keep their original spiritual beliefs to themselves. Catholic saints were substituted for deities when oppressors didn't allow those deities to be mentioned, let alone worshiped.[362] Thankfully, with the expanding consciousness happening around the world, many of these important teachings are now coming to light. There is much work yet to be done in this regard; however, some progress has been made.

---

362. Ford, *Hero with an African Face.*

Chapter Six

The enchanting myths and tales we've covered here are but a small fraction of the wealth of spirituality available throughout Africa. I hope this brief glimpse at goddesses has opened your heart to explore more of these amazing cultures.

## Recommended Reading

*African Mythology A to Z* (Second Edition) by Patricia Ann Lynch

*Encyclopedia of African Religion* by Molefi Kete Asante and Ama Mazama

*Hero with an African Face* by Clyde Ford

*Chapter Seven*

# East Asian Goddesses

The concept of Asia began with the Greeks, who divided their known world into two expansive parts: Europe and Asia. Where today we consider Asia to encompass China, Japan, Korea, Vietnam, and the like, the Greeks believed Asia to be the Persian Empire, much of which is now in modern-day Turkey.

East Asia is officially described as encompassing the totality of China, Taiwan, Singapore, Vietnam, Korea, and Japan.[363] With incredible cultural diversity within these regions, I will focus on goddesses from China and Japan and the common belief systems shared by people in this region through Confucianism, which has no deities, Buddhism, and the traditional folk religions, customs, and beliefs from these areas.

Stories of deities found within East Asian mythology share common themes, including the influence of water, either as a force of destruction or simply as the backdrop to the physical world, social order, and the importance of structured society as a path to piety and goodness with particular emphasis on family and the virtue of sacrifice of self in favor of the collective society.

## East Asian Cosmology

Goddesses will be explored through several of the religious and cultural groups within China, Japan, and Asia.

---

363. Holcombe, *History of East Asia*, 3, 5.

## Ainu

Ainu are Indigenous people from Hokkaidō, Kuril Islands, and Sakhalin.[364] Despite the close proximity to Japan, the Ainu are a distinct people who may be related to the Neolithic period of Japan known as the *Jōmon* culture, a term that referred to the cord pattern discovered in the pottery of the people who lived in a hunting and fishing society and likely practiced ancestor worship.[365] Jōmon culture flourished during the period of 10,500 BCE to 300 BCE and is believed to be the origin for the Ainu or other Indigenous people who lived in Asia in ancient times.[366] Ainu are completely distinct culturally from the Japanese and after years of discrimination have revitalized their cultural beliefs in modern times. Traditional Ainu beliefs are animist in nature. They believe in a creator god and the animating life force found in all things. Additionally, they worship the bear as head of the gods, which they collectively call *kamuy*, and acknowledge their divine ancestor Aioina Kamui. They worship a rich pantheon of gods and goddesses and their divine feminine kamuy.

## Buddhism

Buddhism originated in India by founder Siddhartha Gautama, meaning "one who achieves his goal," who lived between the sixth and fourth centuries BCE. Siddhartha was born in Nepal in a town called Lumbini in the Lumbini Province. The exact date of his birth is a topic for debate; however, most agree the date was likely in 485 BCE. Much of what we know of Buddha came from legends. Siddhartha was born on a full moon to an ancient ruler named Suddhodana. As a son of a ruling class family, Siddhartha enjoyed every privilege imaginable, but became disillusioned and dissatisfied.

At the age of twenty-nine, he left the security of his family home and his wife and child. He ventured beyond the protective walls into the world at large and became astounded by the vast suffering he witnessed. Siddhartha then experienced the Four Sights when he saw old age, death, and disease for the first time and realized that nobody can escape these inevitable circumstances. The final sight came when he met an aesthetic who suggested there was a path to freedom

---

364. Crawford, "Origins of the Ainu."

365. Williams, *Religions of the World*, 146.

366. Department of Asian Art, "Jōmon Culture."

from suffering, only to achieve it would mean renouncing all of life's privileges. Through an incredible act of courage, the prince renounced all his worldly possessions and comforts and set out on a mission to understand the true nature of suffering in the world and find lasting peace. After years of searching and studying, the Buddha realized enlightenment at the age of thirty-five while sitting under the Bodhi tree, in Bodh Gaya, India, and continued to teach up until his death at Kushinagar in Uttar Pradesh, India.[367]

Buddhism is considered a religion by some and a philosophy by others, probably because the founder emphasized the importance of the practice itself rather than any strict dogma or sacred texts.[368] Buddhism includes some goddesses and, in this chapter, we will explore goddesses who emerged from three schools of Buddhism throughout the ages:

1. **Mahāyāna Buddhism:** The Great Vehicle, currently the most widely followed branch of Buddhism that developed in India, has aspirants strive to become a vehicle of enlightenment, or Bodhisattava.

2. **Theravāda Buddhism:** The oldest school known as School of Elders claims to follow the original teachings of Buddha and doctrines through the Pali language.

3. **Vajrayana Buddhism:** The Way of the Diamond. Followers recognize that they already embody all the qualities of a Bodhisattava if they would only quiet the mind and follow the proper procedures to remember their inherent divinity. Through the use of spiritual practices, they hope to shorten the lengthy process of attaining enlightenment after repeated cycles of death and rebirth.[369]

Buddha's teachings are not purported in a single text, but come from shorter stories and myths that offer lessons for how to live a good life. Buddhism is not a religion. There is no god, no doctrine, and therefore the practice has been embraced by practitioners around the world who adhere to the principles alongside other belief systems and religions.

---

367. Skilton, *Concise History of Buddhism*, chapter 2.
368. Liusuwan, "Is Buddhism a Philosophy or a Religion?"
369. Nandakumar, "Female Deities in Vajrayana Buddhism."

## Chinese Folk Religion

Like many mythologies around the world, Chinese myth has an emergence story that begins with a Cosmic Egg that arose from chaos. Primordial being Pan Gu formed within this egg for 18,000 years until he grew the distance between heaven and Earth and emerged to create the world. He used his axe to separate the dual forces of yin and yang, pushing the sky high over the earth, and after his death, his body transformed into the natural phenomena of the world.[370]

Philosopher Han Fei told the story of an early and fearful time in history when humans were afraid and made nests above ground to avoid predators. Mythological hero Fu Xi encouraged humans to come down from the trees and helped them get food and fire and taught them to read and write.[371] Gods and goddesses emerged to help humanity and became fixed in the traditional religion of the Chinese.

## Daoism

Daoism (Romanized through the Wade-Giles system as *Taoism*) began around 500 BCE with the philosopher Laozi who wrote *Daodejing*, the key text of Daoism.[372] According to Daoism, the universe created itself out of chaos and formed the Tao, or way. Chaos divided into the opposite energies of yin and yang, the building blocks of all things in the material world, and formed itself into an egg from which P'an Ku emerged. He held the heavenly yin and earthly yang apart and experienced the expansion of the universe. After his death, his breath became the wind and clouds and stars formed from his hair. The sun came from his left eye, and the moon from his right, and the five sacred mountains of China formed from his body. His bones transformed into jade and pearls and the trees and flowers emerged from his skin.

Whether the world is viewed through the traditional belief systems or the Tao, in both systems, the yin and yang, meaning "dark and light," demonstrates the dual nature of life that many ancient cultures embraced. The recognition of the negative and positive forces evident within yin and yang and the desire to

---

370. Moorey, *Understand Chinese Mythology*, 11–2.

371. Watson, *Han Fei Tzu*, 96.

372. Komjathy, *Daoism*, 1, 95.

achieve greater balance, peace, and stability in life gave rise to the colorful pantheon of goddesses in this chapter.

## Shinto

Shinto is the oldest religion in Japan and was considered the state religion there up until 1945. Current studies suggest at least half the population of Japan still follows Shinto today, although that percentage could be as high as 80 percent. Because Shinto has no founder and no official texts, Shinto practices are so interwoven into the daily life of the Japanese people, almost every single person would follow Shinto to some degree. Earlier we discussed Buddhism, which is the second most followed religion in Japan, and because Buddhism is considered a philosophy more than a religion, many Japanese people follow both Shinto and Buddhism together, a practice called Ryobu Shinto.

Shinto means "way of the kami." Kami are spirits or supernatural forces found in every aspect of life in both animate and inanimate objects. The primary practice of Shinto involves numerous purification ceremonies and cleansing rituals held on a daily and annual basis to wash away evil spirits known as oni. Shinto shrines or alters are set up both in public places and within the home to make offerings and prayers to the various kami. Deity status is indicated by common root words including *no-kami*, a term that designates god status, *Ōmikami*, meaning "great or primary," and *no-Mikoto*, referring to deities given a special duty or task to perform.[373]

Shinto does not recognize any official site for holy occurrences since the sacred dwells within all things. Home altars called Kamindana are quite common and contain sanctified objects blessed by a priest, food offerings, fresh flowers, or anything the family wishes to have there to honor the presence of the kami and provide a focal point for offerings and blessings.[374]

Shinto subscribes to a cyclical form of time, the idea that all time is now, rather than the Western thought that the world will one day come to an end.[375] Helping ancestors ascend into the afterlife is a great concern. Shinto followers believe there are eight million kami, a number that is not to be taken literally,

---

373. Yong, "120 Shinto Gods and Goddesses to Know About."

374. Williams, *Religions of the World*, 78, 90–1.

375. Williams, *Religions of the World*, 10–4.

but refers to the fact that because spiritual energy resides in everything, the exact number is well beyond mortal understanding.

The *Kojiki*, "An Account of Ancient Matters," written in the eighth century, and *Nihongi*, compiled by the Chinese in 720 and also called the *Nihon Shoki* (Chronicles of Japan), are the two texts of Shintoism. The *Kojiki* tells a mythological tale of the creation of Japan before naming several of the gods and describing the early events of imperial Japan. *Nihongi* is one of the earliest sources of Japanese mythology.

## East Asian Goddesses

The following is a listing of some of the potentially millions of deities found within the Ainu, Chinese, Buddhist, Daoist, and Shinto pantheons.

## Aki-Bime-no-Kami

**Keyword:** Autumn

**Categories:** Shinto, Personification

She personifies the autumn season and is one of the many daughters of food goddess Uke Mochi.[376]

## Amaterasu Ōmikami

**Keywords:** Sun, Daylight, Protection

**Categories:** Shinto, Personification, Tutelary, Ancestral

Amaterasu is the major kami of Shintoism as the goddess and personification of the sun. Followers believe their emperor and his family are direct decedents of Amaterasu, who is by far the most revered kami and a central figure of Shintoism. One of the Three Precious Children, Amaterasu is the daughter of creator god Izanagi and goddess Izanami. Her consort, Tsukuyomi, is god of the moon and night. Considered the ancestor of the imperial house and all Japanese people, Amaterasu bestowed three sacred objects on the royal family of Japan—the sword, mirror, and jewel piece, which are now considered the Three Imperial Regalia.[377] She gave birth to three goddesses who emerged from her brother

---

376. Coulter and Turner, *Encyclopedia of Ancient Deities*, 482.

377. Kinsley, *Goddesses' Mirror*, 82.

Susanoo's sword. She is a protector of the Yamato clan and considered the ancestor of all the emperors.[378]

## Ame-no-Sagume

**Keywords:** Heavenly Advisor

**Category:** Shinto

In Shinto, there were three heavenly messengers sent to claim the earth, including Ame-no-Wakahiko-no-Kami. When a pheasant came to bring him a message, Ame-no-Sagume encouraged him to shoot it because she saw the bird as an evil omen. He fired the arrow, but it turned back toward him and killed him.[379] Her name implies she was an advisor, but in this case, her advice wasn't very good.

## Ame-no-Uzume

**Keywords:** Heavenly Dancer

**Category:** Shinto

**Also Known As:** Ame-no-Uzume-no-Mikoto

Known for happiness, mirth, and the arts, she performed a dance that returned the sun to Earth. After storm god Susanoo killed sun goddess Amaterasu's seamstress, the sun goddess retreated to a cave. Ame-no-Uzume lured Amaterasu out of hiding by performing a dance and brought light back to the earth. Sarutahiko, leader of earthly gods, is her consort. Ceremonial music and dance in temples are dedicated in her honor to reenact this dance and please the gods.[380]

## Ban Zhen Niangniang

**Keyword:** Protector

**Category:** Daoism

**Also Known As:** Banzhen

---

378. Williams, *Religions of the World*, 159.

379. Herbert, *Shinto*, 339.

380. Herbert, *Shinto*, 175.

She is a Daoist goddess who cures rashes.[381] She is associated with smallpox, measles, and scarlet fever and protects children from these dreaded diseases. The term *Niangniang* means "goddess" and can be attached to any number of female deities with different functions relating to women and childbirth.[382]

## Benzaiten

**Keyword:** Knowledge

**Categories:** Shinto, Mahāyāna Buddhist, Personification

Hindu goddess Sarasvati was carried into Buddhism in Japan and evolved into the deity known as Benzaiten, who is associated with water and is among the most worshiped deities in Japan. She represents knowledge, eloquence, and music and the arts, and became the only woman among the *Shichifukujin* (Seven Gods of Luck). She personifies business, artistic talent, and commercial success.[383]

## Bixia Yuanjun

**Keyword:** Mother

**Category:** Daoist

Goddess of Morning Clouds and Dawn, she was a human who ascended to her deified status through prayer and was officially granted this status during the Tang and Ming Dynasties by emperors.[384] She is connected with the sacred Mount Tai in Shangdong Province and presides over fertility and serves as a guardian of mothers and children. She is particularly helpful with assisting those who wish to have a male child.[385] She was widely revered in the twentieth century by healers and wives with many festivals celebrated in her honor.[386]

---

381. Harvard Art Museums, *Paper God.*

382. Sharma and Young, *Annual Review of Women in World Religions*, 149.

383. Ludvik, *Sarasvati.*

384. Kohn, *Daoism Handbook*, 393.

385. Jestice, *Holy People of the World*, 66, 128.

386. Monaghan, *Encyclopedia of Goddesses and Heroines: Africa, Eastern Mediterranean, Asia*, 112.

# Chang'e

**Keyword:** Moon

**Category:** Chinese Folk

**Also Known As:** Chang-O

According to legend, Chang'e is the consort of Hou Yi, an archer who shot down nine of the ten suns during an especially hot summer to keep the earth from being scorched. As a reward, an immortal gave Hou Yi the elixir of immortality, but he did not want to leave Chang'e to become immortal, so he asked her to keep the elixir safe. Fengmeng tried to coerce Chang'e into giving him the elixir, so she drank it herself on August 15 and immediately ascended to the moon. In some stories, Hou Yi kills himself and joins her, while in other stories, she remained forever separated from her beloved. Her only companion on the moon was Yu Tu, the Jade Rabbit. To this day, mid-autumn celebrations are in her honor.[387]

# Changxi

**Keywords:** Moon/Lunar Energy

**Categories:** Chinese Folk, Ancestral

Mother of the twelve moons, she is consort of ancestor Emperor Di Jun, the god of the eastern sky. She bathes the moon, which alludes to a common theme within Chinese mythology about the sun and moon needing bathing to clear dust from them and make them brighter in the sky. Some scholars believe she may be an older version of Chang'e.[388]

# Chinnamunda

**Keyword:** Sacrifice

**Category:** Vajrayana Buddhist

Similar to the Hindu goddess Chinnamasta, she is depicted with a severed head, which relates to the idea of ultimate sacrifice and generosity as she gives her life force or blood to assist others. She also represents the idea of the illusory

---

387. Yang, An, and Turner, *Handbook of Chinese Mythology*, 90.
388. Yang, An, and Turner, *Handbook of Chinese Mythology*, 88, 91.

nature of the body as we transcend from life to death and the advanced notion that by shedding the ego, one can attain ultimate perfection in enlightenment.[389]

## Chiwash ekot mat

**Keyword:** Water

**Category:** Ainu

She is the primary member of the Wakka-ush Kamui, who personifies different bodies of water, and represents the mouths of rivers.[390] Female personification of the places where the fresh and salt waters mingle, she ensures salmon are properly released into the streams so the people can catch them during salmon season.

## Cundī

**Keywords:** Good Fortune, Mother of Buddhas

**Category:** Mahāyāna Buddhist

Known as the Goddess of Seventy Million Buddhas, she is shown with eighteen arms and sitting atop a lotus flower. She has a Dharani, or chant, that people can say to clear karma and bring goodness into past, present, and future found in the Karandavyuha Sutra and is considered the source of the well-known and beloved chant *Om Manipadme Hum*.[391] She is associated with Avalokitesvara, who is among the most venerated bodhisattvas, or enlightened beings, within the Mahāyāna tradition.

## Dian Mu

**Keywords:** Lightning, Mother

**Category:** Chinese Folk

Consort of Lei Gong the thunder god, she creates lighting by holding up flashing mirrors. Known as Mother of Lighting, she works with several gods, to bring about various weather patterns.

---

389. Klasanova, "Chinnamunda."

390. Batchelor, *Ainu-English-Japanese Dictionary*, 499, 83.

391. Roberts with Yeshi, "Basket's Display," 200a–247b.

# Doumu

**Keyword:** Mother

**Category:** Daoism

Deity associated with the seven stars of the Northern Dipper, she is called Queen of Heaven, Empress of Heaven, or Mother of the Great Chariot. She is a protective force comparable to the Hindu goddess Marici.[392]

# Ehuang

**Keyword:** River

**Category:** Chinese Folk

**Also Known As:** E Wang

She is one of two sisters who both served as goddesses of the Xiang River. They are collectively called Xiang Shui Shen and are the daughters of Emperor Yao. Both daughters married Emperor Shun, and when he died, Ehuang drowned herself.[393]

# Feng Popo

**Keyword:** Wind

**Category:** Chinese Folk

**Also Known As:** Feng Pho-Pho, Feng Po Po

Known as Madame Wind, she personifies the wind and rides a tiger in the clouds and rules over storms and moisture. The tiger is a symbol of the crone, which is why she is often portrayed as an old lady. She calmed storms by collecting the high winds in her bag.[394] Initially she was called Feng Bo, the Earl of Wind, and then the earl became a woman.[395]

---

392. Kohn, *Daoism Handbook.*

393. Monaghan, *Encyclopedia of Goddesses and Heroines: Africa, Eastern Mediterranean, Asia,* 113.

394. Monaghan, *Encyclopedia of Goddesses and Heroines: Africa, Eastern Mediterranean, Asia,* 113.

395. Campbell, *Gods and Goddesses of Ancient China,* 100.

# Guanyin

**Keywords:** Compassion, Mercy

**Categories:** Mahāyāna, Theravāda, Vajrayana Buddhism

**Also Known As:** Kuan-Yin, Kannon

The Buddhist deity of compassion and mercy cares for all beings and is widely worshiped in China, Japan, and throughout the world in all branches of Buddhism. In Japan, she is known as Kannon, the Japanese Divine Mother who protects people from war, disease, and bad weather, such as tsunamis and hurricanes.[396] Large white statues of Kannon called Avalokiteshvara, a compassionate enlightened being who postpones their own salvation to help all sentient beings achieve liberation, are seen throughout Japan. Interestingly, the male Avalokiteshvara transformed into the female deity who embodied the traits of grace and became one of the most beloved figures in Buddhism.[397]

# Hariti

**Keywords:** Protector, Childhood

**Categories:** Mahāyāna Buddhist, Vajrayana

**Also Known As:** Karitemo (Japan), Yakshini, Kunti, Nata, Bhatta, Revati, Tamasuri, Alika, Magha, Benda

In Chinese tradition, Hariti is one of the Twenty-Four Protective Deities of Mahāyāna Buddhism and protectress of the Dharma.[398] In Vajrayana tradition, she was known as Yakshini. She and consort Yaksha were venerated in India before the time of the Buddha.[399] In mythology, Hariti had five hundred children she could not feed, so she turned to cannibalism. When Buddha took one of her favorite children, she asked him for help, so he returned the child and converted her and her family to the Dharma. She became known as a fierce defender and protector of children. Her consort is Pañcika, a nature spirit. Her myth is similar to the Hindu goddess Sasthi.

---

396. Reid, *Changing Face of Guanyin*, 5.

397. Yu, *Kuan-Yin*.

398. Simon, "Dictionary of Chinese Buddhist Terms," 1070–2.

399. Nandakumar, "Female Deities in Vajrayana Buddhism."

# Hashinau-uk Kamuy

**Keyword:** Hunting

**Category:** Ainu

Sister of the hearth goddess, she is goddess of the hunt who guides hunters to game, and the hunters give offerings to her to ensure success. She is known as bring down game woman.

# He Xiangu

**Keyword:** Immortal

**Category:** Daoism

**Also Known As:** Ho Hsien-Ku

She is a virginal goddess who had long hairs on the top of her head at birth, and when she became a teenager, a spirit appeared to her and told her to eat mother-of-pearl so she could become immune from death. She is the only official female deity among the members of the Eight Immortals of Daoism, although Lan Tstai-Ho had undetermined gender and often dressed like a woman.[400] She also vowed to remain a virgin and stopped eating as much food, so she raised her frequency and ascended to heaven as an immortal.

# Hou Tu Nainai

**Keyword:** Earth

**Category:** Chinese Folk

An earth goddess, she helped legendary King Yu drain excess water from the Yellow River during the Great Flood by sending messenger birds to him to let him know how to proceed. She began as a harvest and soil god named Hou Tu but changed to a goddess in the fourteenth century. She embodied the spirits of the dead emperors and empresses.[401]

---

400. Monaghan, *Encyclopedia of Goddesses and Heroines: Africa, Eastern Mediterranean, Asia*, 115.

401. Campbell, *Gods and Goddesses of Ancient China*, 94.

# Huchi

**Keyword:** Crone

**Categories:** Ainu, Personification

**Also Known As:** Kamui-huchi, Abe huchi

The word *huchi* or *fuchi* means "old woman or grandmother," but is also the Ainu word for *fire*, and as such, she is the goddess of fire.[402]

# Inari Ōkami

**Keyword:** Fertility

**Category:** Shinto

She is an important fertility goddess who presides over any agricultural endeavors, including rice and tofu, and is symbolized by a fox. Although she is a goddess in modern times, she was previously cited as androgynous. Worshiped since 711 CE, her shrine is on Mount Inari.[403]

# Izanami-no-Mikoto

**Keywords:** First Woman

**Category:** Shinto

Izanami is the Divine Mother and Creator Goddess of many of the Shinto kami and consort of Izanagi. She died giving birth to the fire god Kagutsuchi. After her death, her husband went to retrieve her from the Underworld called the land of Yomi and broke a taboo by looking at her corpse.[404] So disgusted by her horrible appearance, Izanagi ran away, so in retaliation for his disloyalty, Izanami cursed his descendants.

# Janguli

**Keywords:** Healer, Snakes

**Category:** Vajrayana Buddhism

---

402. Batchelor, *Ainu-English-Japanese Dictionary*, 157.

403. Koshikidake and Faulks, *Shugendo*, 87.

404. Philippi, *Kojiki*, 61.

Known as the remover of poisons, she was primarily worshiped in India as the Hindu goddess Manasa and revered for curing people who had been poisoned. She became known as the Subjugator of Snakes. She can also be conflated with goddess Tara as Janguli-Tara and is shown with four arms carrying a lute and protection mudra.[405]

## Jingū-kōgō

**Keywords:** Legendary Empress

**Categories:** Shinto, Ancestral

**Also Known As:** Okinaga-Tarashi-Nime-no-Mikoto

Known for her beauty, wisdom, and virtue, according to Book IX of the *Nihongi*, she assisted her husband, the legendary Emperor Chūai, in battle after receiving divine guidance from the gods.[406] Chūai did not believe or follow the advice she gave him and died soon thereafter. In 200 CE, she became empress and subdued rebels, went on to conquer the Korean Peninsula, and was venerated after her death. During her reign, she was pregnant with a son who became the legendary Emperor Ojin, considered the divine essence of the Shinto war god. Some credit her son Ojin's presence in her womb for her success.[407] There are tombs dedicated in her honor in the cities of Nara and Osaka, Japan.

## Jiu Tian Xuan Nü

**Keywords:** Sky, Stars, Heavens

**Categories:** Daoism, Ancestral

The word *Tian* refers to heaven, and as such, she is known as Mysterious Lady of the Nine Heavens, a woman who appeared as a human-headed bird. She served as an essential advisor to Yellow Emperor Huang Di during a confrontation and defeat of war god Chi You. Considered a legendary ancestor of the Chinese, she helps with new concepts, creativity, and overall problem-solving.[408] She

---

405. Klieger, "Tara—An Example of Buddhist-Hindu Syncretism," 46–52.

406. Aston and Barrow, *Nihongi*, 224–53.

407. Griffis, *Mikado's Empire*, 76–9.

408. Raines and Maguire, *What Men Owe to Women*, 247–8.

had the gift of invisibility and people believed she could move the northern stars around to protect the empire.

## Kamu-Oichihime-no-Kami

**Keyword:** Mother

**Category:** Shinto

Called Mother of the Great Year, she is the daughter of warrior god Ōyamatsumi, consort of Susanoo, god of seas and storms, and the mother of Ōtoshi-no-Kami, who is known as the Great Year god and father of many of the Shinto deities.[409]

## Kanakhala

**Keywords:** Dancing, Devotion, Sacrifice

**Category:** Vajrayana Buddhism

Known as Younger Mischievous Girl, she is a Mahasiddha of Vajrayana Buddhism. She and her sister Mekhala were so devoted to their guru, they severed their heads and danced for him. They are often shown holding swords above their heads.[410] As part of the group of self-sacrificing deities, the sisters are listed among the Mahasiddhas, meaning "great adepts of Vajrayana Buddhism."

## Kukuri-Hime-no-Kami

**Keyword:** Peacemaker

**Category:** Shinto

**Also Known As:** Kikuri-Hime-no-Kami

She binds fates together as a goddess of mediation who assisted during a conflict between creator god Izanagi and creator goddess Izanami. She is revered as a peacemaker as suggested by her name *kiku*, meaning "hearing," and *ri*, "truth." Her name may also relate to the chrysanthemum flower, which relates to the imperial family. She is considered a mediator between heaven and Earth.[411]

---

409. Cali and Dougill, *Shinto Shrines*, 299.

410. Shaw, *Buddhist Goddesses of India*, 413.

411. Herbert, *Shinto*.

# Konohanasakuya-Hime

**Keyword:** Earth

**Categories:** Shinto, Ancestral, Personification

Called the Blossom Princess, she personifies the earth and is especially connected to Mount Asama, located north of Mount Fuji, and all the volcanoes in Japan, and she is symbolized by the cherry blossom. Her father, the warrior god Ōyamatsumi, would not allow Ninigi, ancestor of the imperial family, to marry her and offered one of his other daughters instead, but when Ninigi refused, he received a curse and became a mortal.[412] Ninigi later accused Konohanasakuya-Hime of cheating on him. This infuriated her, and in retaliation, she gave birth to their children in a burning hut and said her children would not be harmed if they were his, and when they were all born without incident, she proved her fidelity.

# Kushinada-Hime

**Keywords:** Harvest, Fertility, Rice

**Categories:** Shinto, Personification

**Also Known As:** Kushinadahime, Inadahime

She became the wife of the god of seas and storms Susanoo after he rescued her from the evil eight-tailed dragon serpent of kosi.[413] She is the personification of rice, which makes the pair a good match since Susanoo is in charge of the rains that help the harvest.

# Luo Shen

**Keywords:** Yellow River

**Category:** Chinese Folk

Famed Chinese poet Cao Zhi's poem "Nymph of the Luo River," written in 222 CE, describes her as a daughter of the god Fu Xi.[414] She drowned and became a river deity for the Luo River, which is a tributary stream or river that flows into the larger Yellow River. The term *shen* refers to a spirit.

---

412. Herbert, *Shinto*.

413. Philippi, *Kojiki*, 509.

414. Smithsonian Institution, "Nymph of the Luo River."

# Mahāpajāpatī Gotamī

**Keywords:** Mother of Buddhism

**Category:** Mahāyāna Buddhism

Buddha's mother Maya died shortly after his birth, so his aunt Mahāpajāpatī Gotamī, Maya's sister, adopted Siddhartha and raised him until he eventually became the Buddha.

After Buddha attained enlightenment, Mahāpajāpatī Gotamī asked Buddha to allow women into the priesthood. He initially refused, but eventually she became the very first *bhikkhuni* (nun) whom Buddha ordained into the *Sangha* (Buddhist community).[415]

# Mārīcī

**Keywords:** Sun, Warrior

**Categories:** Mahāyāna, Vajrayana Buddhism

**Also Known As:** Marishiten

She is pictured with several heads, including one of a boar. She is the Buddhist version of Doumu, a Chinese goddess and mother of the Big Dipper. She personifies the dawn. As Marishiten, she is worshiped in Japan as healer and patroness and protectress for samurai warriors.[416] Called Lady of Brilliant Light Rays, in some of her more militant forms, she is seen sitting atop a lotus wearing a skull necklace.[417]

# Maya

**Keyword:** Mother

**Categories:** Mahāyāna, Theravāda, Vajrayana Buddhism

Gautama Buddha's birth mother, who died after his birth, ascended to a blissful afterlife where she was deified. She is known as Queen Maya and has various names in Tibet and China. The meaning of her consort Suddhodana's name

---

415. Tin, *Dhammapada*, 462.

416. Hall, *Buddhist Goddess Marishiten*, 1–9, 21–4.

417. Shaw, *Buddhist Goddesses of India*, 203.

implies he was a ruler. Myths name him as a king, although Buddha himself never wanted an elaborate origin story to supersede his teachings.[418]

## Mazu

**Keywords:** Mother, Protector

**Categories:** Chinese Folk, Daoism, Tutelary, Ancestral

Called the Queen Mother of Heaven, she is a patron saint of sailors, fishermen, and travelers and merchants. It is believed Mazu may have been a real-life villager from Fuji who saved three of her brothers from a shipwreck. She is now seen as a protector and ancestral spirit who roams the sea and intercedes to protect people. She was adopted into the Taoist pantheon in 1409.[419]

## Mekhala

**Keywords:** Dancing, Devotion, Sacrifice

**Category:** Vajrayana Buddhism

Known as Elder Mischievous Girl, she and her sister Kanakhalawere so devoted to their guru, they severed their heads and danced for him and were elevated to goddess status.[420] The sisters have associations with the other severed-head goddess Chinnamunda. Iconography relating to severing the head represents the ultimate sacrifice in order to serve others and shed the ego self.

## Meng Po

**Keywords:** Reincarnation, Forgetfulness

**Categories:** Chinese Folk, Chthonic

In stories about the Chinese hell, she serves a broth so people won't recall hell or their previous lives after they're reborn. She wipes the slate clean so souls can reincarnate properly into the next incarnation. If for some reason someone fails to sip the broth, they will be born with knowledge of the past.[421]

418. Gombrich, *How Buddhism Began*, 82.

419. Kohn, *Daoism Handbook*, 394.

420. Dowman, *Masters of Mahamudra*, 317, 321.

421. Graves and Guirand, *New Larousse Encyclopedia of Mythology*, 400.

# Midzu-ha-no-me

**Keywords:** Water, Harvest, Fertility

**Categories:** Shinto, Personification

Before she gave birth to the fire god who killed her, creator goddess Izanami gave birth to Midzu-ha-no-me, who emerged from Izanami's urine.[422] She became a water goddess and the personification of proper irrigation.[423]

# Nairatmya

**Keywords:** Air, Sky

**Categories:** Vajrayana Buddhism, Primordial

As a primordial sky goddess, Nairatmya is said to have no self because she embodies the air and the life force that animates all things. She is called Lady of Emptiness as a divine yogini who is one with universal consciousness. Hevajra, the namesake of the *Hevajra Tantra* that describes worship in a circle or mandala, is her consort.[424]

# Nakisawame-no-Kami

**Keywords:** Spring Water

**Categories:** Shinto, Personification

After the creation goddess Izanami died giving birth to the fire god, her consort Izanagi's tears created Nakisawame-no-Kami, who is the personification of spring water.[425]

# Nü Gua

**Keywords:** Mother, Fertility, Creation

**Categories:** Chinese Folk, Ancestral, Primordial

Mother of the Chinese belief systems, Nü Gua's consort Fu Xi is considered one of the Three Sovereigns, Three August Ones, and humanity's original ances-

---

422. Astonand Barrow, *Nihongi*, 21.

423. Philippi, *Kojiki*, 521.

424. Shaw, *Buddhist Goddesses of India*, 387, 398–9.

425. Philippi, *Kojiki*, 55.

tor who invented the I Ching. Nü Gua and Fu Xi are often depicted together with conjoined dragon tails and tools to help humanity. Fu Xi holds a compass, and Nü Gua carries a compass. Together, they are credited with creating people from clay and repopulating the world after a flood.[426] She repaired a damaged heavenly pillar with a five-colored stone and is still venerated today in temples as the patroness of Earth who mended the broken world. Nü Gua's marriage to Fu Xi balanced yin and yang.

# Nuying

**Keyword:** River

**Categories:** Chinese Folk, Personification

She is one of two sister goddesses who personify the Xiang River and both married Emperor Shun. When the emperor died, her sister Ehuang drowned herself, which may stem from a practice of sacrifice to ensure good harvests and protection from famine or drought.[427]

# Pet-etok-mat

**Keyword:** River

**Categories:** Ainu, Personification

She personifies the source of rivers and is one of Wakka-ush Kamui, a group of female goddesses similar to nymphs of other cultures who embody and personify all the various kinds of flowing water—springs, ponds, rivers, waterfalls, and so forth. Collectively, they are known as the Watery Gods.[428]

# Pet-ru-ush mat

**Keyword:** River

**Category:** Ainu

She is goddess of courses of rivers and one of a group of nymphlike female deities called Females of the Waterways, or Wakka-ush-kamui, who look out

---

426. Lewis, *Flood Myths of Early China*, 116.

427. Monaghan, *Encyclopedia of Goddesses and Heroines: Africa, Eastern Mediterranean, Asia*, 113.

428. Batchelor, *Ainu-English-Japanese Dictionary*, 499.

over the rivers that flow into the ocean.[429] Fishermen ask them for bountiful catches and to protect them from harsh conditions.

## Prajñāpāramitā Devi

**Keywords:** Wisdom, Great Mother

**Categories:** Mahayana, Theravāda Buddhism

She is the Great Mother who personifies the essence of wisdom and subject of forty texts known as the *Prajñāpāramitā Sutras* composed between 100 BCE and 600 CE in India.[430] She is the personification of the Perfection of Transcendent Wisdom.

## Simhamukha

**Keyword:** Wisdom

**Category:** Vajrayana Buddhism

She is a wisdom goddess depicted with a lion face and is considered comparable and similar to Sekhmet in Egypt. Her fierce energy is said to assist people in transmuting the energy of anger into an enlightened state, and as she has achieved this level of consciousness, she is considered a fully enlightened dakini, or female embodiment of the divine.[431]

## Sitātapatrā

**Keyword:** Protector

**Categories:** Mahāyāna, Vajrayana Buddhism

A powerful protector, she guards people from malevolent supernatural forces. She is a divine being who emanated from the ball on the top of Buddha's head, which is called an Ushnisha. Most people see the Buddha and assume the ball is a knot of hair tied atop his head; however, he is actually bald, and this ball is one of what is called the thirty-two marks of the Buddha. She has many forms and

429. Batchelor, *Ainu-English-Japanese Dictionary*, 499.

430. Conze, *Perfect Wisdom*.

431. Klasanova, "Simhamukha."

can appear with one head or up to a thousand heads and a thousand hands. She is called the One with the White Parasol.[432]

## Sunü

**Keywords:** Sexuality, Fertility, Music

**Category:** Daoism

Goddess of music and sexuality, her songs could pacify wild animals and change the seasons. Called Immaculate Girl, she is the first female harp player who shared her sexual expertise with the Yellow Emperor, who wrote the book *Su Nü Jing*, a book of Daoist sexuality.[433]

## Tamayori-Hime

**Keyword:** Sea

**Categories:** Shinto, Ancestral

Daughter of sea god Owatatsumi-no-Kami and younger sister of Toyotama-Hime, she is mentioned in both the *Kojiki* and the *Nihongi*. After her sister turned into a sea monster during childbirth and left her husband, she took care of their baby, her nephew Ugayafukiaezu-no-Mikoto, and eventually married him. Their son became the first legendary Emperor Jimmu.[434]

## Tara

**Keywords:** Star, Mother

**Category:** Vajrayana Buddhism

Known as Mother of Liberation, the name *Tara* comes from the Sanskrit word for *star*. Tara is featured in Tibetan Buddhism as a female aspect of Avalokiteśvara, a Buddha who encompasses the passion of all Buddhas created by his tear. She is represented in several colors considered to be different forms of the same deity who address various challenges in life. Green Tara called Shyama represents abundance, prosperity, and the earth. Blue Tara, Ekajata, is a fierce protective Tara comparable to Kali in Hinduism. White Tara is called Sita

---

432. Porció, *One with the White Parasol*.

433. McMahon, *Misers, Shrews and Polygamists*, 43.

434. Aston and Barrow, *Nihongi*, 94–110.

and represents purity and perfection. Yellow Tara, Bhrikuti, assists with wealth creation. Red Tara, Kurukulla, is a protective Tara who removes obstacles and assists in magnetizing things to people.[435]

## Tian Hou

**Keywords:** Protection, Power

**Category:** Chinese Folk

A champion for unmarried women, she chose to remain single and became a seer and deity. She also protects sailors as a patroness for their safety.[436]

## Toyotama-Hime

**Keywords:** Luck, Prosperity

**Category:** Shinto

Mentioned in both the *Kojiki* and the *Nihongi*, she represented luck of the sea and luck of the mountain. In her myth, hunter Hoori misplaced his brother's lucky fishing fetish, and on his journey to find it, he met the beautiful princess, daughter of the sea god Owatatsumi-no-Kami, who lived in a sea house. With her father's blessing, she became the wife of Hoori, the grandfather of the first emperor of Japan. She turned into a sea monster during childbirth.[437] When Hoori spied on her during childbirth after promising he would give her some privacy, she left him.

## Uke Mochi

**Keywords:** Abundance, Food, Home, Hearth

**Category:** Shinto

**Also Known As:** Uke-Mochi, Uke-Mochi-no-Kami, Ogetsu-Hime-no-Kami

Known as the Goddess Who Possesses Food, her myth in the *Nihongi* says she created food by spraying it from her orifices. The moon god Tsuki-Yomi became so offended by her actions, he killed her. Sun goddess Amaterasu became

435. Nandakumar, "Female Deities in Vajrayana Buddhism."

436. Sharma and Young, *Annual Review of Women in World Religions*, 149.

437. Aston and Barrow, *Nihongi*, 93, 98.

infuriated by the murder and refused to ever gaze on the moon again, separating day and night.[438]

# Vajrayogini

**Keywords:** Love, Passion

**Category:** Vajrayana Buddhism

She is a goddess of passionate dance and movement who assists people with great passion to transmute and raise the frequencies of their ecstatic devotion to higher-leveled consciousness.[439] The fervor she embodies is universal and reflects a selfless love for all beings. Through this perspective, she may assist people in turning the mundane activities of the material world into higher ideals.

# Vasudhārā

**Keyword:** Wealth

**Categories:** Mahāyāna, Vajrayana Buddhism

Her name means "Stream of Gems" and she is called the Bountiful Lady, associated with the creation of abundance, wealth, and prosperity. Her myth is included in the *Vasudhara Dharani* in a tale called *The Inquiry of the Layman Sucandra* about a man who needed to create wealth to feed his large family.[440]

# Wakahirume-no-Mikoto

**Keywords:** Divine Seamstress

**Category:** Shinto

She sat in a sacred weaving hall creating garments on a loom for the deities. Storm god Susanoo flung a horse into the sacred hall, startled her, and caused her to fall and cut herself. She died of her injuries and the incident angered sun goddess Amaterasu so much, she retreated into a cave, taking the sun and daylight with her.[441]

---

438. Coulter and Turner, *Encyclopedia of Ancient Deities*, 482.
439. Shaw, *Buddhist Goddesses of India*, 360.
440. Suzuki, *Essays in Zen Buddhism*.
441. Aston and Barrow, *Nihongi*, 45.

# Wakasaname-no-Kami

**Keywords:** Harvest, Prosperity

**Category:** Shinto

She is Otoshi-no-Kami's granddaughter and a fertility goddess of harvests, grain, prosperity, and good crops. She presides specifically over the agricultural phase of transplanting new rice in fields.[442]

# Wakaukanome-no-Kami

**Keyword:** Water

**Category:** Shinto

Agriculture and water goddess, she personifies streams. Known as a kami of cereals, she is enshrined in Nara Prefecture at Hirose Jinja as a gracious kami.[443]

# Xihe

**Keyword:** Sun

**Categories:** Chinese Folk, Ancestral

With her consort Emperor Di Jun, the sacred ancestor, she is the mother of the ten suns that scorched the earth.[444] The suns appeared as ten three-legged crows perched in Fusang, a sacred mulberry tree. Each day, Xihe picked one of the crows to ride around the world with her in her carriage. Later in history, Xi and He became two male gods.[445]

# Xiwangmu

**Keywords:** Queen Mother of the West

**Category:** Daoism

**Also Known As:** Xiwang Mu

The Northwest is considered a mythological utopia in Chinese myth and the location of Kunlun, the mythical mountain of Daoism and home to goddess

442. Herbert, *Shinto*.

443. Picken, *Historical Dictionary of Shinto*, 112–3.

444. Gu, *Cultural History of the Chinese Language*, 124.

445. Monaghan, *Encyclopedia of Goddesses & Heroines*, 72.

Xiwangmu, who rules over immortals and possesses the elixir of immortality and a peach tree that bears fruit once every three thousand years.[446] Toward the end of the Han Dynasty, a peasant cult emerged around the Queen Mother of the West, quite possibly as a reaction to a life-threatening drought that caused people to become obsessed with the idea of attaining immortality.[447] The movement is considered by some scholars to be the first documented mass religious movement in history.[448]

## Yamatohime-no-Mikoto

Keyword: Priestess

Category: Shinto

Known as Emperor Suinin's daughter and legendary High Priestess, she is founder of the Ise Grand Shrine. In the *Nihon Shoki*, she is a servant of sun goddess Amaterasu.[449]

## Yaśodharā

Keywords: Divine Mother

Categories: Mahāyāna, Theravāda, Vajrayana Buddhism

She was the princess who became Siddhartha Buddha's wife before he left his royal life to become the Buddha. She became a Buddhist nun and achieved enlightenment during her lifetime and is worshiped as a goddess known as Bearer of Glory.[450]

## Zhi Nu

Keywords: Love, Marriage, Harvest

Category: Chinese Folk

Also Known As: Weaving Maiden

446. Hsun, *Brief History of Chinese Fiction*, 33.

447. Cahill, *Transcendence & Divine Passion*, 21.

448. Lagerwey and Kalinowski, *Early Chinese Religion*, 580, 976, 1062.

449. Tanaka, *Japan's Orient*, 160.

450. Mahathera, *Buddha and His Teachings*.

Zhi Nu is known for one of the most enduring tales in Chinese mythology. Cattle herder Niu Lang had a special cow that spoke and encouraged him to go to heaven and marry Zhi Nu, the weaving maiden, daughter of the Jade Emperor who weaved her father's robes from clouds. Her father allowed her to go to Earth and marry the herd boy. She loved him so much, she abandoned her duties in heaven, so the gods came and took her back to heaven. When Niu Lang tried to follow, the gods threw up a wall of stars to stop him, now known as the Milky Way. Once a year, magpies form a bridge from heaven to Earth on the seventh night of the seventh lunar month so the lovers can reunite. The Double Seventh Festival is celebrated annually.[451] As agricultural deities, the tale describes the real-life condition of the separation of Chinese men and women during the planting and harvest seasons.[452]

## Zhu Sheng Niang Niang

**Keywords:** Fertility, Childbirth

**Categories:** Daoist, Ancestral

Called Maiden Who Brings Children, she helps with all aspects of conception and birth to all activities dedicated to protecting both mother and child. She is seen holding a book with a brush to record the child in the family ancestry register.[453]

## Summing Up

I hope you've enjoyed our exploration of East Asian goddesses. Religion and spirituality within the Chinese belief systems are a complex mix influenced by several factors: Confucianism, Daoism, Buddhism, and what is known as traditional folk religion, all of which are polytheistic with followers who recognize the divinity in all things, including natural phenomena and ancestors.

Like many Indigenous cultures, Ainu fought for rights within Japan and seem to be making good progress in that goal. On May 24, 2019, a new law went into effect to officially recognize the Ainu as the Indigenous people of Japan. As with all efforts to honor and respect diversity and early peoples, the journey contin-

---

451. Campbell, *Gods and Goddesses of Ancient China*, 117.

452. Granet, *Chinese Civilization*.

453. Eng, *Understanding Chinese Culture in Relation to Tao*.

ues and will hopefully lead to improving conditions and promote healthy human rights into the future.

The impact of Buddhism around the world cannot be understated. With deities such as Tara and the other feminine goddesses becoming more prevalent in society, women are encouraged more than ever to follow this path knowing they can achieve what their male predecessors did in the past and more.

As a former state religion, Shinto is infused into the personal, political, and social lives of the Japanese people with the belief system embedded into everything, including the imperial house. Followers choose to either worship at public shrines, with or without the presence of priests, or they may enlist the help of shamans to perform various sacred rites, or practice and worship within the privacy of home.[454]

I hope this brief exploration of East Asia left you with curiosity about this amazing part of the world and the goddesses beloved by the diverse peoples there.

## Recommended Reading

*Introduction to Buddhism* by the Dalai Lama

*Encyclopedia of Goddesses and Heroines: Africa, Eastern Mediterranean, Asia* (Volume 1) by Patricia Monaghan

*Buddhist Goddesses of India* by Miranda Eberle Shaw

*A History of East Asia* by Charles Holcombe

---

454. Williams, *Religions of the World*, 17–22.

## Chapter Eight
# Hindu Goddesses

Hinduism is the world's oldest religious tradition with roots in the Indus Valley Civilization dating back from 3000 to 1700 BCE.[455] Although the Hinduism faith boasts a billion followers, the people only recently used that word themselves.[456] The term *Hindu* originated during the Persian Empire when Persian leaders attempted to describe one of the boundaries to their territories along what was then called the Sindhu River. Today, the word *Hindu* is used to describe the people who live south of that same river, which in modern times is called the Indus, who share the beliefs that originated in the sacred texts of that land.

Imperialism and British colonization cemented the term *Hindu* into the collective minds of people around the world. Even the word *India* was not used until British colonization. Prior to British arrival, there were no geographical boundaries in place. The British consolidated the regions within the subcontinent under one rule and called the area India. In antiquity, the region known as Bharat was described as being located south of the snowcapped mountains and north of the sea.[457]

India is the largest democracy in the world. A region that embodies diversity, India has over sixteen languages, hundreds of dialects, and openness to all manner of faiths. Like many of the cultures described in this book, followers of

---

455. Keay, *India*, 1.

456. Sengupta, *Being Hindu*, 18, 24.

457. Sengupta, *Being Hindu*, 36–9.

Hindu faith do not subscribe to the idea of religion because their practices are wholly integrated aspects of daily life.

# Cosmology

Hindu cosmology is often difficult for outsiders to understand, in part because Hindus do not believe in one true god. Brahma is considered the supreme god who has multiple embodiments as both gods and goddesses. Hinduism has no founder as it is believed that Brahma always existed and has no beginning or end. The purpose of life is to acknowledge oneness with all, to pursue your unique talent or *dharma*, action or *karma*. By so doing, you can achieve a state of oneness with all that will help you eventually avoid the constant recycling of your soul through death and rebirth known as *samsara* to attain oneness with the divine. Eternal Order or *Sanatan Dharma* exists because Brahma created the universe, and that is how it has always been and always will be. To properly practice the Sanatan Dharma, followers can participate in daily devotionals called Puja, which is accomplished through prayer, ritual, or sacrifice. Puja can be performed either in homes or public temples or through making contact with a deity by close proximity to a statue, image, or religious artifact.

Hinduism recognizes the one Supreme God Brahma as a triad of different aspects called the Trimurti, which includes Brahma the creator, Shiva the destroyer, and Vishnu the preserver, who maintains the world between creation and destruction. Lesser gods and goddesses animate various aspects of the known world. Individual practitioners of Hinduism may choose to follow any of these deities and recognize one of them as their primary god of choice depending on which denomination they follow. Hinduism has four main traditions or denominations: Shaivism, worship of Shiva (or Siva) as the Supreme God; Vaishnavism, worship of Vishnu as Supreme God; Smartism, recognition of God in one of six forms (Shiva, Vishnu, Ganesha, Shakti, Surya, and Skanda); and Shaktism, belief in the Divine Mother as supreme.[458]

The fighting that occurs throughout the world in the name of a true God is astounding, so Hindus do not subscribe to that idea, and therefore avoid conflict by allowing individuals to embrace their own inner ideal of the Supreme Being.

---

458. Editors of Hinduism Today, *What Is Hinduism?*

For that reason, there are no heretics or unbelievers to ostracize.[459] Hinduism honors all truth seekers. Because Hinduism does not focus on converting others to their faith or evangelizing their beliefs as is common in Christianity and other religions, this gives rise to the wide misconceptions about their beliefs. What we do know of India and Hinduism is based on several Sanskrit manuscripts including the *Vedas*, considered among the oldest texts in the world that date sometime before the first millennium BCE; the *Brahmanas*; and the two great epics, the *Mahabharata* and the *Ramayana*.[460]

Hinduism recognizes the divine feminine power as an active force embodied in the term *Shakti*. The major Hindu denomination Shaktism is of particular interest in this exploration of goddesses because believers recognize the primary divine being as a Great Mother goddess called Mahadevi or Devi from which all the other goddesses originate. The term *devi*, when uncapitalized, refers to anything heavenly while still denoting a feminine energy. Male deities and counterparts would be called *Deva* or *deva*.[461]

Perhaps the simplest way to categorize Hindu goddesses would be to place them into one of two groupings:

**Duo:** A goddess joined to a husband or consort. Such goddesses are revered as the Hindu faith honors the divine feminine and her life-giving abilities that assist her husband in a totality of creation. They are two halves of a whole, united in the sanctity of marriage. These goddesses are beautiful, kind, and pleasant women who bless their followers with different aspects of divine love.

**Solo:** A goddess who is on her own as an individual representation of the divine who have no husbands or consorts. They are most often depicted as terrorizing, bloodthirsty warriors. Unlike other pantheons where we might categorize such fierce ladies as Chthonic or Underworld beings, the Hindu goddesses are not necessarily dwellers of the Underworld. Their fierce appearance is used to frighten off demons and dark forces and they are revered and beloved protectors of humanity.

---

459. Sengupta, *Being Hindu*, 71.

460. Keay, *India*, 2.

461. Das, *Complete Illustrated Guide to Hinduism*, 9; Hawley and Wulff, *Devi*, 51.

# Hindu Goddesses

Although Hinduism recognizes one Supreme God, the full pantheon of gods and goddesses is said to number anywhere from 33 to 33 million, or all the way up to 330 million, depending on the scripture.[462] Obviously, there is no way to explore all the incredible deities within Hinduism, but here, you can discover a few of the best-known Hindu goddesses.

## Aditi

**Keyword:** Infinity

**Category:** Duo

As a Divine Mother figure, she is mentioned in the *Vedas* over eighty times.[463] As a protective, cosmic, divine, and all-encompassing being, she represents infinity and personifies the vast cosmos and the *akasha*, or infinite realm of space. She is mother to the god Indra and every celestial deity collectively called the Adityas with her consort, the Hindu sage Kashyapa.

## Agneya

**Keyword:** Fire

**Category:** Duo

Agneya is mentioned in the *Vishnu Purana* and gets her name from the fact she is the daughter of Vedic fire god Agni. Her name means "originating from fire."[464] Her mother is Vedic sacrifice goddess Svaha. Agneya is mentioned in Vedic literature for her power from being born of fire. She presides over the southeast direction. Her consort, Uru, is a descendant of Vedic rishi Angiras. According to the Sanskrit text *Harivamsham*, they are parents to several kings, including Agna, Sumanas, Khyaati, Kratu, Sibi, and Gaya.[465]

---

462. Dasa, "33 Million Gods of Hinduism"; Dudhane, "How Many Gods Are There in Hinduism?"

463. Kinsley, *Hindu Goddesses*, 9.

464. Vyasa, *Vishnu Purana*, 199.

465. Dutt, *Prose English Translation of Harivamsha.*

# Ammavaru

**Keyword:** Mother

**Categories:** Solo, Primordial

**Also Known As:** Ankamma

She is a primordial mother described as coming into being long before the four yugas (ages) began. She laid the cosmic eggs that birthed the triad of gods—Brahma, Shiva, and Vishnu.[466]

# Aranyani

**Keywords:** Forest, Animals, Protector

**Categories:** Solo, Personification

**Also Known As:** AraNyaanii

*AraNyam* means "forest." In chapter 10 hymn 146 of the *Rigveda*, Aranyani is attested as a goddess of the forest who may be the earliest example of a forest goddess in the world. The hymn describes her as quiet and elusive with the exception of the tinkling bells on her anklets and describes how she protects the forest and creatures who live there.[467]

# Bagalamukhi

**Keywords:** Magic, Courage, Power

**Category:** Solo

Gifted with the power of attraction, she can assist people in attracting right circumstances into their lives or the right people to help create optimal outcomes. She helps people free themselves from delusion. Yellow is her color, which is associated with the solar plexus chakra center and personal strength and power. She is depicted with lions. In one myth, she stops a demon by grabbing his tongue. She doesn't kill him, but converts him with her power into a devotee. In another, Vishnu calls upon Parvati, who calls Bagalamukhi forth as a powerful form of her divine energy. She is one of the ten Dasha Mahavidya, goddesses of the Hindu yoga tradition.

---

466. Whitehead, *Village Gods of South India*, 124.

467. Harish, "Hymn to a Forest Nymph in the Rig Veda."

# Bhairavi

**Keyword:** Fertility

**Category:** Duo

Like Kali, she wears a garland of heads and can be depicted as a consort to Bhairava, an avatar of Shiva worshiped in the Shaivism denomination of Hinduism. Associated with a crescent moon and smeared with blood, she is related to menstrual cycles as she who dwells in the *yoni* (vagina). She is revered within Shaktism as a higher-leveled deity than even Brahma, Shiva, and Vishnu.[468] She is one of the ten Dasha Mahavidya, goddesses of the Hindu yoga tradition.

# Bhramari

**Keyword:** Bees

**Category:** Duo

During a battle, a demon threatened to destroy the earth and heavens, and Shiva called upon Bhramari, who rose up behind him as a giant tower that blocked the demon army. She then sent hordes of black bees, wasps, hornets, mosquitoes, and flies from her hands and the sides of her body toward the demons and defeated Arunasura's demon army.[469] She is considered a divine partner or counterpart of Lord Shiva.

# Bhuvaneshvari

**Keywords:** Earth Mother

**Category:** Duo

**Also Known As:** Prapanceshvari

She embodies the physical world, is symbolized by the crescent moon, and is fourth on the list of ten Dasha Mahavidya goddesses of the Hindu yoga tradition. Her twenty hands hold various items, including a lotus, and she is typically depicted as seated in a yogic stance. In the *Bhagavatam*, she is described for her beautiful lotus face and her tinkling jeweled ornaments and golden arm bangles.

---

468. Jonesand Ryan, *Encyclopedia of Hinduism*, 120.
469. Vijnanananda, *Srimad Devi Bhagavatam*, 764, 765, 1054.

Her face is compared to the moon, her three eyes to lotus leaves, and the crown on her head to the sun and moon.[470] She is associated with Shiva.

# Chhaya

**Keyword:** Shadow

**Categories:** Duo, Personification

She is the personification of shadows that cling to the sun and the mother of the planet Saturn. Sun god Surya is her consort, and she is also considered the reflection of Surya's first wife, Saranyu.

# Chhinnamasta

**Keyword:** Sacrifice

**Category:** Solo

As one of the ten Dasha Mahavidya, goddesses of the Hindu yoga tradition, she is a goddess of life and death who is shockingly depicted with her head in one hand and her weapon used to decapitate herself in the other. Despite this violent appearance, she is not associated with battle.[471] An important goddess of the Shaktism denomination of Hinduism, when her hungry followers beg for food, she cuts off her own head to nourish them with her blood, so her action is seen as self-sacrificing. While she is sometimes associated with aspects of Shiva, she is typically considered a fierce aspect of the Devi, or mother goddess.

# Dhumavati

**Keyword:** Crone

**Category:** Solo

She is one of the ten Dasha Mahavidya, goddesses of the Hindu yoga tradition, and is considered akin to a crone deity who is depicted as old, wrinkled, and angry. With only two arms, she is accompanied by a crow. Some mythological accounts say she was cursed by Shiva, but she offers protection to worshipers

---

470. Vijnanananda, *Srimad Devi Bhagavatam*, 1186.

471. Kinsley, *Tantric Visions of the Divine Feminine*, 144–7.

who bring her offerings of food and drink. In the Sanskrit text *Umasahasram*, she is described as ageless.[472]

# Durga

**Keywords:** War, Protection

**Categories:** Solo or Duo, Primordial

Durga is one of the major mother goddesses of Hinduism who was created by the Trimurti of Brahma, Shiva, and Vishnu to fight off a buffalo demon named Mahish. She received two legs from Brahma, light of Shiva, and six arms from Vishnu. Aside from her duties as a protector and war goddess, she is also associated with motherhood and destruction of evil and anything that threatens peace and the greater good. She helps devour the unwanted influences that disturb inner peace within individuals. Due to her divine origins, she is beyond defeat, never afraid, and known as The One Who Eliminates Sufferings, which is among the many reasons why she is beloved around the world.[473] In some traditions, she is seen as a consort of Shiva, while in other traditions she is a celibate solo goddess.[474]

# Ganga

**Keyword:** Purification

**Categories:** Duo, Personification

She is the personification of the holy Ganga or Ganges River. As the daughter of the personification of the Himalayan Mountains, she is mentioned in the *Rigveda* and known for purification and forgiveness. Her consort varies depending on denomination. She is sometimes considered as the consort of Lord Shiva.

# Gayatri

**Keyword:** Wealth

**Categories:** Duo, Personification

---

472. Leela and Manohar, *Umasahasram English Translation*, 385.

473. Patel, *Little Book of Hindu Deities*, 40.

474. Sullivan, *A to Z of Hinduism*, 72.

A consort of Brahma, she appears with five heads and five hands sitting on a lotus. She is the personification of the beloved Vedic hymn called *Gayatri Mantra* from book 3, hymn 62 of the *Rigveda* and represents wealth and prosperity. Also known as *Savitri Mantra*, *Gayatri Mantra* is a devotional prayer to Savitr, an aspect of sun god Surya and personification of the sun prior to sunrise.[475] Puja recited before dawn often include this mantra.

## Jyestha

**Keyword:** Misfortune

**Category:** Duo

**Also Known As:** Moodevi

Mentioned in the *Baudhdyanagrhya Sutra* dating from 600 to 300 BCE, she is the older and often called ugly sister and counterbalance to Lakshmi the goddess of wealth. Jyestha was born when the oceans contained poisons and her sister Lakshmi emerged from the milk sea as a beautiful embodiment of blessings. In early times, people worshiped Jyestha to keep undesirable and inauspicious things away from themselves and their homes. Sage Dussaha is her consort and myths describe his discovery of his wife's inability to be around anything auspicious or blessed. In one village, her image was placed facedown because it was believed if it turned upright, death would occur. Women made offerings to her before eating to protect them from an ill fate or being sent to hell after death.[476]

## Kali

**Keywords:** Destruction, Death, Time, Change

**Categories:** Duo, Primordial

We are currently living in the Kali Yuga, the fourth and final era in Hindu cosmology where chaos and depravity abound.[477] As a goddess, Kali relates to time and is known as The Black One, a black goddess who shot out of the forehead of Durga when she became angry. She wears a garland of human heads and feeds on death. She is considered a consort or form of Shiva because she emerged from

---

475. Griffith, *Hymns of the Rig Veda*, 163.

476. Leslie, *Roles and Rituals for Hindu Women*.

477. Sullivan, *A to Z of Hinduism*.

him, yet she still embodies a primordial quality. Despite her startling appearance, she helps people break free of illusions and emerge from the constant cycle of death and rebirth to achieve *moksha*, or liberation.[478] She is often seen dancing atop Lord Shiva and is listed among the ten Dasha Mahavidya, goddesses of the Hindu yoga tradition.

## Kamadhenu

**Keyword:** Mother

**Category:** Duo

**Also Known As:** Surabhi

An abundance goddess, she is said to have emerged in the same churning of the cosmic sea of milk that gave life to the goddess Lakshmi. Kashyapa the Hindu sage is her consort. According to the epic *Mahabharata*, Surabhi is one of sixty daughters of the god Daksha, a creation deity. She is known as mother of all cows and goddess of plentiful bounty who grants wishes.

## Lakshmi

**Keyword:** Wealth

**Category:** Duo

**Also Known As:** Kamala

Goddess of prosperity, wealth, and abundance, Lakshmi is one of the most important goddesses in all of Hinduism. During a great flood, Lakshmi hid in the sea of milk and emerged as a stunning beauty whom all the gods loved. Shiva wanted her, but she loved Vishnu and chose him. She is never far from Vishnu's side. Her four arms hold gifts for the prosperity of humanity, including the lotus flower and the Aum symbol.[479] The protective god of law and order, Vishnu, is her consort who takes on physical form and comes to Earth to help people during especially difficult times with Lakshmi by his side. Just as Brahma, Shiva, and Vishnu are collectively called the Trimurti, as consort of Vishnu, she is one of the Tridevi with her sisters Parvati and Sarasvati, who are consorts to the other Trimurti. Lakshmi carries coins to symbolize wealth as well as lotus flowers to

---

478. Patel, *Little Book of Hindu Deities*, 48.

479. Patel, *Little Book of Hindu Deities*, 43.

remind seekers of the importance of the spiritual aspects of life. Another form of Lakshmi, who is pictured sitting on a lotus while elephants pour water over her, is Kamala, who is included within the ten Dasha Mahavidya goddesses.[480]

# Mahadevi

**Keywords:** Mother, Fertility

**Categories:** Duo, Primordial

**Also Known As:** Devi

Similar to the way Brahma, Shiva, and Vishnu are all aspects of one god, Mahadevi is seen as the totality of the goddess and the primordial mother. She is the key figure of the Hindu denomination Shaktism. A very early form of the Divine Mother, her counterpart would be the Mahadevas, or great gods. She began as a fertility goddess in the Vedic times and evolved into several other goddesses over time, including the river goddess Ganga, Parvati, Kali, and Durga.[481]

# Matangi

**Keyword:** Prosperity

**Categories:** Solo, Primordial

**Also Known As:** Uccista-Matangini

In her singular form as Matangi, she spreads music and education to assist with advancing wisdom. Other myths cite her most common form as Uccista-Matangini, a fierce goddess sitting atop a corpse, wearing red items, holding a sword and skull.[482] In her origin myth, the gods and goddesses Shiva, Parvati, Vishnu, and Lakshmi were eating and some food fell to the ground. Matangini was born from those leftovers and Shiva declared she will help people control their enemies and receive their heart's desires. She is one of the ten Dasha Mahavidya, goddesses of the Hindu yoga tradition. Depending on the denomination, she can be the consort of Shiva.

---

480. Kinsley, *Tantric Visions of the Divine Feminine*, 14.

481. Patel, *Little Book of Hindu Deities*, 36, 81.

482. Kinsley, *Tantric Visions of the Divine Feminine*, 21, 213.

# Parvati

**Keyword:** Devotion

**Category:** Duo

**Also Known As:** Uma, Guari, Shakti

Parvati is one of the Tridevi with her sisters Lakshmi and Sarasvati. She represents the divine energy between a man and a woman, motherhood, devotion, fertility, harmony, and nourishment. She is the reincarnation of Shiva's first wife, who burned in the fire ritual of *yajna*, which means "offerings to gods." Shiva, the god of pure being and consciousness, is often depicted dancing in a ring of fire, which symbolizes the return to ash and pure being that occurs within the life cycle. Parvati fell in love with the reclusive Shiva, who did not notice her because he was too deep in meditation, so she went into her own meditative state and became so energetically appealing, Shiva emerged from his cave to marry her. She is the mother of the peacock-riding demigod Karttikeya and Lord Ganesh, the elephant-headed demigod who removes obstacles.

# Periyachi

**Keywords:** Protection, Childhood

**Category:** Solo

She is a fierce Hindu goddess and aspect of Parvati; as Periyachi Kali Amman, she is an aspect of Kali. She protects and guards mothers and newborn children against the evil eye. In the Tamil diaspora and state of Tamil Nadu in southern India, she is worshiped in a protection ceremony done during the third month of pregnancy called Pumsavana.[483] During the seventh month, she is honored to ask for an easy labor, and after birth, offerings are made to the goddess to continue to bless the newborn.

# Pratyangira

**Keyword:** Protection

**Category:** Duo

---

483. Bloomfield, *Sacred Books of the East*, 97.

One of the goddesses of Shaktism, her consort is the lion-headed god of protection Narasimha, who is the fourth incarnation of Vishnu. She has a lion head and human body like her husband and is considered the divine feminine aspect of those same protective qualities. She is known for warding off evil and helping people reverse baneful magic attacks.

# Radha

**Keyword:** Compassion

**Category:** Duo

Radha is an avatar (or reincarnation) of the wealth goddess Lakshmi, and female counterpart to Krishna, the eighth avatar of the god Vishnu. Their story is immortalized in the important text the *Brahmavaivarta Purana* that states she was given her name because she was born of dance.[484] Radha embodies divine love, tenderness, and compassion. She is also featured in several other texts, including the *Gita Govinda*, a twelfth-century poem by Jayadeva that describes the love story of Krishna and Radha.[485]

# Ratri

**Keyword:** Night

**Categories:** Solo, Personification

She is the Vedic goddess mentioned in the *Rigveda* who is the divine personification of the night. She is mentioned as the sister of Ushas, the personification and goddess of the dawn. She is typically viewed as helpful and assisting people with protection and safety during the night, but during passages in the *Rigveda*, she is asked to leave in favor of the day and light.[486]

# Saranya

**Keywords:** Clouds, Dawn

**Categories:** Duo, Personification

**Also Known As:** Sanjna

---

484. Nagar, *Brahmavaivarta Purana*, 21.

485. Miller, *Jayadeva's Gitagovinda*.

486. Griffith, *Complete Rigveda Book 1*, hymn 113.

Mentioned in the *Rigveda*, she is among the oldest-known Hindu goddesses. As the personification of the clouds and the dawn, she is noted as the first and most important wife of sun god Surya. One of her most notable myths describes a time when she left Surya to create *Chhaya*, the shadows.

## Sarasvati

**Keywords:** Wisdom, Arts, Music, Literature

**Categories:** Duo, Solo

Sarasvati was the very first goddess worshiped in Hinduism. As consort to Brahma, she is one of the Tridevi with her sisters Lakshmi and Parvati. She is the goddess of wisdom, motherhood, the arts, music, literature, and speech who is mentioned in the *Rigveda*. She is special in that she was once a consort who became an independent deity when her husband, Brahma, became upset by her disinterest in him and kicked her out of his house. Sarasvati cursed him and ensured he had no followers, which is why you rarely see the two of them pictured together. She became a champion for independent unmarried women.[487] Because of her freedom from a husband, she is the muse of Hinduism who inspires musicians and artists. Clothed in white, she holds a book of knowledge, prayer beads, and a musical instrument called the vina, which is similar to a sitar.[488] Writers, creators, and artists pray to her before beginning their work or performances, and students worship her before tests to ensure success.

## Sasthi

**Keywords:** Fertility, Protection

**Category:** Duo

**Also Known As:** Devasena, Shashthi

Worshiped in Nepal and India, Sasthi is an early Vedic fertility goddess who originated with folk traditions whose fertility aspect extends to crops, harvests, and vegetation to bring forth food. In *Vayu Purana*, she is noted as being born of Brahma's mouth and forming half of Shiva's body.[489] She is a nurturing figure

---

487. Patel, *Little Book of Hindu Deities*, 39.

488. Das, *Complete Illustrated Guide to Hinduism*, 123.

489. Tagare, *Vayu Purana*, 83.

who protects children and is sometimes pictured holding up to eight children in her arms. She rides a cat and nurses infants. She is often worshiped by those who have difficulties conceiving. In mythology, she initially devoured children until her legend evolved and she became the protector of children. Her story is similar to the Buddhist goddess Hariti. She is also known as Devasena and is the wife of war god Kartikeya.[490]

## Sita

**Keywords:** Virtue, Sacrifice, Earth

**Category:** Duo

Born of the earth, Sita divinely emerged in a plowed field and is considered the daughter of the Great Earth Mother. The harrowing story of her abduction is featured prominently in the *Ramayana*. The story is about Sita and her marriage to Rama, the seventh incarnation or avatar of the god Vishnu. Sita was abducted and held prisoner by the demon king Ravana for several months. When she was rescued, Vishnu questioned her fidelity, so Sita threw herself into fire, saying that if she had remained loyal to her husband, she would not burn. When she survived the fire, she became highly regarded for her virtue, purity, self-sacrifice, and courage.[491]

## Tara

**Keywords:** Rebirth, Reincarnation

**Category:** Duo

Tara is a well-known Buddhist goddess. In Hinduism, the *Padma Purana* tells the story of Tara and her husband Brhaspati and her affair with the moon god Soma that resulted in the birth of a boy who personified twelve suns. When the gods asked Tara whose son this was, she admitted it was Soma's, so he named the boy Budha (not to be confused with Siddhartha), who became the ancestor of the lunar race of kings. Brhaspati tried to curse Soma, but all those attempts failed, and since he still loved Tara, he asked the moon god to return her, which he did. Still, the affair gave rise to a great war between Rudra and Soma called

---

490. Nagar, *Brahmavaivarta Purana*, 28, 388–9.

491. Patel, *Little Book of Hindu Deities*, 47.

the Tarakamaya War.[492] Tara is linked to cremations and is known as she who takes one across the ocean of birth and rebirth.[493] In her Hindu aspect, she is included as one of the ten Dasha Mahavidya, goddesses of the yoga tradition.

## Tripura Sundari

**Keywords:** Love, Playfulness, Transcendence

**Categories:** Duo, Primordial

**Also Known As:** Lalita or Sri Lalita

This gentle goddess of love and seduction is worshiped during the full moon. She is one of the ten Dasha Mahavidya, goddesses of the Hindu yoga tradition. She represents pure consciousness and transcendence. She is mentioned in the *Satya Yuga* and is considered one of the primary aspects of creation.[494] She is also seen as an aspect of the Great Goddess Mahadevi and is worshiped in Shaktism as an aspect of Shakti, or all goddesses in existence, whether fierce or gentle. She is also one of many consorts of Lord Shiva.

## Tulasi

**Keywords:** Holy Basil

**Categories:** Duo, Personification

Tulasi is the personification of the Holy Basil or Tulsi plant worshiped as a goddess in Hinduism. She is seen as an avatar or element of the wealth goddess Lakshmi. In the *Brahma Vaivarta Purana*, she is described as an ornament or consort of Vishnu as she remains at his feet, and one can receive salvation by looking at her or touching her.[495]

## Ushas

**Keyword:** Dawn

**Categories:** Duo, Personification

---

492. Vyasa, *Padma Purana*, 105.

493. Jones and Ryan, *Encyclopedia of Hinduism*, 119.

494. Kulkarni, *Satya Yuga*.

495. Nagar, *Brahmavaivarta Purana*, 141.

She is the personification of the dawn, consort to sun god Surya and sister of Ratri, the personification of night. Ushas is often depicted riding across the sky to usher in the new day. Mentioned more than almost any other god or goddess in the *Rigveda*, she is described as Daughter of the Sky and Lady of the Light who brings riches and prosperity to her followers.[496]

## Vac

**Keywords:** Mother of the Vedas

**Categories:** Duo, Personification

Vac personified the speech used in the reciting of the Vedas. She is considered the power of the sacred words to bring forth truth and is said to inspire artists.[497] For that reason, she has associations with the patron of artists, goddess Sarasvati. Vac is named as consort of Prajapati, a very early Vedic creation god who is associated with Brahma. Some scholars believe his name may be related to the name Pajapati, the Buddha's aunt and foster mother.

## Yamuna

**Keyword:** River

**Categories:** Duo, Personification

She is the personification of the sacred Yamuna River, a tributary to the holy Ganges River. Bathing in her waters removes sin, and the river was important to Krishna, so she is noted as one of his consorts. She is shown as a beautiful woman on a tortoise with a water pot in her hand. She is daughter of the sun god Surya and his consort, dawn and cloud goddess, Saranya.

## Summing Up

The colorful goddesses of the Hindu faith encompass the belief in reincarnation and the continuation of the soul to ultimately transcend the constant cycle of death and rebirth. Teachings that promote good works in relation to all living beings while giving individuals the room to explore their faith as they see fit is a wonderful philosophy to carry from the ancient times to the modern world and

---

496. Griffith, *Complete Rigveda Book 1*, hymn XLVIII, 65.

497. Kinsley, *Hindu Goddesses*, 11.

into the future. With the potential of up to 333 million deities in the Hindu pantheon, there is much more to learn and experience about the Hindu goddesses. I hope this brief look at the complexities of this amazing faith will encourage you to discover more in the future.

## Recommended Reading

*Hindu Goddesses* by David Kinsley

*The Little Book of Hindu Deities* by Sanjay Patel

*Being Hindu* by Hindol Sengupta

*Chapter Nine*
# Indigenous Goddesses

The term *Indigenous* is commonly used to refer to over 370 million people around the globe who belong to diverse cultural, political, social, and ethnic groups that vary greatly from the dominant societies where they live. The United Nations recognizes Indigenous groups by several factors: self-identification as Indigenous; historical community that existed prior to colonial settlers; links to territories and natural resources; distinct social, economic, and political systems; distinct language, culture, and beliefs; nondominant society; and the determination to maintain their ancestral environments.[498]

Today, great effort is being made by the United Nations and other organizations around the world to finally right the wrongs done to the earliest peoples by settlers who simply dismissed them as being one and the same, destroyed their homes and structures, and forced them to publicly abandon their faiths in favor of other religions. It is no wonder that the study of the spirituality of these groups remains elusive. Much of what is known came after the colonization of these areas and even the names given to deities or other aspects of certain societies was put upon them by settlers who knew nothing about their true beliefs. This travesty is a disgusting remnant of early history around the world and must be remedied.

While efforts are being made, this is still a long process that will involve much healing and a new way of viewing our world. In this important section, I will

---

498. United Nations, "Who Are Indigenous Peoples?"

attempt to do my best to honor these great cultures with verified sources of what scholars do know about goddesses worshiped by these groups. Yet with all living religions, you and I must keep in mind that we simply cannot fully understand or comprehend the vast complexities of any belief unless it is our own, particularly within groups and peoples as diverse as the Indigenous populations.

## Indigenous Cosmologies

Another huge area of contention within Indigenous cultures has to do with the names used to describe them. In the United States, for example, American Indian, Indian, Native American, or Native are used frequently and considered acceptable. Still, we must be sensitive again to the fact that the groups are so diverse, it is always best to ask people their preferences. Tribe and Nation are unacceptable in some circumstances because when Europeans landed in the Americas, they renamed people, inaccurately grouped them together, or mispronounced names already in existence.[499] Everyone in society has a part to play in rectifying this long open wound to heal and bring forth greater understanding and respect for others in the future. With that in mind, several goddesses from living religions from several diverse geographic regions will be discussed. Names used by those people to describe themselves collectively as well as proper deity names will be considered at all times.

### United States

The United States is home to several diverse Indigenous groups, and we will explore goddesses from several cultures:

Gabrielino-Tongva: A Californian nation of Tongva people who have inhabited the San Gabriel Valley in Los Angeles and Orange County for thousands of years.

Hopi: A sovereign nation located in northeastern Arizona who began the village of Oraibi dating back to 1150 CE, making it the oldest continuously

---

499. Smithsonian Institution, "Impact of Words."

inhabited site in the United States.[500] Hopi believe we live in the Fourth World, having destroyed the prior three.[501]

**Keresan:** Describes several groups, including Acoma, Cochiti, Kewa, San Felipe, Santa Ana, and Zia Pueblos.

**Navajo:** Navajo refer to themselves as the Diné, meaning "the people." Navajo Code Talkers assisted the United States during World War II by creating codes to help communicate top secret information. The sacred Navajo Nation in Utah, Arizona, and New Mexico encompasses 27,000 square miles.

**Lakota Sioux:** Indigenous people originally from North and South Dakota, Minnesota, and Wisconsin with some presence in Iowa.

**Shawnee:** Official peoples of the Oklahoma area, they originally migrated from the Ohio River basin.

**Zuni:** The ancestral home of the Zuni is called the Zuni Pueblo, which is located about 150 miles west of Albuquerque, New Mexico.

### Canadian First Nations and Inuit

The term *First Nations* is used to describe Indigenous Aboriginal people of Canada who are ethnically different from *Métis*, the term used to describe unique cultures that emerged from the union of Aboriginals and Europeans in Canada. First Nations people also differ from the Inuit, who inhabit the subarctic regions of Greenland, Canada, and North America. We will explore goddesses from the Inuit and some of the Canadian First Nations:

**Inuit:** Indigenous people from the far northern reaches of Canada who ethnically differ from other First Nation groups.

**Iroquoian First Nations/Haudenosaunee:** First Nations people from southern Canada and northeast North America who lived in New York from the Hudson River all the way north to the St. Lawrence River and west to Genesee banned together and formed the Iroquois Federation, "People of the Longhouse," sometime in the fifteenth century. Members included

---

500. Biggs, "Hopi."

501. Courlander, *Fourth World of the Hopis.*

the Cayuga, Mohawk, Oneida, Onondaga, and Seneca. The Tuscarora joined the federation in the early eighteenth century. The tribes integrated as both a protective measure and to stop fighting between them and attempted a lofty goal of uniting under a unified belief system to share culture and support each other. Dream interpretation was an important aspect of the Iroquoian religion as the information received through the dream state was seen as valuable and needing to be acted upon.[502]

**Maliseet:** The Indigenous people who live in the area between Maine and New Brunswick, Canada.

**Mi'kmaq:** First appeared ten thousand years ago in the area around New Brunswick, Nova Scotia, and Prince Edward Island.

**Nuxalk:** First Nation people Indigenous to the Pacific Coast of British Columbia in Canada.

**Passamaquoddy:** Live in the northeast part of North America.

I cannot cover every one of the diverse groups who inhabit these areas, but I will explore some fascinating goddesses of the incredible people listed.

## Oceanic

*Oceania* is a broad term used to describe around 10,000 Pacific Ocean islands that spread between the Americas and Asia. Goddesses from the following areas within the Oceania region will be discussed:

**Hawaii:** Although Hawaii is a territory of the United States, the Hawaiian people are descendants of Polynesians who live within the area of Oceania. If you've been to Hawaii, you know the islands are one of a kind—a fascinating mix of the ancient world and modern conveniences. While the goddesses once worshiped by ancient Hawaiians theoretically belong to the past, superstitions and reverence for the deities who embody elements of the natural world are still clearly honored and followed to this day.

Ancient Hawaiians began with two creator deities, Ku and Hina—the sun and the moon, masculine and feminine. Ku's name meant "rising

---

502. Krober, *Artistry in Native American Myths*, 21.

upright" and referred to the fact that he rose in the east. Hina meant "leaning down," referring to the west.

**Indigenous Australians:** We will explore the incredible goddesses worshiped by the earliest settlers of Australia. Indigenous Australians is the proper term used to describe the Aboriginal Australians and the Torres Strait Islanders of Australia and their spiritual practices. Current science suggests that this group is the oldest population in the world outside of Africa as studies indicate they inhabited Australia as early as 70,000 years ago.[503]

**Māori:** The Indigenous peoples from New Zealand originated from the ocean of Kiwa and arrived in Hawaiki, a mythological homeland.[504] The Māori also have ancestral ties to the Polynesians. Like the Hawaiians, Māori worshiped a goddess known as Hine, which means "girl" in Māori.[505] The alternate spelling is *Hina*, widely known throughout Polynesia.

Most Māori goddesses have hyphenated names that include *Hina* or *Hine* to denote the different aspect of what is likely the same deity in all her manifestations. *Hina* denotes a powerful female energy and is often depicted as a princess or queen. She is widely worshiped around the entire region with slightly different versions of her gifts and talents. She is typically paired with the trickster god Maui as both a consort and sister. We will explore her energy in her various forms as well as other goddesses the Maori deify.

**Tahiti:** Tahitians worship a rich pantheon of deities, and we will look at their goddesses. Tahitians' supreme god is Oro, and they also worshiped the taro and plant god Ro'o, hunting god Tu, and forest god Tane, as well as their own version of Hina.

Within the goddesses of Oceania, *Hina* is an incredibly common name used throughout Polynesia that will be repeated in the sections on Hawaii, Maori, and Tahiti. The name *Hina* is Japanese with the word *Hi* meaning "light, sun, or day"

---

503. Blakemore, "Aboriginal Australians."
504. Ruckstuhl, Velasquez Nimatuj, and McNeish, *Routledge Handbook of Indigenous Development*, 328.
505. Behind the Name, "Hine."

and *Na* referring to greens or vegetables.[506] Hina as a goddess is known as a tutelary deity and protector for women, and the idea of green vegetables may somehow denote her ties to fertility for both females as well as for the land. Hina is revered in several areas throughout Polynesia.

# Indigenous Goddesses

Let's get started exploring goddesses of the Indigenous cultures around the world.

## A'akuluujjusi

**Keywords:** Creation, Animals

**Category:** Inuit

The Great Mother, she created the animals for the people, including walruses and caribou.[507]

## Aiaru

**Keyword:** Guardian

**Category:** Tahitian

She is one of the Seven Guardians of the World along with Fa'a'ipu, Fa'aipo, Nihoniho-tetei, Orerorero, Tahu'a, and Tamaumau-'orere.[508]

## Ai-tupuai

**Keyword:** Warrior

**Category:** Tahitian

Called head eater, she is the sister of Mahu-fatu-rau and To'i-mata and one of the three daughters of the Supreme God Oro who helped him in battle.[509]

## Akycha

**Keyword:** Sun

**Categories:** Inuit, Personification

---

506. Behind the Name, "Hina."

507. Tsing et al., *Arts of Living on a Damaged Planet*, chapter 7.

508. Craig, *Dictionary of Polynesian Mythology*, 3–4.

509. Craig, *Dictionary of Polynesian Mythology*, 193.

She is the personification of the sun who, according to legend, lived on Earth. She and her brother the moon lived in a village before ascending to the heavens.[510]

# Anjea

**Keyword:** Reincarnation

**Category:** Indigenous Australian

She kept the souls of the deceased so they could rest between lives. When the soul was ready to incarnate, she crafted their new body from mud and placed her handiwork into their mother's womb for the soul to enter upon rebirth.[511]

# Awitelin Tsta

**Keyword:** Mother

**Category:** Zuni

Awonawilona is the dual creator deity who split into two: Awitelin Tsta, Earth Mother, and her consort Apoyan Tachi, Sky Father. She is a pregnant mother goddess who birthed everything in the universe through four wombs.[512]

# Birrahgnooloo

**Keywords:** Fertility, Floods

**Category:** Indigenous Australian

She is a fertility and water goddess considered the Divine Mother who breathed life into all things on earth along with her consort, creator god Baiame. When needed, she sends floods and rain.[513]

# Chehooit

**Keywords:** Earth Mother

**Category:** Gabrielino-Tongva

510. Monaghan, *Women in Myth and Legend*, 9.

511. Jordan, *Dictionary of Gods and Goddesses*, 20.

512. Cotterell, *Dictionary of World Mythology*.

513. Ash, Giacon, and Lissarrague, *Gamilaraay, Yuwaalaraay & Yuwaalayaay Dictionary*.

The creator Quaoar created the god Weywot, known as Father Sky. The two danced, and Chehooit emerged as Earth Mother, who was initially lifeless until several beings assisted her in creating the earth over time.[514]

## Eingana

**Keywords:** Dreamtime Snake

**Category:** Indigenous Australian

She is a creation goddess who holds the thread of life, and if she severs it, the person passes. She is a snake goddess who has no ability to give birth physically, yet she made everything in the physical world and is seen as the divine creator of all that is.

## Fa'a'ipu

**Keyword:** Genealogy

**Category:** Tahitian

She is one of the guardians of the world along with Aiaru, Fa'a'ipo, Nihoniho-tetei, Orerorero, Tahu'a, and Tamaumau-'orere.[515]

## Gnowee

**Keyword:** Sun

**Categories:** Indigenous Australian, Personification

Her torch personified the sun. Once a mortal woman, her baby wandered away and she now carries her torch and searches for her lost son in the sky daily by following him around the world.[516]

## Godasiyo

**Keyword:** Chief

**Category:** Haudenosaunee/Iroquois

She became the original mythological chief of the Iroquois people. According to myth, she and her constant companion, a white dog, were on a canoe, and

---

514. Falkner, *Mythology of the Night Sky*, 190.

515. Craig, *Dictionary of Polynesian Mythology*, 34.

516. Hathaway, *Friendly Guide to Mythology*, 83.

the people got into a disagreement about whether to row to the left or right and sank the vessel, drowning their amazing chief and dividing the people into many nations.[517]

# Grandmother Woodchuck

**Keyword:** Protection

**Categories:** Maliseet, Passamaquoddy

**Also Known As:** Nuhkomoss Munimqehs

She is a wise old grandmother who raised Glooskap, the main hero of Passamaquoddy mythology who taught the people to hunt and cared for them.[518] Like many Grandmother figures in mythology, she is a protector and helper who remedies problems rather than acting as a creator goddess.

# Haumea

**Keywords:** Earth Mother

**Category:** Hawaiian

Mother of Pele and other deities, she became the Divine Mother for many of the gods known in the Hawaiian pantheon. She had seven sons and six daughters, including the volcano goddess Pele with her consort Moemoe-a-aulii. Some Hawaiian chants list her as an ancestral spirit, or *'aumakua*, who had once been a mortal woman who lived on the island of Oahu, while others mention her as a deity. As an Earth Mother, she is a fertility goddess and offers help with childbirth because she had so many children herself. Her children emerged from her body. She also helped a female chief give birth painlessly, which is why she is considered the divine midwife.[519]

# Hi'iaka

**Keywords:** Growth, Healing

**Category:** Hawaiian

---

517. Hodge, *Smithsonian Institution Bureau of American Ethnology*, 538.

518. Fee and Webb, *American Myths, Legends and Tall Tales*, 419.

519. Cunningham, *Hawaiian Religion & Magic*, 28–9.

Born in the shape of an egg, her older sister Pele tucks her under her arm. Hi'iaka is a healing goddess who could bring the dead back to life, fend off danger, and perform magic. Kahuna, who specialized in herbs, often enlisted her help. She was considered an ancestral deity who was personified by certain flowers and ferns. She received the fury of her sister Pele when she fell in love with one of Pele's chiefs—an epic tale that is still performed in hula performances today.[520] She has several other iterations depending on her healing intent: Hi'iaka-i-ka-maka-o-ka-'opua, personification of rainclouds; Hi'iaka-i-ka-wai-ola, her healing qualities; Hi'iakmakole-wawahi-wa'a, she appears as a red rainbow who warns fisherman of dangers; Hi'iakanoho-lani, seen in the skies and heavens.[521]

# Hina

**Keywords:** Moon, Fertility, Power

**Categories:** Hawaiian, Maori, Tahitian, Ancestral

In Hawaiian legend, Hina is among the oldest goddesses in the pantheon known as one of the important ancestors of all the people who is linked to the moon and presides over all female 'aumakua, or ancestors. Associated with the sun god Ku, people prayed to Hina in the west and Ku in the east. In the western direction, she is Hinaalo, mother of the Hawaiian people, and when worshiped in the east, she was Hina-kua who helped future generations. She could also appear as Hina'ea to embody both sunrise and sunset. In her Hinahele form, fisherman worshiped her.[522] Hina is the mother of demigod Maui. She is known as Hina-i-ka-malama (Hina in the moon), and in myth, she travels the rainbow bridge up to the sun, which was far too hot for her, so she climbed higher toward the moon. Hina can still be seen in the full moon.[523]

The Tahitian Hina is a fertility goddess who represents feminine power, creativity, and the moon. She is the god Oro's mother. She left her first husband Te Tuna for Maui, and after a battle, Maui tore off Tuna's head and created coconut trees.

520. Cunningham, *Hawaiian Religion & Magic*, 33.

521. Cunningham, *Hawaiian Religion & Magic*, 34.

522. Cunningham, *Hawaiian Religion & Magic*, 34–5.

523. Cunningham, *Hawaiian Religion & Magic*, 29–30.

# Hina-Ika

**Keyword:** Fish

**Categories:** Māori, Tutelary

Called Lady of the Fish, this version of Hina protects the oceans and all life living in it as the people believe the world emerged from the sea. For the Māori, she teaches the people to make clothing from bark. Her husband Irawaru, a half man half fish god, makes fishing nets from her hair.[524] In Hawaii, she is mother of the island of Molokai.

# Hina-Keha

**Keywords:** Pale Moon

**Categories:** Māori, Personification

Hina-Keha personifies the full moon and in this form also represents pregnancy, fertility, and childbirth. Maui is her consort.

# Hina-Nui-Te-Po

**Keyword:** Underworld

**Categories:** Māori, Chthonic

Called Great Lady of the Night, she guides the deceased into Rarohenga, the Māori Underworld, after death.[525] She became an Underworld goddess after discovering that she mated with her father Tāne. She is often invoked by Tahitian fire walkers who put themselves in trance to walk across hot coals as an exercise of mind over matter.

# Hine-ahu-one

**Keywords:** First Woman

**Categories:** Māori, Primordial

Called Earth Maiden, she is the first woman created out of soil by her father Tāne.[526] She is a consort of Maui.

---

524. Knappert, *Pacific Mythology*, 115.

525. Craig, *Dictionary of Polynesian Mythology*, 167.

526. Craig, *Dictionary of Polynesian Mythology*, 70.

## Hine-Tengarumoana

**Keywords:** Fish Lady of the Ocean Waves

**Categories:** Māori, Personification

This version of Hina is her fish form where Hina represents the fertility and abundance of the ocean to provide. Her consort is Māori hero Tinirau.[527] She is called Lady of the Ocean Waves.

## Hine-Titama

**Keyword:** Dawn

**Categories:** Māori, Ancestral

She is the goddess of the dawn and ancestor of the Māori.[528] She used this name until she discovered that she married her father Tāne and then she changed her name to Hina-Nui-Te-Po and descended into the Underworld.

## Huruing Wuhti

**Keyword:** Creation

**Category:** Hopi

**Also Known As:** Sea Woman

Known as Sea Woman, she owns all turquoise stones and shells and lives in a turquoise house surrounded by seashells. She is associated with a creation story where the Hopi people traveled across the sea into their current land and emerged from a boat. The tale contradicts other Hopi legends about Spider Grandmother, so Sea Woman is known as Deity of the West to represent the direction of the ocean.[529]

## Iyatiku

**Keyword:** Mother

**Category:** Keresan

**Also Known As:** Corn Mother

---

527. Craig, *Dictionary of Polynesian Mythology*, 71.

528. Craig, *Dictionary of Polynesian Mythology*, 352.

529. Courlander, *Fourth World of the Hopis*, 204.

She is a corn and agriculture goddess. All people emerged from the earth, from Iyatiku herself, through a northern hole called Shipap. They emerged in darkness, faced east, and she brought the light into the world. Ambiguity exists on whether she created the sun or simply caused the male sun to rise.[530]

# Julunggul

**Keywords:** Rainbow Serpent

**Categories:** Indigenous Australian, Primordial

The primordial creation being appears as a serpent and is sometimes considered either male or female and is credited with creating all life.[531] The Rainbow Snake is said to appear to help boys go through the initiation into manhood.

# Ka'ahupahau

**Keyword:** Protector

**Categories:** Hawaiian, Ancestral

Born of human parents, Ka'ahupahau transformed into a shark and lived with her son, who was also a shark, in a cave near the entrance of Pearl Harbor where she guarded the area, saving people from shark attacks. Sharks were important 'aumakua—spirits of ancestors who emerged and embodied many forms in the natural world including birds and animals.[532]

# Kaiona

**Keyword:** Forest

**Category:** Hawaiian

Worshiped on Oahu Island, she helped people find their way out of the forests when they were lost. To help them, she would send a small bird to guide them toward trails that would lead them out of the woods.[533]

---

530. Tyler, *Pueblo Gods and Myths*, 105, 140.

531. Berndt, *Australian Aboriginal Religion*, 4.

532. Cunningham, *Hawaiian Religion & Magic*, 31–2.

533. Cunningham, *Hawaiian Religion & Magic*, 35.

# Kalamainu'u

**Keyword:** Lizard

**Category:** Hawaiian

She imprisoned her lover Puna-ai-koa'e in her cave and tried to hide her identity as a lizard. When her lover escaped and learned about her, he returned and loved her despite her lizard form.

# Kapo

**Keyword:** Fertility

**Category:** Hawaiian

Kapo is another of Haumea's daughters and a sister of Pele. She is a fertility goddess who created *hula halau*, a dance school, on all the islands and helped Laka with the sacred dance. She may be a version of Laka. She is Wākea's consort and love goddess Laka's mother. Followers sometimes worshiped her for good purposes and other times evoked her to do harm by sending evil energies back to those who sent them.[534]

# Kapu-alakai

**Keyword:** Healing

**Category:** Hawaiian

A healing goddess, she assisted the medical profession and was worshiped by medical professionals and healers.[535]

# Kiha-wahine

**Keyword:** Ancestor

**Category:** Hawaiian

An ancestral deity of the Hawaiian people, she was venerated on Maui before being promoted by King Kamehameha I and worshiped throughout Hawaii.[536]

---

534. Cunningham, *Hawaiian Religion & Magic*, 36.

535. Cunningham, *Hawaiian Religion & Magic*, 37.

536. Cunningham, *Hawaiian Religion & Magic*, 37.

# Kokumthena

**Keyword:** Grandmother

**Category:** Shawnee

**Also Known As:** Cloud Woman

She is the primary hero and creator goddess in Shawnee mythology who helps transform the people through her good works. Many Indigenous cultures have a male transformational figure, so she is uniquely powerful as the feminine divine catalyst for good.

# Kunapipi

**Keywords:** Mother Nature, Fertility

**Category:** Indigenous Australian

She is the mother of many of the gods in the pantheon, mother of plants and animals, Mother Nature. She gave birth to people and animals and could transform herself into the Rainbow Serpent.[537]

# Laka

**Keywords:** Love and Beauty, Fertility

**Category:** Hawaiian

Laka is Haumea's daughter and Pele's sister. She is also the sister and sometimes consort of Lono, the peaceful god of fertility and agriculture. Laka is associated fertility as a reproduction goddess also known for love and beauty. Credited with being the creator of the sacred hula dance, Laka is honored by those who learn the sacred dance up to the present day. As a fertility goddess, Laka assists the forests with growth and lush vegetation. In Laka's temple on the island of Kaua'i, dances are performed and old chants are still used. At one time, hula had been banned, but after reinstatement, it remains among the most important pieces of Hawaiian cultural heritage.[538]

---

537. Berndt, *Australian Aboriginal Religion*, 4.

538. Cunningham, *Hawaiian Religion & Magic*, 31.

# La'ahana

**Keyword:** Cloth

**Category:** Hawaiian

She made bark used for clothing and was the daughter of the god Maikoha, the kapa maker. Kapa was the cloth that was crafted from this bark she created.[539]

# La'ama'oma'o

**Keywords:** Storms, Winds

**Category:** Hawaiian

Mother of wind and storms, she gave her son Paka'a a bowl containing his grandmother's bones that allowed him to control wind and storms to help sailors with navigation.[540]

# Lea

**Keyword:** Canoe

**Category:** Hawaiian

Goddess who helped people build the canoes that were a huge part of Hawaiian culture. She took on a *kinolau* (spirit form) as a bird and would go test the trees to find the best and strongest ones to craft the canoes.[541]

# Lilinoe

**Keywords:** Moisture, Mist

**Categories:** Hawaiian, Personification

Younger sister of Poliahu the snow goddess, Lilinoe personifies moisture and fine rain and lives in the Haleakala Volcano in Maui. Other myths say she stayed with her sister on Mauna Kea, which is on the island of Hawaii and is now home to one of the best astronomical observatories in the world and home to Hubble Telescope.[542]

---

539. Cunningham, *Hawaiian Religion & Magic*, 37.

540. Cunningham, *Hawaiian Religion & Magic*, 37.

541. Cunningham, *Hawaiian Religion & Magic*, 209.

542. Cunningham, *Hawaiian Religion & Magic*, 38.

# Mahu-fatu-rau

**Keyword:** Warrior

**Category:** Tahitian

She is the sister of 'Ai-tupuai and To'i-mata and is one of the three daughters of the supreme god Oro who helped him in battle. Her name means "escape from a hundred stones."

# Manisar

**Keyword:** Harvest

**Category:** Gabrielino-Tongva

Wife of Iuichepet, she is the oldest daughter of a chief who helps with creating an abundant harvest by providing corn to people.[543]

# Nā-maka-o-ka-ha'i

**Keywords:** Water, Sea

**Categories:** Hawaiian, Personification

Pele's older sister who embodies and personifies the ocean. In one famous myth, she caused Pele and her siblings to leave their home in Tahiti and relocate to Hawaii because she constantly bombarded Pele with ocean water that snuffed out her flames.[544]

# Nerrivik

**Keywords:** Sea Mother

**Category:** Intuit

A mortal woman who was taken up by a seabird became deified into a goddess who provides food for the people and serves as a patron for fishermen.[545]

---

543. Kroeber, *Handbook of the Indians of California*, 623.

544. Cunningham, *Hawaiian Religion & Magic*, 42.

545. Coulter and Turner, *Encyclopedia of Ancient Deities*, 392.

# Nihoniho-tetei

**Keyword:** Genealogy

**Category:** Tahitian

She is one of the guardians of the world along with Aiaru, Fa'a'ipo, Fa'a'ipu, Orerorero, Tahu'a, and Tamaumau-'orere.[546]

# Nu'akea

**Keyword:** Fertility

**Category:** Hawaiian

She was a fertility goddess who created the milk for nursing mothers to feed their children.[547]

# Nukumi

**Keywords:** Protector, Grandmother

**Category:** Mi'kmaq

**Also Known As:** Kisikuskw, Kesegoocskw

She is a wise old grandmother formed from a rock by the sun god Nishkam. She is similar to the Passamaquoddy goddess Nuhkomoss Munimqehs because she also raised Glooskap and adopted him after his mother died in childbirth.[548]

# Oniata

**Keyword:** Corn

**Categories:** Haudenosaunee/Iroquois, Personification

**Also Known As:** Onatah

One of three sister goddesses of agriculture collectively known by the Iroquois as De-o-ha'-ko, she and her sisters personified life-supporting spirits of corn, squash, and beans. In Iroquoian and Algonquian myth, twin culture heroes emerged—one good and one evil. The evil twin Flint (or Tawiscara in the Iroquois language) killed his mother in childbirth by cutting his way out rather

---

546. Craig, *Dictionary of Polynesian Mythology*, 34.

547. Cunningham, *Hawaiian Religion & Magic*, 39.

548. Mi'kmaq Spirit, "Coming of Nukumi."

than waiting to be born. Corn was originally said to spring forth from the twin's mother after her death and burial. In one legend, Tawiscara causes a blight of the corn crops, and Oniata must be rescued to bring corn back to the people.[549]

# Papahānaumoku

**Keywords:** Earth Mother

**Categories:** Hawaiian, Primordial

**Also Known As:** Papa

Primordial goddess of creation, she embodies Mother Earth. Wākea is her consort who some say is a human. She gave birth to the gourd, called an ipu. Wākea covered the gourd with a blanket and threw it into the air, creating the sky. The insides of the ipu became the sun, the seeds became the stars, the lining became the moon and clouds. Wākea turned the juice from the ipu into the rain. One of Papa's children was born with defects and, after being buried, emerged as the taro plant, which is used to make poi. To this day, poi is considered sacred for that reason. Papa is also credited with birthing each of the Hawaiian Islands.[550]

# Papatūānuku

**Keywords:** Earth Mother

**Categories:** Māori, Primordial

She is the Earth Mother, and the term *Papatūānuku Kokiri Marae* refers to an urban space in Aotearoa, New Zealand.[551] She and her husband, Ranginui, created all life. Often called by their more affectionate names of *Papa* meaning "earth" and *Rangi* meaning "sky," they were the primordial couple who gave rise to all beings in one of the Māori creation myths.

# Pele

**Keywords:** Fire, Volcano

**Categories:** Hawaiian, Personification, Ancestral

---

549. Stevens, *Flint Chips*, 532–3.

550. Cunningham, *Hawaiian Religion & Magic*, 39.

551. Ruckstuhl, Velasquez Nimatuj, and McNeish, *Routledge Handbook of Indigenous Development*, 328.

Pele is a key goddess in the creation myth of Hawaii. A daughter of Haumea, she and her brothers came from Tahiti. Pele personified Kilauea Volcano and is known as she who shapes the sacred land. She is honored as an 'aumakua or ancestor and appears in human form. The subject of many popular myths, Pele often appears as a beautiful woman who hitchhikes along the highway. When kind strangers give her a ride, she mysteriously disappears. She also appears as a white dog that warns people when the volcano is about to erupt.[552] People who dare take the volcanic stones from the lava beach in Hilo, Hawaii, near Kilauea are said to be subject to her curse and report bad luck and often mail the rocks back to the post office on the island.[553]

## Poli'Ahu

**Keyword:** Snow

**Categories:** Hawaiian, Personification

Lilinoe's sister is the personification of snow and the snowcapped mountain of Mauna Kea on the Big Island of Hawaii.[554] She is known for a sledding competition. She is often depicted wearing the snow and being physically cold because, at times, despite what one might think, it snows on the top of the peaks in Hawaii. Her name means "pretty sister."

## Pukkeenegak

**Keywords:** Home, Hearth, Fertility

**Category:** Inuit

She is a goddess for childbirth, the home, hearth, and making clothing. Her face is tattooed and she obtains food for the people.[555]

## Sedna

**Keywords:** Mother of the Sea

**Category:** Inuit

---

552. Cunningham, *Hawaiian Religion & Magic*, 41–3.

553. Russo, "Mysterious Reason Tourists Keep Mailing Rocks Back to Hawaii."

554. Cunningham, *Hawaiian Religion & Magic*, 40.

555. Coulter and Turner, *Encyclopedia of Ancient Deities*, 392.

She presides over marine animals and the sea, and shamans make offerings to her to ask her to release food for the people. Her father threw her into the sea as a sacrifice and that action transformed her from a beautiful maiden to a one-eyed hag. Those who wish to visit her must make a perilous journey into the underworld and back.[556]

## Sky Woman

**Keyword:** Mother

**Categories:** Iroquois/Haudenosaunee, Cayuga, Wyandot

**Also Known As:** Ataensic, Ata-en-sic, Ataentsic

The Iroquois creation myth is the story of a sick woman who was pushed down to Earth from a hole in the sky and gave birth to twins—one good and one evil—and after her death became the source for food in the world.[557] The tale is told with various versions, including the story where the Sky Woman comes from the heavens and lands on a turtle and made her home on Turtle Island, the Indigenous name for North America.

## Spider Grandmother

**Keywords:** Grandmother, Creator

**Category:** Hopi

**Also Known As:** Gogyeng Sowuhti, Kokyangwuti

Known as the Spider Grandmother, she is credited in some myths for helping create the world with Tawa, the spirit of the sun, and his nephew, Sotuknang. Spider Grandmother also crafted humans from clay, and she led them into the Fourth and current world. She taught the people how to take long and successful migrations across the land. Hopi call her Deity of the East because she is associated with *sipapuni*, the place from which the Hopi emerged located in the Grand Canyon in Arizona.[558] According to Hopi cosmology, Hopi emerged through a hole in the top of sipapuni and inhabited the mesas where they live today.[559]

---

556. Laugrand and Oosten, *Sea Woman*.

557. Krober, *Artistry in Native American Myths*, 17.

558. Courlander, *Fourth World of the Hopis*, 32, 204.

559. Biggs, "Hopi."

Spider Grandmother was a seer and had a crystal she used to foresee events and locate lost people.

## Spider Woman

**Keywords:** Protector, Harvest, Agriculture

**Category:** Navajo

**Also Known As:** Na'ashjeii Asdzaa

One of the most important Navajo deities, she is a savior for humanity rather than a creator. She assists humankind and taught people the arts of agriculture and weaving. Children were taught to behave or Spider Woman would carry them into the clouds and eat them and that the white face of Spider Rock was created from bones of misbehaved children.[560]

## Tahu'a

**Keyword:** Protector

**Category:** Tahitian

Called The Artificer, she is a very old goddess and one of the guardians of the world along with Aiaru, Fa'a'ipo, Fa'aipu, Nihoniho-tetei, Orerorero, and Tamau-mau-'orere.[561]

## To'i-mata

**Keyword:** Warrior

**Category:** Tahitian

Oro's third daughter known as Axe Eye helped her father fight along with her sisters 'Ai-tupuai and Mahu-fatu-rau.[562]

## Uli

**Keyword:** Sorcery

**Category:** Hawaiian

560. Walker, "Spider Rock."

561. Craig, *Dictionary of Polynesian Mythology*, 252.

562. Craig, *Dictionary of Polynesian Mythology*, 193.

Uli was used by the Kahuna 'ana'ana who used sorcery against their enemies to pray people to death. Uli could also bring people back to life and heal people.[563]

# Ungud

**Keyword:** Fertility

**Category:** Indigenous Australian

Ungud is another version of the Rainbow Serpent who is both female and male and appears as a snake. She is considered either a god or goddess who is equated to the penis of the shaman.[564]

# Waka

**Keyword:** Lizard

**Category:** Hawaiian

She is a lizard, called a *mo'o*, worshiped by female chiefs. In one legend, she was transformed into a beautiful woman to distract Lono from reaching land.[565]

# Wala

**Keyword:** Sun

**Categories:** Indigenous Australian, Personification

Sun goddess Wala traveled across the sky each day with her sister Bala until she realized that the two of them together were making the earth too hot, so she sent Bala home and hid herself away so that the soil could become fruitful and abundant.

# Whaitiri

**Keyword:** Thunder

**Categories:** Māori, Personification

---

563. Cunningham, *Hawaiian Religion & Magic*, 40.

564. Buchler and Maddock, *Rainbow Serpent*, 16.

565. Beckwith, *Hawaiian Mythology*, 526–8.

She personified thunder and had a fierce personality. Her chant separated Earth and sky.[566] She married the mortal Kaitangata but didn't like his calm nature and eventually returned to the heavens.

## White Buffalo Calf Woman

**Keywords:** Seven Sacred Rites, Prophecy

**Category:** Lakota Sioux

**Also Known As:** Ptesan-Wi, Ptesanwi

White Buffalo Calf Woman brought the peace pipe to the Sioux people and is one of the most important mythological figures of the Sioux.[567] She is known for her powers of prophecy and alerting people to answered prayer. She first appeared to the Sioux as a beautiful woman dressed in white buckskin who met with the elders and presented them with the sacred pipe and instructions for caring for the earth. She transformed into a red and brown buffalo calf and then into a white buffalo calf.[568]

## Wuriupranili

**Keyword:** Sun

**Categories:** Indigenous Australian, Personification

Personification of the sun, she is known as the Sun Woman. Her bark torch is the sun. She is the dawn or, when stained with ochre, she is a red dawn.

## Yhi

**Keywords:** Light of Creation

**Category:** Indigenous Australian

She lived in the dreamtime as goddess of light and creation. When she woke up, light came to the earth and plants began to grow. She is the embodiment of the divine spark.

---

566. Craig, *Dictionary of Polynesian Mythology*, 326.

567. Dooling, *Sons of the Wind*, 136.

568. Brown, *Sacred Pipe*, 3–10.

## Summing Up

The plight of the Indigenous peoples around the world has been an incredible blight on humanity that is slowly being addressed and rectified. The material within this chapter is but a small fraction of the knowledge kept by the ancient ones that the public at large will likely never have access to, nor should they. When trust is eroded, only time, understanding, and willingness to accept and change can bring about healing.

## Recommended Reading

*Sacred Pipe* by Joseph Brown Epes

*The Fourth World of the Hopis* by Harold Courlander

*Artistry in Native American Myths* by Karl Krober

*Hawaiian Religion & Spirituality* by Scott Cunningham

*Part Three*

# Goddess Discovery
# and Guided Journeys

## Part Three

Now that you've discovered goddesses from around the world, I will share several guided journeys designed to help you bring greater peace and balance into your body and connect with goddess energy. You'll hopefully receive greater understanding about how you may have interacted with goddesses in your past lives. You will also explore your ancestral lineage to honor goddesses worshiped by your ancestors.

*Chapter Ten*

# Preparing for Goddess Discovery

Before you go on any guided journeys, there are some basic preparations I always recommend. These will help you better receive insights from the experience. These preparations include activities like recording and journaling, setting sacred space and an altar, and using your imagination.

## Recording Journeys

For best results, I suggest you get a recording app or device and read the guided processes aloud. When you're ready, put your headphones on and listen to the journeys so you can experience the insights in a more relaxed way. Aside from the ease of listening without having to memorize the words, your subconscious mind loves the sound of your voice. You can also keep those recordings handy to use again in the future if you want to do journeys again a second or third time. Thanks to technology, you can download recording apps for free or for a small fee then use them again and again.

## Keeping Ideas in Journals

I am a huge fan of journaling and I highly recommend you make use of a journal to document all the potentially life-changing insights revealed during our time together. Each exercise includes journaling exercises. Down the road, the future you will thank current you for taking time to take stock. There are lots of options:

**Recording App:** Record your thoughts with the same app you use for guided imagery.

**Paperbound Book:** If you like putting pen to paper, use a paper journal.

**Notebooks:** A simple notebook works well for recording thoughts and ideas.

**Apps:** A text app or Word document is a perfect place to record thoughts and ideas.

Above all, pick something you will actually use. What do you like? What feels easy? Experiment and find what you love.

## Imagination is Key

Before you do any guided journeys, it's important to fully embrace and acknowledge the power of your imagination. The key to any kind of healing is opening yourself to the realm of your imagination so that images, thoughts, and feelings can bubble up from the depths of your soul. How this may show up for you is unique and comes in three main ways:

**Visions:** You may be able to easily visualize concepts and notice images appear in your mind during guided journeys and exercises.

**Feelings:** You may not see anything but you have a deep sense of inner knowing or an emotion that emerges as you go. You've learned how to trust your gut and you can use that same wisdom to gain insights into yourself.

**Sounds:** You may hear the inner voice guiding you with clear insights and directions for how to proceed or what lessons to take away from different situations and you can use that gift to get the most out of meditations and guided journeys.

**Thoughts:** You may receive insights in your mind as complete thoughts already formed. This can happen either when your own higher self and soul present hidden wisdom to you for review or when your guides, angels, and unseen helpers share their wisdom with you. Be on the lookout for those helpful bursts of inspiration and insight.

I'll do my best along the way to encourage you to recognize and embrace your unique gifts and talents during these journeys by tuning in to the way that you best receive information. Know that if you're not somebody who sees visions, that's okay. Each of these methods for perception is equally valid. Trust your process and give yourself the gift of allowing your imaginative insights to come forth during your journey work.

## Creating Sacred Space

One way to support your imagination and feel comfortable taking journeys is to actively create your own sacred space within your home or office where you can go consistently to do your spiritual work. The familiarity of using the same comfortable place will help your mind and imagination soar. There are two kinds of sacred space you'll need to focus on: the external world around you and the interior space within your mind. Once your spaces are established, you will begin to explore the inner realm of your mind and you will meet with a trusted guide to help you along the path. Let's explore each of these topics now.

### External Sacred Space

Once you've got your journal and recording devices in place, you will want to pay attention to your personal space. Creating your own external sacred space begins in your home. It's important to have a special place, even if it's a tiny one, where you can sit and meditate, do past-life regressions, or do other inner work. This doesn't need to be anything elaborate. You could literally find a chair or a specific place on a couch or sofa where you feel the best and enjoy meditating. It's highly possible if you share your home with others or if you don't have a lot of space that this won't be any huge area. That's fine. It doesn't need to be. The most important thing about this space is how you feel when you're there. Once you designate a place to connect with Source energy and use it frequently, you'll build up a special and supportive force field around you that is similar to the amazing energy you feel at a holy site. In this first exercise, you will explore your own space to find out what area is best for you.

## EXERCISE: LOCATING YOUR SACRED SPACE

Try this quick and revealing process to find the best place to use for your spiritual work.

Take a moment and walk around your home. Consciously notice which chairs, sofas, couches, or other places you normally sit in. Do you have favorite places or chairs you gravitate to? If so, take a moment to consciously bring those spaces to mind. As you're moving about your home, notice them. Sit for a moment in each place. Notice how you feel with every new location. Which one do you like best, or are they equal?

Next, walk around your home a second time and notice what areas you avoid. When possible, take a moment and go sit in some of the places you typically avoid. How does that feel?

Now go back to your favorite place and sit for a moment. Consciously tune in to the difference.

Finally, settle in on the one place you feel would be best for your meditation and spiritual practices if you don't have that place set up already. Consciously begin to go to that space any time you need alone time to connect with your inner wisdom and higher self.

## JOURNAL PROMPT: LOCATING YOUR SACRED SPACE

Sit in the space you've chosen and reflect. Pull out your new journal you're using for this book and notate the following:

1. Which place did you love best and why?
2. What places do you avoid? Were you surprised by what you noticed?
3. Why did you select the place you did for your spiritual work?

That exercise doesn't take long, but it is quite revealing. We have so many distracters in our modern lives, it's hard to get in touch with how we really feel about our space unless we take a second or two to do so. I practiced doing that very exercise earlier in the year and have since found another nice secondary vortex where I now do some of my meditations. It's like opening a whole new world of possibility within your old familiar surroundings.

I asked you to notice the places that are not currently on your list of favorites to help you get in touch with the places that don't feel as good so you can begin to spend more of your time connecting with the most supportive energies in your home. We don't need to make excuses or try to change places we don't like. Whenever possible, when you're doing meditation or other journey work, retreat to one of the places you love. Recognizing on a more conscious level why you love that space more than another location makes your connection all the stronger. Not utilizing a place isn't necessarily a bad thing either. Perhaps another family member has dibs on certain rooms, chairs, or spaces, or perhaps you don't like the energy as much. It's an interesting exercise to make note of the subtleness in energy that exists in our own homes.

Throughout history people recognized the special energy that emanates from the core of the earth in certain sites. All people can sense those good vibes, and they've been doing so since the beginning of time. The other phenomenon that happens when people begin to congregate in these energy vortexes and create monuments or sites where they can worship the gods is that the positive vibrations from all the people who love the place builds up over time so that everyone can feel it and it becomes stronger and stronger. When you start building that place up for yourself within your own home, no matter what challenges exist in the outer world, you will have carved out a beautiful spiritual space where your soul will feel calm, protected, and embraced. There, you will find comfort and solace in the space you created for yourself. As you move through the material, that's the space where I recommend you go to every time you do any of the experiences and exercises in this book.

## Decorating Your Space

Once you find your special place, you will want to adorn it with objects of devotion that not only make you feel good, but that represent the deities or energies you're trying to connect with daily. Before you add in your spiritual décor, you'll want to begin with the basics to ensure the exterior space is comfortable. Make note of the following:

**Furniture:** Even if you live with others or have a smaller space, hopefully you can find a special chair or sitting area that's comfortable and comforting where you can sit and become so relaxed that new thoughts and ideas flow freely.

**Accessories:** You'll want to accessorize this space with throw pillows, comfy blankets, and whatever you need to feel supported. When you do journey work and meditation, your inner body temperature can rise and fall in unpredictable ways, so blankets are great to have around.

**Incense, Sage, and Oils:** You may be able to deepen your meditations and guided journeys by consciously adding certain scents into your space, which you can do using essential oils, incense, or sage. The olfactory sense is one of the strongest primal forces human beings have within them to send signals to our brains. Scientific research shows that the sense of smell is intricately linked to our memories and emotions. Because of the way our brains are wired, smells go straight into the brain and help us recall the past.[569] That's why you can smell a freshly baked stack of gooey chocolate chip cookies and suddenly have a flashback to grandma's kitchen during your childhood. When selecting smells for your space, pick something you love so that the mind can relax and go into the state of consciousness you want to achieve. If you used the same scent all the time, let's say every time you meditate, that would also help trigger the brain that it's time to do your work and could easily send you into the proper mental space to achieve optimal results. A few recommendations include the calming scent of lavender, which helps open your mind to inner vision; energizing peppermint, which helps focus energy; or earthy patchouli, for a sense of grounding and connection to the earth. Experiment and pick the scents you love and enjoy.

**Music:** Supportive music can work wonders on altering the frequencies around you and supporting deep spiritual insights. Music is clinically proven to support our overall happiness and health and can actually stim-

---

569. Walsh, "What the Nose Knows."

ulate our brains to move into various brainwave frequencies such as the alpha state, which supports health, healing, and meditation.[570]

The sky's the limit as to what you can do or create. Do what you love, include what you like, and find a space that reflects your unique style and personality that makes you feel embraced and empowered. The bottom line is to do whatever makes you happy. Sounds easy enough, I know, but everybody becomes so busy in life, at times, you may forget what you love, so take a little "me time" and set your space up in a way you love. And also remember, creating a sacred space doesn't mean you have to hire an interior decorator to do things perfectly. "Perfect" should be something different for everyone and should reflect your own unique brand of tastes, styles, and comforts.

## Creating Your Altar

Once your space is chosen and you've found comfy seating, smells, and items to create the perfect ambiance, it's time to create an altar, a place where you can focus your spiritual energy and intent to place within this supportive environment. The thought of setting up such an important site within your home may sound daunting, but it doesn't have to be. Altars can vary person to person. Your altar should reflect your inner being. Within that comfortable space you located earlier, your altar could be a bookshelf, tabletop, windowsill, or special space outside. There's no right or wrong on location, size, or how you want to create your altar. All you need is a flat surface to place items you love in a way you enjoy, and as you love and pay homage to the goddess or deities in your own way, the positive energy will flow to you, and you will feel blessings enter your life.

Another idea to keep in mind is that you may not want to set up a permanent altar. You may prefer to create something you can easily remove after each seating. That may be a better practice to follow if you have roommates, family members, or others who share your space. You could place your items on a table; do your prayers, meditations, or inner work; and then store the items in a secure place until you're ready to use them again. I've created such pop-up altars in hotel rooms in the past by placing a small cloth atop a hotel desk and placing my sacred items there. That may work better for you.

---

570. Budson, "Why Is Music Good for the Brain?"

## Items to Place on Your Altar

Once you decide on your altar, you have unlimited options on what you can place there. Here are a few ideas:

**Statues:** Goddesses or deity statues are perfect for your altar.

**Photos:** Pictures of your ancestors or deities either framed or lying flat can help you connect.

**Flowers:** Fresh flowers or silk flowers add color and magic to your space.

**Books:** Sacred books or spell books can be useful on your altar.

**Candles:** You may wish to keep candles lit or use artificial candles to engage the element of fire.

**Water:** If you choose to call upon the water element, you might enjoy a bowl of water in your space.

**Cards:** If you have tarot or other divination cards, you may keep those on the altar for easy access when you're ready to give yourself a reading.

**Crystals:** Stones and crystals amplify energy and easily shift the vibrations of your space to a higher level. They also add beauty and create a connection with Mother Earth.

**Handwritten Affirmations or Prayers:** Amplify the energies of prayer or things you would like to create more of in your life by placing handwritten notes in with other sacred items.

Again, there are no limits to what you can create. Experiment and do what you enjoy.

## Prayers and Affirmations

You will likely want to include prayers or affirming words to say either to yourself or aloud during your sacred practice. That could be as simple as thanking the higher power, divinity, or source energy of your choice for your many blessings, or you may choose to recite a mantra or other prayer for healing and peace. As we put together our own rituals, the words that matter most are those you speak from your heart that best reflect your inner state of being at any given moment. Those speeches or prayers could be more reflective, or you might be appealing to your higher power to intercede on your behalf or to help you achieve a fortunate outcome. Speaking from the heart and knowing the unseen realm is listening and can respond can bring great comfort in times of need. As you strive to create greater connection to source in your life, speak from the heart and go from there. One exercise that's great to do first thing in the morning is to go to your altar and begin your day with a heartfelt expression of gratitude. Let's explore that one now.

## Approaching and Working with Your Altar

Obviously if you're taking the time to carefully set up an altar and consider prayers or affirmations to recite there, you'll want to approach your altar with a sense of respect and reverence. There are several ways you can work with your altar to bring more meaning and sacredness to any spiritual work you do. There's no right or wrong way to use your altar so long as that sense of respect is maintained. You may enjoy lighting a candle each day to respect or honor a certain deity, anniversary, or rite of passage. You may like to honor your deities by placing flowers or other offerings before them.

### EXERCISE: APPROACHING AND WORKING WITH YOUR ALTAR

Once you've prepared your altar, go there, and use the following to explore gratitude.

Stand in quiet contemplation before your altar and quiet your mind. Breathe in through your nose and exhale out of your mouth while envisioning yourself becoming more relaxed. If you feel tension, breathe into those areas, and use your inner power and imagination to release any stresses from the outer world. If you're guided, you may say a prayer or affirmation aloud to express thanks for your many blessings.

Think of all you have to be thankful for in your life. Think of family, friends, your work, and any other areas you are grateful for and continue to expand that sensation by taking your time to think of all the many areas of your life until you feel greater peace in every single cell of your being.

Whenever you feel ready, end in prayer by either saying aloud or to yourself, "And so it is. *Higher Will be Done*," or some other affirming statement that feels meaningful to you. There is no right or wrong on the words themselves or whether you choose to speak them aloud or say them to yourself. Your intent is what matters, so do what feels right and good to you. Once you finish, go about your day experiencing those blessings fresh in your mind and knowing that the more you think of all you have to be grateful for, the more blessings you will experience.

### JOURNAL PROMPT:
### APPROACHING AND WORKING WITH YOUR ALTAR

Sit quietly with your thoughts as you reflect on your altar. When you're ready, take a moment to consider the following as well as any other important thoughts that pop into your mind:

1. How did you feel standing before your altar?

2. Did you find yourself able to be more centered there?

3. What intentions did you set or prayers did you create there?

That little process is but one of endless possibilities you could do with your altar. There's no right or wrong in how you approach your altar, but I do find that standing in some kind of quiet contemplation a few minutes before settling in to meditations or guided journey work makes your inner practices more meaningful and effective. In your next journey, you will explore your inner world sanctuary.

## Finding Your Interior Sacred Space

Now that you've successfully established your exterior sacred space, you'll need to move on to create a supportive interior space where you will do your work. While I may be no interior decorator, I can help you with the most important interior you can consider—*your mind*. It's incredibly helpful to consciously create your own special place within the realm of your subconscious mind where you can find refuge, comfort, and solace and where you can go to launch your spiritual journeys such as the ones you'll find later in this book.

The awesome news about your interior sacred space is that it can be anything and it can be filled with everything your heart desires, or nothing at all. You can find a space in…space, as in outer space, floating among the stars, or you might find a more grounding wooded forest is your go-to. If you want fancy luxurious items, you can envision having anything you want within the interior of your mind. Once you find this special place, you will go there often to begin your guided journeys and to find an inner sense of peace and harmony within yourself.

In a moment, you'll take a journey to find your own special place. Your space might be in nature or elsewhere, so I'll be encouraging you to allow your place to reveal itself and I will remind you to be open to whatever emerges. Your space just might be far more amazing than anything you could consciously create. Wherever your space is, it's intended to be a wonderful area where you can feel most at ease. Because you will return here again and again, you will be able to use the site well beyond the exercises and experiences of this book as your personal go-to place, your unique inner vortex to help you launch into the places where you can receive the most helpful information for your soul's journey.

## EXERCISE: FINDING YOUR INTERIOR SACRED SPACE

Now that you've hopefully decided on how to record journeys to play back to yourself and you've found your own special sacred place to write down and record your thoughts, you're ready to do a quick exercise to help you locate your special place in your mind's eye, knowing you will return here again and again throughout the course of the book once we begin doing other exercises.

With all that in mind, when you're ready, go to your sacred space, the place you selected earlier to do your spiritual work. Before you begin, make sure you're as comfortable as can be. Do you need music or incense? Blankets or pillows? Make yourself feel nurtured and embraced. Settle in your seat and place your hands comfortably on your lap or to your side with your feet flat on the floor. Gently close your eyes and breathe.

Imagine you can feel a beautiful beam of pure white light moving down through the top of your head. Feel that light moving into your forehead, your eyes, nose, and jaw and moving down, down, down, and into your neck and shoulders, into your arms, elbows, wrists, hands, and fingers. Allow the white light to lovingly move through your shoulders, into your heart, your stomach, and all the way down your spine and into your legs. The light moves through your thighs, knees, calves, ankles, and heels and into the soles of your feet.

Allow the light to pour through you now from head to feet, removing any tensions and allowing those tensions to move down, down, down and out the soles of the feet and into the earth where those tensions are instantly transformed into a peaceful loving light for our planet. The light is getting stronger and stronger now and it begins to pour out of your heart center, creating a beautiful golden ball of light that surrounds you by about three feet in all directions. Feel yourself floating inside this golden light, safe and secure, totally carefree, knowing that within the golden ball of light you are protected and only that which is of your highest good can come through.

Now I want you to imagine a doorway in front of you. See the door, feel the door, or just know the doorway is there. In a moment, when I count to three, you will open that door and step inside your own sacred space, a place where your soul will feel energized, refreshed, safe, and invigorated. Ready? One, two, and three; open the door now. Walk or float through that door into your sacred space. Be there now. Notice what's happening. Where are you? Are you indoors or outdoors? How do you feel? Notice the peaceful energy of this special place and take your time to look around, feel the feelings, hear the sounds, and notice whatever you can about your special place.

PAUSE HERE.

Imagine you can notice that your soul feels alive in this space. You sense that you've gained new energy from being here. Allow the supportive and loving vibrations of your special space to continue to affect and strengthen you. Know that you can bring this supportive energy with you now as you turn around and walk or float back through the door you came through. Open that door now and go back out to where you began. Be there now and close the door to your sacred space, knowing you will be here again very soon.

Standing back where you began, feeling energized and refreshed, you notice you are still surrounded by that golden ball of protective light. Keep this heightened sense of well-being with you today and always. In a moment, when I count back from three, you will return feeling awake, refreshed, and better than before. Three, grounded, centered, and balanced; two, energized and refreshed and being careful and safe in every activity; and one, you're back!

## Journal Prompt: Finding Your Interior Sacred Space

Take a moment to record a few details about your journey.

1. What did your space look or feel like?
2. Were you able to see anything, or did you experience more of a feeling?
3. Make note of any details about the area or space that really impacted you.

Wonderful job! Know that you will become quite familiar with this place as we go because it will be the launchpad for your other journeys. If you didn't sense much that first time, don't worry. More will be revealed over time, and whatever you received today is perfect for this moment.

## Meeting Your Trusted Guide

All people have an army of unseen helpers who assist them throughout their soul's journey. Through my many years of working with clients, I discovered their journeys are enriched by consciously making that connection. Next, you will meet with your helpful guide or angel, a being who loves and supports you. Call them what you will, but you are deeply loved by many on the unseen realm. You will return to the sacred space you created and meet with your special friend who will accompany you through all the journeys in this book. For the sake of simplicity, I will refer to this helper as your guide even though the energy that shows up for you might be more of an angel or an energy you would describe as a light being.

## Exercise: Meeting Your Trusted Guide

Prepare yourself with music, blankets, or anything you need to feel supported and return to your sacred space. Sit and relax. Close your eyes. Breathe. Breathe in peace, and healing and love, and exhale any tensions or concerns. Feel the loving bright white light move through the top of your head and move down, down, down through your arms and hands, down your torso, and into your legs and feet. Allow the light to pour from your heart and surround you in a golden shield of love and light. Feel yourself floating in the bubble of golden light and know that within the light, you are safe, secure, and protected.

Notice the doorway you saw earlier that leads into your sacred space. You can see that door, you may feel or sense it there, or have an inner knowing that the door is there. When I count to three, you will return to your sacred space. Ready? One, two, and three; open the door and be there now. Take a look around; feel the supportive and loving energy of your special place. Listen to any sounds, and as you do, find yourself feeling relaxed and totally at ease.

As you reflect on the peaceful energies of your special sacred space, imagine there's a beautiful angel, spirit guide, or being of light who is floating down from above to join you. Imagine they can be there with you right now. Feel their loving energy as they greet you and know that this special presence is your personal guide who has been with you and your soul since the beginning of time. They know every single thing there is to know about you, your soul, and your soul's journey. Feel the unconditional love and high regard they have for you. Take a moment now to ask them any questions and allow them to share any information you need at this moment. You may ask them their name, how they would like to work with you, or any other question and allow them to share helpful information with you.

PAUSE HERE.

Thank your loving guide for joining you today and know that they will be here to meet you the next time you arrive in your sacred space to assist you with your spiritual journeys. Go ahead and say goodbye for now and imagine your guide floats away. Turn around and walk or float back through the door you came through, closing the door behind you. Be there now, back where you began. You're still surrounded by the golden light, safe and secure, and when I count back from three, you will return feeling better than ever before. Three, you're grounded, centered, and balanced; two, benefitting from this supportive energy throughout your day; and one, you're back!

### Journal Prompt: Meeting Your Trusted Guide

Sit quietly and consider your new guide and all you learned today. Make note of important details your guide shared. Here are a few ideas to get you started:

1. Did you meet with your special guide?
2. If so, did you notice an angel, light being, or spirit guide?
3. Had you encountered this guide before, or are they new to you?

Take notes about any other important insights that came up during your first meeting. Remember, you'll be getting to know your guide quite well over the course of the upcoming exercises.

## Summing Up

Now that you've prepared your external environment to support you energetically on your journey to connect with Goddess and you've established a go-to place within the inner sanctuary of your mind, you can continue to explore the multidimensional goddesses from around the globe.

*Chapter Eleven*

# Goddess Discovered

Like many, I believe a great societal shift is occurring now that will ultimately bring equality to all people from all walks of life, the likes of which has not been seen in millennia. Being denied opportunity based on biology, including gender, race, and so forth, is wrong. One of the fallouts from forcing oneself to operate in the world of the past is how many people felt obligated to change their behaviors or suppress their true feelings to fit in. The effort to conform could involve any number of compromises, including downplaying natural intuition or talent, perhaps, or avoiding emotions at all cost and sticking to the cold hard facts. In one way or another, most people experience some form of that dynamic at some point in life. If this ever happened to you, over time, your true essence gets shoved so far down, it becomes hard to recall how you really feel or think about anything. How can you open and expand your energy to embrace who you truly are and discover your own inner goddess? Here are a few ideas.

## Open to Your Emotions

While we certainly don't want to be unprofessional in the workplace or elsewhere, the fact that people were taught to avoid emotions at all costs ultimately took a toll on our mental well-being. These days, the schools of thought that embrace emotional intelligence help change those old ways and show people why our feelings and intuition represent strength rather than weakness. To embrace goddess power or personal strength in general, learning to open to what you're feeling and expressing your feelings in a healthy way will improve your life.

## EXERCISE: OPEN TO YOUR EMOTIONS

Prepare for your journey. Stand near your altar, light candles, and do whatever you need to help you feel energized and focused. Close your eyes and breathe. Breathe in through your nose and exhale out your mouth. Imagine feeling a beautiful light pouring down through the top of your head. Feel the loving light moving down through your head, neck, shoulders, and arms, moving through your torso, down your spine, and into your legs and feet. Breathe. Breathe in love and peace and harmony. Exhale any tensions. As you continue to breathe, turn your attention to any tense places within the body. Where are they? Rather than avoiding those areas, move into them instead. Imagine now you can go into tense places. As you do, notice if there are any emotions there. If so, what are they? Notice the first thoughts that come into your mind. As you notice any emotions or stress, go ahead and send love, light, and acceptance into those areas. Allow that love to open your energy and release tension and any unwanted emotions. Continue to breathe. Breathing in love and joy and peace and happiness, and exhaling any residual tensions. Take your time to move through any areas of tension sending love and releasing any unwanted emotions. Imagine you can easily fill your entire body with love and light. Continue working for as long as you're guided. When you're ready, open your eyes, feeling lighter, brighter, and better than you did before.

## JOURNAL PROMPT: OPEN TO YOUR EMOTIONS

Sit with your feelings for a bit, and when you're ready, consider taking out your journal.

1. How do you feel right now?

2. What emotions did you discover and what emotions are you hiding from yourself?

3. What emotions are easier to express?

If you ever find yourself feeling something less than positive, take time and write about the circumstances that caused you to feel that way. You may also benefit from engaging in physical movement to help release stuck emotional energy from the body. A good brisk walk can have a great healing effect.

## Balancing Energy

Everything in nature has an opposing force. Where there's hot, there's cold, happiness or sadness, peace or unrest, and so forth. These dual forces were personified by deities in pantheons as early people tried to explain various phenomena. Trying to survive in a dangerous world meant understanding that opposing forces must be honored and acknowledged. Opposites are everywhere in our world. Our constant and evolving need to reduce stress and find balance is experienced by everyone, but bringing peace and harmony into our physical bodies is often easier said than done. In the upcoming exercise, you will do some deep breathing and acknowledge the dynamic forces within your body to emerge with a greater state of peace and balance.

### EXERCISE: BALANCING ENERGY

Find some time when you won't be disturbed to begin this exercise. You may want to be near your altar and include music, scents, crystals, or other tools to aid your journey. When you're ready, sit in your sacred space with your feet flat on the floor and your hands in your lap or resting on each knee. Close your eyes and breathe. Fill your lungs with light and joy and peace and exhale any tensions. Continue to breathe, and with every breath you take, you feel more and more at ease and relaxed. Imagine now that you can notice your dominant hand, whether that is your right or left hand. Notice that hand now, the one you use most often for writing and doing physical activities. Put all your energy and awareness into that hand. Allow your consciousness to move from that hand, up your arm, imagining all the cells in your hand and fingers and arm are beginning to become alive and awake. Bring that energy into that whole side of your body. Feel and sense the shoulder on your dominant side, half of your neck and body, and the leg and foot on that side. Bring your full awareness into that half of your body that you use the most. Breathe into it and allow yourself to become fully awake and aware of this energy. Very good.

Now consider your opposite hand. Bring all your energy and awareness into your other hand. Allow your full awareness to be in your second hand. Feel how the energy differs there and notice each of your fingers, your palm, and continue to bring your awareness of your supporting hand up through your wrist and into your supporting arm, into that half of your neck and body and into the leg on that same side of your body. Feel that entire side of your body. Notice now how you can easily sense the way that the feeling differs from your more dominant side. Place both of your hands on your knees. As you do, bring your awareness into both hands at the same time—the dominant and the supportive. Notice the differences in the energy. Notice all you can about these two energies and how those energies flow within your entire body.

When you're ready, allow your supportive hand to receive some of the excess energy from your more dominant hand. Imagine one side can give to the other. Feel that happening now as you ask that equal amounts of energy move into each of your hands. As you do, imagine the equal flow of life force can now move up through your hands, into your wrists and arms, and into your body. Start with the top of your head. Feel the two sides of your forehead and allow the energy there to become fully balanced as that energy flows equally through every cell into your forehead, your eyes and ears, your nostrils and mouth, and down into your neck.

Balance energy from the top of your head through your body and into your legs and feet. Allow a pure white light to come through your head and travel easily through your body, removing any stuck energy, and flow freely now as this loving light flows through your neck and arms and through your body and legs and moves into your feet. Imagine you can feel any extra energy you don't need flowing into the earth as a loving offering to the planet. Continue to breathe and release any tensions into the earth as you move toward this serene sense of balance and peace. Take your time.

Deepen this practice by tuning into specific areas. If one side of your neck feels tension, allow the other side to send some of its energy there so you can relax and balance every cell within your body. The light continues to move through you into your shoulders. Both your left and right shoulders are experiencing an equal balance of energy now. Tensions are moving out and away as the balancing continues through your ribcage, your lungs, to the base of your spine. Feel this light moving into both legs equally.

As you do this process, take your time. You may now be aware that one side of your body needs more energy than the other. That's perfectly okay. Just imagine you can direct your energy easily so that both sides of your body feel equal now. Continue to notice the shifts in energy as this flow of loving light moves through every single cell in your body.

As the light travels from head to feet, begin now to think the following affirmations:

> *I now invite my body to become balanced.*
> *I now invite my mind to become balanced.*
> *I now invite my spirit to become balanced.*

As you state these intentions, sit and enjoy the sensations of increased energy that flows into perfect balance within your body. Your light is now becoming lighter and lighter and lighter, brighter and brighter and brighter. Take your time to receive. When you feel this balancing is complete, you may open your eyes, feeling awake and refreshed and better than ever before.

## Journal Prompt: Balancing Energy

Continue to sit and breathe for as long as you like as you reflect on new sensations of balance. If you would like to make a few notes on your experience, here are ideas to help.

1. Once you paid conscious attention to your body, could you sense a difference between the two sides of your body?
2. Which side felt more tension and how did you address that?
3. How did you feel after focusing on a feeling of greater balance?

The more you consciously bring awareness into one side overdoing it or tension within certain parts of the body and make a conscious effort to relax in a uniform way, the less time this practice takes.

## Awakening Personal Power

One of the big keys to goddess power involves awakening and acknowledging your own inner personal power. That doesn't necessarily mean you need to go from being a shy but kind person to an obnoxious bully, but instead, you want to own your personal space and embrace who you are in the spirit of self-acceptance and knowing that you matter. In this next short exercise, I invite you to expand your consciousness and allow yourself to fully embrace who you truly are in all your glory.

### EXERCISE: AWAKENING PERSONAL POWER

Stand in front of your altar and say, think, or feel any prayers you're guided to. When you're ready, take a deep healing breath in through your nose and raise your hands up toward the sky. Breathe in light and power and healing, and as you exhale, bring your arms down and imagine that any fearful, insecure energy is pushed out of the body and down into the earth where it can be transformed into a loving light for the planet. You will do a few repetitions of this exercise, and as you do, think, feel, or say the following aloud or to yourself:

*I am powerful!*
*I awaken to my full potential!*
*I accept who I am!*
*I am an awesome cocreator with the universe!*

Lift your arms as you breathe in love and light and say or think, *I am powerful!*

Exhale and release tension and any unwanted energy.

Lift your arms again as you take a deep breath and state, *I awaken to my full potential!*

Exhale and release anything less than your brightest and most beautiful self.

Lift your arms and say, *I accept who I am!*

Exhale anything keeping you from full self-love and acceptance right now.

Lift your arms, breathe, and say, *I am an awesome cocreator with the universe!*

Exhale any remaining tensions.

Now stand before your altar feeling refreshed, energized, and awake to your incredible personal power. Take that energy out with you today as you make positive decisions and work with others for the betterment of all concerned. Amazing work!

## Journal Prompt: Awakening Personal Power

I would absolutely love for you to do that exercise daily for a week and even beyond that to see how you change and feel as you consciously remind yourself of your awesome goddess self. For now, when you're ready, write down the following:

1. How do you feel after doing the breathing exercises compared to how you felt before?

2. Could you feel tensions and uncertainties flowing away from you?

3. Would you be able to commit to doing this for a week to see improvements?

The conscious practice of affirmations, releasing stuck energy, and deep breathing can be truly transformational. When you begin to control the narrative on what you're telling yourself, you begin to expand yourself into the goddess you've always been and deserve to be now and in the future.

## Meet a Goddess

During the guided journeys earlier in the book, you may have encountered a goddess or two, but if not, use the upcoming journey to meet with a goddess of your choice. A big part of the benefits you receive from meditation or journey work depends on the intentions you set beforehand. You can decide upfront which specific goddess you want to meet with, or you might choose a geographic location or time period within ancient history. Another option would be to allow for your highest good to emerge and be surprised by who shows up. All options are on the table, so decide, and when you're ready, settle in your sacred space and see what happens.

### EXERCISE: MEET A GODDESS

Find and prepare your sacred space and altar where you want to work, sit down, and relax. Close your eyes and breathe, breathing in love and peace and joy and happiness, and exhale any tensions and concerns. Continue breathing in love and light through your nose, exhaling tension. Imagine there's a beam of pure white light coming down through the top of your head. Feel this loving light moving down, down, down, into your forehead, moving into your eyes, your nose, and down into your mouth and jaw. Allow this loving light to move into each vertebra in your neck and travel down into your shoulders, moving into your arms, your elbows, your wrists, hands, and fingers.

Breathe in peace and harmony and exhale tensions. Allow the white light to continue moving down, down, down into your spine, moving through your shoulder blades, into your heart center, moving into your stomach, your lungs, and going all the way down to the base of your spine. Continue to breathe. Breathing in love and peace and joy, and exhaling any tensions. Feel that light moving down through the base of your spine and into your legs, moving into your thighs, knees, calves, ankles, heels, and toes and down into the soles of your feet. Feel the light traveling through the soles of your feet and moving down, down, down, into the core of the earth.

Imagine feeling the light moving through the top of your head, traveling down your spine, and moving out the soles of your feet. Allow that light to become stronger and stronger and pour out of your heart center, creating a beautiful golden ball of healing light that surrounds your body by about three feet in all directions. Feel yourself floating inside this golden healing light, safe and secure, totally carefree, and know that within this golden ball of light, only that which is of your highest good can come through.

Now imagine there's a doorway in front of you. See this door, feel it, or just have an inner knowing that the door is there. In a moment, when I count to three, you will open the door and step inside your beautiful space where you feel safe and totally secure. Ready? One, two, and three; open the door now. Walk or float into this sacred space. Be there now, inside this beautiful place. Take a moment to feel the loving and supportive energy of this space where you are safe, secure, and totally carefree.

As you continue to enjoy the loving and supportive energies of your special place, I want you to imagine your beautiful angel or spirit guide floats down from above to join you. You can see your special guide, feel their presence, or allow yourself to have an inner knowing that your guide is there. As you greet your special guide, tell them about your intentions for today, and let them know you would like to meet with a goddess whom you've known in ancient times or a goddess whom your ancestors worked with and worshiped in ancient times. Take a moment and let your guide know the specifics about your intentions today.

PAUSE HERE.

Very good. Now imagine you can take your guide by the hand and walk or float over to the other side of your sacred space where you notice a doorway in front of you. In a moment, when I count to three, you and your guide will walk or float through that door, and you will find yourself in a very early time. Ready? One, two, and three; you're opening the door. Open that door now and be there now in this early time period. Where are you? Notice the first thought that comes to your mind. How do you feel? Imagine you can look around at the surroundings. Notice what you notice. As you do, you sense a presence is walking or floating up to you now. As they get closer, you see this is a goddess.

Notice this goddess now. Where is she from? Notice the first thought that pops into your mind. You might see her, and if so, what does she look like? Notice any special jewelry, amulets, or other adornments. If you cannot see her, what does it feel like she's wearing? You may also hear her speaking. What is she saying? Or you may simply feel her presence. As you experience this goddess, ask her name. Who is she? Take your time and allow all these insights to come through.

PAUSE HERE.

Ask the goddess what connections you have from ancient times. Have you encountered her in your past lives, or do you sense that you may be meeting on behalf of your ancestors, or is this the first time you've met? Imagine she can explain this connection to you now.

PAUSE HERE.

Why has she emerged at this time in your soul's history? What special message does she have for you today? Take all the time you need to have this conversation.

PAUSE HERE.

When you're ready, thank the goddess for meeting with you today. Imagine she is walking or floating away. Go ahead and turn around and walk or float back toward the door you came through and walk back into your sacred space. Be there now. Feel the supportive energy of your special place.

Go ahead now and allow your guide to clarify anything or answer any questions you may have about this experience.

PAUSE HERE.

Very good. Thank your guide for joining you today. Again, feel the unconditional love and high regard they have for you. Say goodbye and watch them float away. When you're ready, walk or float through the door and go back out to where you began your journey.

Be there now, back where you started. In a moment, when I count back from five, you will return to full waking consciousness, feeling awake, refreshed, and better than you felt before. Ready? Five, you're grounded, centered, and balanced; four, you're continuing to process this information in your dreams tonight, so by tomorrow morning, you will be fully integrated into this new energy and awareness; three, you're driving safely and being completely safe in all your activities; two, grounded, centered, and balanced; and one, you're back!

## JOURNAL PROMPT: MEET A GODDESS

Take a moment of reflection to consider the journey you just experienced. When you're ready, you may want to record a few thoughts in your journal.

1. What goddess did you meet today and where was she from?
2. Did you sense knowing this goddess from a previous lifetime or through an ancestral connection?
3. What information or insights did the goddess share that will help you later?

You could repeat this journey and meet the same goddess again, or you may find a totally new deity emerges.

## Summing Up

I hope these fun journeys help you embrace your goddess self and create greater self-confidence and personal power. Keep in mind that with any of these journeys, you could do them again later down the road and receive a totally different outcome. Many of the relaxation processes could be integrated into your daily spiritual work to help you experience greater clarity, strength, and balance in your life. The more specific experiences could be used during different stages of life when you have big questions that need answers. Because the information received will vary over time, that's one of the many reasons why taking notes is such a good practice. You never know what helpful insights may emerge.

*Chapter Twelve*
# Discovering Ancient Goddesses

Now that you've had a chance to meet with a goddess directly, you can explore some fun exercises by venturing into different parts of the ancient world to connect more specifically with some of the goddesses you encountered in the first section of the book. Your goal will be to meet with goddesses from antiquity. Out of respect, this section will not feature any goddess journeys dealing with living religions. That said, in guided imagery, anything can happen. It is possible that during these journeys, you may meet a goddess from a living religion. This could happen because of a past-life or ancestral link or due to a connection your soul has with a certain religion or deity. If you experience a goddess from a living culture, treat her with great respect and ask her what she wishes to share. I'll include guidance for this as you go along. In the meantime, prepare to have an amazing exploration of the great goddesses of the ancient world and get to know yourself better in the process.

## Celtic Otherworld

You can now do a fun exercise to celebrate the Celtic goddesses by journeying to the supernatural realm known as the Otherworld to the ancient people of Britton and Ireland. The Otherworld is a fantastical realm where you may encounter goddesses, deities, and energies of love and joy. In Irish mythology, the Otherworld is the origin place for the Tuatha Dé Danann, and is called Annwn in Welsh mythology.

For this journey and all the others in the book, you will go through your relaxation through the doorway into your sacred space, meet with your guide, and go from there.

## EXERCISE: CELTIC OTHERWORLD

Prepare your altar, say your prayers, and do any of your rituals as guided. When you're ready, settle in to take this journey to the Otherworld. Sit in your space, close your eyes, and breathe. Allow healing, white, pure light to move through the top of your head and travel down your spine, arms, and legs and into your feet. The light pours through you, cleansing every cell, raising your vibrations, and removing any tensions. The light becomes so strong, it pours forth from your heart center and surrounds you in golden light. Feel the warm protective embrace of this familiar golden ball of light. Notice the doorway that leads into your sacred space. When I count to three, you will walk or float through that door. Ready? One, two and three; open the door now.

Be there now, inside your sacred space. Take a moment to look around and feel the supportive energy. As you do, you notice your special guide is floating down to join you. Say hello and let your guide know that today you would like to journey into the heavenly realm of the Celtic Otherworld. As you explain this, take your guide by the hand, and the two of you will walk or float to the other side of this room where you'll notice a doorway. In a moment, when I count to three, you and your guide will open the door and step into the Otherworld. One, two, and three; open the door now. Step through the door and find your-self in the Otherworld. Notice the beautiful surroundings as you look around. Feel the heavenly energy of this realm. Go with your guide and float through the Otherworld. Notice everything about this place. As you do, you notice beings of love and light are there to greet you as well as goddesses and other high-frequency energies. Take a moment to experience this realm and take in all you can.

PAUSE HERE.

Very nice. As you continue to absorb the heavenly energy, you notice a goddess emerges who wishes to speak to you. Imagine she is floating up and wants to share information with you. Who is she? Allow her to share her identity and any other information, and when you're ready, you can ask her questions.

PAUSE HERE.

Thank the goddess for joining you today. Allow her to float back to where she came from and turn to your trusted guide. When you're ready, take your guide by the hand, turn around, and go back toward the door you came through and go back to your sacred space. Close that door and be back now, inside your sacred space. Take a moment and ask your guide what other lessons and learning about your soul or helpful information for your continued journey through life you can receive from the Otherworld. Imagine your guide can share that with you now.

PAUSE HERE.

Thank your loving guide for helping you today and notice them float away. Turn and go back out to where you began this journey and close the door to your sacred place. Be back now, surrounded by golden light and filled with the heavenly energy of the Otherworld. When I count back from three, you will return to waking reality, feeling better than ever before. Three, you are grounded, centered, and balanced; two, processing this new energy in your dreams tonight so by tomorrow morning, you will be fully integrated into this new Otherworldly energy; and one, you're back!

## JOURNAL PROMPT: CELTIC OTHERWORLD

Although your journey is over, take your time to sit and continue to breathe for as long as needed to help you return to full waking consciousness. Make notes about your trip to the Otherworld and keep track of anything that may be useful to you down the road of life. Here are a few ideas to start:

1. What did you see in the Otherworld?

2. Describe how you felt in the Otherworld and any beings you encountered.

3. What goddess did you meet, if any; where was she from and what did she share with you?

Remember to add anything you would like to your notes and take your time reflecting on the experience.

## Egyptian Healing Temple

In this fun guided journey, you will have a chance to visit an ancient temple either to give or receive healing. I won't make any of these journeys too specific to give you a chance to experience what you will. It's likely if you lived in Egypt in a prior lifetime that those kinds of memories may emerge. As per usual, prepare for your journey and retreat to your special space to begin.

### EXERCISE: EGYPTIAN HEALING TEMPLE

Prepare your altar and other sacred items before you begin your journey. When you're ready, sit in your comfortable space in whatever way makes you most comfortable. Close your eyes. Allow the familiar beam of pure white healing light to move through the top of your head and journey down through your head, neck, and shoulders and into your arms and hands. Feel that light moving into your shoulder blades, your heart center, your stomach and lungs and continuing down your spine and into your legs, your knees, ankles, heels, the soles of your feet, and your toes. Allow the light to carry away any tensions as it moves from head to feet. Feel that light pouring forth from your heart center, surrounding you with a golden ball of light. Know that as usual, within the light you are safe and secure.

Notice your doorway leading into your sacred space. Open the door and walk or float into your space and notice your guide is there waiting for you. Let them know that you would like to visit an Egyptian healing temple either to participate in any proceedings or to receive a healing. Take your guide by the hand now and walk or float over to the door you walked through before. When I count to three, your guide will open the door, and it will lead you to ancient Egypt where you will go into the temple. Ready? One, two, and three; open that door now. Go with your guide and find yourselves in the Egyptian desert standing in front of the healing temple. Imagine you can know where the temple is located. Notice the first thought that pops into your mind. Walk up to the structure and go inside and be there now. Notice what you see.

Are you alone in the temple or with other people? If so, who are they? Allow yourself to walk slowly through the temple and find your activity. You will meet now with others who will either give you a healing or you will assist in the ceremony. Be there now and notice who is with you. Take your time to go through the activities and receive what is for your highest good.

PAUSE HERE.

As you experience the energy of this healing, you may notice goddess statues or sacred objects that are revered by the people there. Which goddesses do you notice? What offerings are made to this deity or others and how do you participate?

Take a moment to thank anyone you've met and finish up your session, and then turn around and go with your guide all the way back out of the temple, paying attention to any other adornments or deities you see within that temple. Go to the door you entered and walk back out into the desert. See the door to your sacred space and walk through that door now, going back into your room. Be there now.

Take a moment to thank your guide for assisting you today. Ask your guide now for further clarity about the healing you participated in today and know that your guide knows all the answers. Are you a reincarnated Egyptian, yes or no? Had your soul participated in any activities like these in prior lifetimes or did your ancestors live in ancient Egypt? How can you use this experience to further your soul purpose in your current lifetime? Take your time to understand this and anything else your guide needs to share with you.

PAUSE HERE.

Thank your loving guide again for all their help and know you will see them again soon. They're floating away, and you are now walking or floating back out the door you first entered, closing that door behind you. Go back to where you began. Grounded, centered, and balanced; in a moment, when I count back from three, you will return. Three, grounded, centered, and balanced; two, processing your healing in your dreams tonight and becoming fully integrated in this new energy by tomorrow morning; and one, you're back!

## JOURNAL PROMPT: EGYPTIAN HEALING TEMPLE

After you've had time to process the Egyptian healing experience, write down any insights you received during your trip to the temple.

1. Were you able to perceive yourself at a temple in Egypt?

2. Describe ceremonies, rituals, or healings and any sacred items or statues of gods or goddesses. How did you feel during this process?

3. Did the experience feel familiar to you as though you lived there before, or did you sense any ancestral connection?

Record any other details including what it looked like, how you felt, and so forth that may be important to you down the road.

## Greek Festival

Ancient Greeks loved honoring their gods and goddesses during numerous festivals held throughout the year. In this next journey, you will travel back in time and find yourself at a festival where you can encounter goddesses.

## Exercise: Greek Festival

Prepare yourself by lighting candles, infusing your space with essential oils, or doing any other activity you find nurturing. Find your sacred space and sit down at a time when you won't be disturbed. Close your eyes and breathe. Connect to the healing white light that moves from your head to your feet and surround yourself with a golden protective shield; know that within that golden light, you are safe, secure, and that only that which is for your highest good can come through. Notice your doorway leading into your personal sacred space. Open the door and step inside where you find your wonderful guide waiting for you. Let them know you would like to participate in a Greek festival. Take your guide by the hand, and the two of you will walk back to the door you went through before. This time, as you open this door, you will be floating above a scene from ancient Greece. Ready? Three, two, and one; open the door. Be there now in ancient Greece. Where are you? Notice the first thought that comes into your mind.

Imagine you and your guide are floating above an enormous gathering of people celebrating a deity or goddess. Imagine you can float with them now as they walk through the festivities. Notice all you can and take your time. What goddess or goddesses do you see? Who is being honored and what activities are going on to commemorate this special occasion? See what you see, hear what you hear, and feel the exciting energy of this happy time.

PAUSE HERE.

Imagine now that you have arrived at the main part of this festival where most people are gathered. You may notice merchants selling goods, musicians playing music, dancing, singing, and people eating and drinking. Take a moment to take it all in. Take your time to enjoy these festivities.

PAUSE HERE.

When you're ready, imagine you can quickly float over the proceedings and go back toward the area where you began. Notice your doorway is there and float through that now, returning to your sacred space. Close that door behind you and speak with your trusted guide. How did you feel there? Did you sense any ancestral or past-life connections to ancient Greece? What other insights can your guide share with you today?

PAUSE HERE.

Thank your guide again for accompanying you on this important journey. Taking all the energy and support you need from your sacred space, notice your guide floats away and you can turn now and walk or float back toward the door where you came from. Open the door and go back out where you began, closing that door behind you.

Still surrounded by that golden protective shell, when I count back from three, you will return, feeling refreshed and better than before. Three, grounded, centered, and balanced; two, processing your journey in your dreams and being completely integrated by morning; and one, you're back!

## JOURNAL PROMPT: GREEK FESTIVAL

Whenever you feel ready, you can make a few notes about your experience at the Greek festival.

1. How did you feel floating above the ancient Greek festival?
2. What goddesses or deities did you see?
3. Describe some of the thoughts, feelings, and sensations you observed. Can you describe the general mood of the people there?

You may receive further insights in your dreams and meditations over the next few days, so be open to receive, and if guided, keep your journal handy.

## Maya World Tree

The Maya believed the World Tree Yaxche stood in the center of Earth as a bridge between thirteen layers of heaven that led up to the mythical land of Tamoanchan and passed down through the human body into the nine layers of the Underworld called Xibalba. The spiritual world had several components:

**Middle World:** The earth.

**Xibalba:** Underworld for Quiche Maya of the south.

**Mitnal:** Underworld for Yucatec Maya of the north.

The god Itzam-Ye sat in the World Tree and embodied secrets of all three dimensions. In this journey, you will have a chance to visit the World Tree to receive insight and wisdom.

### EXERCISE: MAYA WORLD TREE

Find your sacred space and go within. Breathe through your nose and relax as a healing light moves through your body from head to feet, removing obstacles and creating a vast sense of peace and calm within you. Allow the loving light to pour forth from your heart center, embracing you in a blanket of golden light, shielding you from the outer world and allowing only that which is for your highest good to come through. Notice your doorway leading into your inner sacred space. Open the door and walk or float into your sacred space now. Feel the amazing and supportive energy here and allow that loving vibration to move into every single cell in your body, healing you, bringing you peace and greater harmony than ever before.

As you enjoy your special place, notice your guide is floating down to greet you. Say hello and let your guide know you would like to visit the Maya World Tree to receive insights and guidance. Now take your guide by the hand and the two of you will float over to a doorway. When I count to three, you and your guide will float through the door and into the land of the ancient Maya. One, two, and three; open the door. Be there now in a magical land. Notice if you are in an environment where it's a sunny day or a cloudy day. Walk or float through the majestic forest until you reach a clearing, and there before you stands the largest, most beautiful tree you've ever seen. Walk or float over to the tree, and you will see Itzam-Ye, the god who holds the secrets to life. You may also meet a goddess there. Take a moment to approach whoever is there and say hello. Ask them for any wisdom or information they would share with you today.

PAUSE HERE.

Thank the gathering for illuminating you with this information. Take your guide's hand and turn around, floating back through the forest toward the door where you entered. Go through the door and back into your sacred space. Be there now and close the door to the World Tree behind you. Take a moment to ask your guide for clarity or further information.

PAUSE HERE.

When you're ready, thank your wonderful guide for another amazing journey and say goodbye for now as they float back to where they came from. Turn around now and walk or float back through the door you came through and go back to where you began. Feeling refreshed and invigorated, in a moment, when I count back from three, you will return, feeling awake, refreshed, and better than ever before. Three, grounded, centered, and balanced; two, processing the information and inspiration received tonight in your dreams and resolving and integrating that information fully by tomorrow morning; and one, you're back!

## Journal Prompt: Maya World Tree

Document your journey to the World Tree by taking some notes. Here are a few suggestions for what to explore:

1. What did the forested area around the World Tree look like?

2. Did you encounter any creatures there? Any animals or birds?

3. Did you meet Itzam-Ye or any Maya goddesses? If so, who?

Make note of any other information the deities shared with you, including any past-life or ancestral connections you felt and anything else that comes to mind.

## Aztec Temples of the Sun and Moon

In modern times, Teotihuacan, known as the place where the gods were created, is widely associated with the Aztecs who settled the area in the 1400s. Earlier, I mentioned the Aztecs' admiration of their Toltec ancestors, whom they credited with building the abandoned site located thirty miles north of Mexico City. Scholars now believe the site to be far older than the Aztecs realized, having concluded the structure had possibly been abandoned for as long as a thousand years by the time they arrived. Currently, scholars estimate the site emerged sometime between the first and seventh centuries BCE.[571]

Spectacular Teotihuacan features the Pyramids of the Sun and Moon and the temple dedicated to the Feathered Serpent Quetzalcoatl.[572] To date, nobody knows for sure who built Teotihuacan, which likely began as far back as 400 BCE. Despite the ambiguous origins, ancient Aztecs made the most of the infrastructure for their religious practices. In this guided journey, you will visit the Pyramids of the Sun and Moon to receive strength and inspiration.

### EXERCISE: AZTEC PYRAMIDS OF THE SUN AND MOON

Say any prayers, stand before your altar, or settle into your sacred place, and whenever you feel prepared, close your eyes, and breathe. Allow the white light of love and peace to move through the crown of your head, through your torso and legs, and down and out the soles of your feet. Allow the light to remove any tensions you feel and surround you in a golden bubble of light that shields and embraces you, allowing only that which is of your highest good to come through. Notice the door to your sacred place and open that now, floating inside the wonderful energy of your special site. As you arrive, your guide is there to greet you. Say hello and let them know that today you would like to visit the Temples of the Sun and Moon. You may also intend that this journey is an aerial view of the modern site, or you may ask to go back in time to experience the site during an Aztec festival. Take a moment now to set your intentions.

---

571. UNESCO World Heritage, "Pre-Hispanic City of Teotihuacan."

572. History.com Editors, "Teotihuacan."

PAUSE HERE.

Very good. Now take your guide by the hand and float toward the door, open that door, and be there now, in Teotihuacan. Soar over the site, over the Avenue of the Dead, and gaze at those dusty streets and monuments, noticing the grandeur of the Temple of Quetzalcoatl and the Pyramids of the Sun and Moon. Notice yourself floating over these vast stone structures. What year is this? Modern or ancient times? What's happening there? See, feel, or sense all you can as you observe this spectacular site. Soar over the tops of the pyramids and see who is there. What are they doing? If you're guided, you may float down into the area and look around, or you may choose to continue your observation as you float over the area. Take your time to experience all you need to learn and observe.

PAUSE HERE.

When you're ready, float back toward the door you came through and go with your guide back into your sacred space. Take a moment to ask your guide for clarification. What lessons can you learn from experiencing this vast complex? Did you have ancestral or past-life connections there? If so, what were they?

PAUSE HERE.

Thank your guide for assisting you with this journey and walk or float back out the door you first entered. Still surrounded by golden light, when I count back from three, you will return. Three, grounded, centered, and balanced; two, processing this information in your dream state so you are clear by morning; and one, you're back!

## Journal Prompt: Aztec Pyramids of the Sun and Moon

Record your impressions from your journey to the Temple of the Sun and Moon whenever you're ready. Consider the following:

1. When you arrived at the site, did this feel like modern or ancient times?

2. Did you notice people there? If so, who were they and what were they doing?

3. Did you float down to the site or observe by floating overhead?

Make note of any other important details of your journey, including any people you saw, feelings you had, and so forth.

## Inca Lake Titicaca

The primary Inca god Viracocha created the universe, including the sun and the moon, on Lake Titicaca in Peru near the Bolivian border. To the people of the Inca Empire, Lake Titicaca represented the origin of the universe. Archaeologists discovered invaluable sacred offerings of gold and silver submerged in the icy waters as homage to the deities and creator gods.[573] In this journey, you will visit this sacred lake with the highest elevation in the entire world where you may encounter goddesses and make an offering in the sacred waters.

### Exercise: Inca Lake Titicaca

Set up your sacred space in your home and sit peacefully. Breathe. Fill your body with love and light as you allow a beautiful beam of pure white healing light to fill your head, your body, your arms and legs, and move through the soles of your feet into the earth. Imagine the light flows around you and creates a familiar protective golden orb that surrounds your energetic field. Know that within the golden orb, you are safe, secure, and protected, and only that which is for your highest and best may come through.

Go to your doorway and walk into your sacred space. Your lovely guide is waiting for you, anxious to take you for a spiritual healing exploration of Lake Titicaca. Take your guide by the hand and float through your sacred space and through the door leading out to the lake. Be there now, standing on the shore of Lake Titicaca. Feel the crisp cool air of the

573. Delaere and Capriles, "Intact Inca Underwater Offering from Lake Titicaca," 1030–41.

Andes and notice if you see any snowcapped peaks off in the distance. Feel the high frequency of the waters there, the holy place where the universe began. You may also notice if there are any people around. If so, notice who they are and say hello.

Imagine you are here in this sacred site to give a gift or offering to the deity. You may perceive any of these deities or goddesses before you or as talismans or statues you are encountering there. What goddess or deity are you honoring? Pay your respects as you will and imagine you are presenting the goddess or deity with an offering. Take your time to pull out your offering and enter it into the lake. If you would like, make a prayer or any other verbal offering to the deity.

PAUSE HERE.

Imagine that as your offering is received, you feel a sensation of vast peace, tranquility, and healing wash over you from head to feet. Sense the high frequencies of this water removing any unwanted influences of lower vibration. You may also request the assistance of any shamans you encounter on your journey. Take your time to receive the needed healing today.

PAUSE HERE.

When you're ready, thank any deities or anyone else who assisted you today. Take one last glimpse of this gorgeous holy lake, and when you're ready, turn around and walk or float back out toward the door. Open that door and go back into your sacred space and close the door behind you. Meet with your personal guide to explore the experience you just had. Did you sense a past-life connection with the Inca or Lake Titicaca region? Did you feel any ancestral connection there? Allow your guide to share any further insights.

PAUSE HERE.

Very nice. Thank your guide again for their assistance and allow them to float away, knowing they will see you again soon. Turn and walk or float back out to the door where you began your journey, closing that door behind you. Still surrounded by golden healing light, when I count back from three, you will return. Three, grounded, centered, and balanced; two, processing and still absorbing the healing energies throughout the next few days and sensing this healing can continue for you for as long as needed; and one, you're back!

## JOURNAL PROMPT: INCA LAKE TITICACA

Document your incredible journey to the healing waters of Lake Titicaca.

1. How did you feel standing on the shore of the highest elevated lake in the world?

2. Were there any people there? If so, who? Did they speak with you? What did they say?

3. What offering did you make to the deities and to whom?

Continue to write down any other important information you received.

## Mesopotamian Ishtar Gate

Once listed among the Seven Wonders of the Ancient World, the Ishtar Gate was the bright blue mosaic-tiled entrance to the city of Babylon in southern Mesopotamia. In modern terms, Babylon was located near Baghdad. Built around 575 BCE by King Nebuchadnezzar II, the bright blue tiles of this grand structure were adorned with symbols of the king's power. Dragons depicted on the gate represented the main Babylonian god Marduk, bulls symbolized the weather god Adad, and lions represented Ishtar, fertility and war goddess.[574]

Incredibly, in the early 1900s, researchers excavated forty-five feet of the original Ishtar Gate, and carefully reconstructed a portion that is now on display in Berlin, Germany, at the Pergamon Museum. On this fun journey, you will travel back in time to take a journey through the Ishtar Gate and stroll down the Processional Way where ancient Babylonians celebrated the New Year and spring planting period.[575] Along the way, you can enjoy the sites of this amazing spectacle to receive insights and information, and you may meet a goddess or two along the way. To have some fun, take the journey and notice what you see or sense and then check the bibliography section in the back of the book for websites with photos of the gate reconstruction to see how you did in terms of visualizing the incredibly gorgeous details.

---

574. Gries, *Ishtar Gate of Babylon.*
575. History.com Editors, "Babylonia."

## EXERCISE: MESOPOTAMIAN ISHTAR GATE

Settle into your beautiful sacred space and prepare in whatever way you wish for this amazing journey back in time. Sit comfortably and breathe. Allow yourself to fill your lungs with peace, tranquility, and light, and allow that loving light to begin moving down through the top of your head, into your neck and shoulders, arms and hands, through your heart, body, and legs, and into the soles of your feet. The loving light pours forth from your center and wraps you in a golden blanket of healing light. Know within this light only that which is for your highest good can come through. See or sense your doorway, open it, and walk or float into your beautiful sacred space. Feel the supportive and loving energies of this special place, and as you enjoy that feeling, your wonderful guide is floating down from above to join you. Say hello and let them know that today you would like to journey back in time to the Ishtar Gate in Babylon to observe a religious festival. As per usual, you may float over these events and observe them, or you may wish to walk and wander the streets and be among the populace as they experience the spring season. Set your intentions and talk this over with your guide, and as you do that, you float over to the door on the other side of your sacred space.

When I count to three, you and your guide will open the door and find yourselves back in ancient Babylon on the shores of the Euphrates River. Ready? One, two, and three; you're opening the door. Be there now, walking in or floating over the spectacular Ishtar Gate. Notice the bright blue tiles and designs on the gate. Sense the people there. How do you feel? Imagine now that you can follow along as the procession slowly moves inside the city walls. You find yourself on the Processional Way. Notice the festivities, sights, sounds, and smells. Notice any signs of the goddess or other deities. Who are they and how are they being honored? Allow the procession to make the half-mile journey into the heart of the city and continue to enjoy the ambiance. Take your time to notice all you can.

PAUSE HERE.

When you're ready, turn around and walk or float back over the Processional Way toward the gate, exit the city, and find your doorway leading into your sacred space. Open the door and go back to your own sacred area and be there now, closing your door behind you. Take a moment to connect with your guide to discuss your experience in Babylon. Did you notice any goddesses? If so, which ones? Do you sense that you lived a prior lifetime in Babylon? What about any ancestors? Were they there? How can you utilize this journey to better your current life experience?

Thank your guide for assisting you today. Say goodbye for now as they float up and away, back to where they came from. Turn and move out of your space, absorbing the positive and affirming energies as you go. Walk out the door you initially came through and go back out to where you began your journey. Surrounded by golden light, safe and secure, energized and refreshed, in a moment, when I count back from three, you will return, feeling awake, refreshed, and better than ever before. Three, grounded, centered, and balanced; two, processing the journey in your dreams and receiving even more insights and information; and one, you're back!

## JOURNAL PROMPT: MESOPOTAMIAN ISHTAR GATE

Take a moment to process all you received today, and when you're ready, document your journey through the Ishtar Gate.

1. Were you able to walk up to the front of the gate? If so, what did you see, feel, or experience?

2. Describe the Processional Way. What were people doing and what deities did you encounter, if any?

3. What insights did you gain about your soul's journey through this visit?

Notate any other important information to help you on your path in the future.

## Norse Yggdrasil

Yggdrasil is the World Tree in Norse Mythology, a sacred ash tree that sprang forth from the void at the beginning of time and stands in Asgard, the home of the Æsir gods and center of the universe as a crossroads between the nine realms that branched off from its roots.[576] In this journey, you will travel to the tree in the void to the center of the universe to meet the goddesses and find inspiration.

## EXERCISE: NORSE YGGDRASIL

Prepare yourself with any rituals, including candle lighting, crystals, oils, or whatever supports you at this moment in time. If you wish, stand before your altar in quiet contemplation. When you feel ready, sit in your comfortable sacred space with your feet and hands resting comfortably and close your eyes. Breathe in peace and light and love and exhale concerns. Bring the healing white light down from the heavens and allow it to flow through the top of your head, into your neck and shoulders and arms, and through your body into your legs and feet. Allow the light to surround you and shield you in a golden ball of protection. When you're ready, notice your door that leads into your sacred space and open the door and go inside your special place. Bask in the supportive energy there as your guide floats down to meet you.

Let your guide know that today you would like to float into the void and stand at the base of the World Tree Yggdrasil for healing and inspiration. When you're ready, take your guide's hand and float across your space to a doorway. When I count to three, the doorway will open, and you will find yourself in a void near the base of this spectacular ash tree. Ready? One, two, and three; open that door and be there now. Notice what you see. Imagine you can float in space and arrive at the trunk of the mighty ash. Allow the healing vibrations of the roots to move up through your feet, your legs and body, and into your arms and head. Allow the energy of creation and source to fill your being, healing you and raising your vibrations to higher levels than ever before. While there, you may notice the branches and roots going off in different directions, and you may encounter a goddess. Take your time to absorb the healing wisdom of Yggdrasil and all this powerful force has to offer you. Receive messages and wisdom from any of the goddesses who wish to meet you today.

PAUSE HERE.

Filled with loving light and healing wisdom, thank the World Tree and any others who joined you today. Take that newfound energy with you as you walk or float back out toward the door you entered and go through that door now, back into your sacred space filled with the light of the beginnings of time. Take a moment to ask your guide for any clarity.

PAUSE HERE.

When you're ready, thank your loving guide for assisting you again today. Imagine they float away and you can turn and go back out to where you began your journey. When I count back from three, you will return, feeling refreshed and rejuvenated and better than ever before. Three, continuing to benefit from this healing energy tonight so by tomorrow morning you will be fully integrated into your new awareness and expansion received from the World Tree; two, grounded, centered, and balanced; and one, you're back!

## JOURNAL PROMPT: NORSE YGGDRASIL

Write down any impressions you received. Here are a few ideas to start:

1. How did you feel at the base of the World Tree?

2. What energy and information did you receive from this journey and how will you use that in your life?

3. Did you encounter any goddesses? If so, who? What did they share?

Record any other thoughts that come to you. Such insights may occur to you in your dreams and float into your mind overnight or in the coming days, so keep track of everything that feels important.

## Roman Lararium

One of the most fascinating aspects of the Roman religion involved the rituals performed within the household in the Lararium, or sacred altar. The Lararium is named for the Lares, whimsical deities that lived in all Roman homes as protective forces that were particularly prevalent in Pompeii. The Lararium looked like a square stone box with an angular roof and columns adorned with paintings of the gods. They look a bit like ancient dollhouses, and we know that because there are many examples that survived from Pompeii. The *paterfamilias*, or eldest male in the home, tended to the household gods that the family placed inside the Lararium. The family also worshiped the *genius*, the spirit or embodiment of the paterfamilias, as well as another genius that represented the entire family as a collective unit and the continuation of the family lineage.[577] As mentioned earlier in the listing on Vesta, the hearth fire remained burning in this area as homage to the household gods and could not be allowed to go out or else it may mean ill health or ill fortune may befall the family. In this next journey, you will visit an ancient Roman home and encounter a Lararium where you can witness the goddesses and other deities and, if desired, pay homage to them.

### EXERCISE: ROMAN LARARIUM

For this exercise, you may wish to prepare your altar, your own version of your Lararium, with special objects, candles, scents, or stones before beginning your inner journey work. Once that is complete, settle into your sacred space, close your eyes, and rest your hands in your lap. Breathe in love and light and peace and exhale any tensions and concerns. Allow a healing white light to pour down from above, through your head, neck, and shoulders, heart, stomach, and lungs, and move through the body into your legs and feet. The light surrounds you in a golden protective glow, and you are safe and secure now and always. See or sense your doorway and walk or float into your sacred space now. Your guide is there to greet you. Say hello and let them know you would like to take a beautiful journey into an ancient Roman home to visit a

577. Descoeudres, Harrison, and Allison, *Pompeii Revisited*.

Lararium, or sacred altar. Take your guide's hand and float across your sacred space to a doorway. When I count to three, the door will open and you will find yourself inside that home. Ready? One, two, and three; open the door now.

Be there now, inside the heart of the Roman home. Walk up toward the hearth and the Lararium and notice what you notice. You may see candles burning, and you may sense the feeling of divinity at this sacred place. You may see statues of goddesses, Lares, or other deities. You may see people there, or not. As you do, notice which deities or goddesses are represented there. How do they make you feel? Take your time to notice all you can and enjoy this quiet journey.

PAUSE HERE.

When you're ready, take your guide by the hand, turn around, and walk or float back through the door into your sacred space. Close the door behind you and be there now. Ask your guide for any clarification about what you experienced. Did you sense a past-life or ancestral connection there? If so, have your guide explain those things or any other information you need.

PAUSE HERE.

When you're ready, thank your guide for once again helping you with this process. Your guide says goodbye and floats away and you can now take all the energy you need to walk or float back to where you began, closing the door to your sacred space as you go. Be there now, back where you started. You're still surrounded by golden protective light, safe and secure within the light; take all the energy you need to feel awake and refreshed and release any excess energy now, allowing that to flow through your body and out the soles of your feet. You are grounded, centered, and balanced, and when I count back from three, you will return, feeling better than ever before. Three, processing this visit to the Lararium in your dreams tonight and becoming fully integrated into any new energies or information by morning, driving and being safe in all activities; two, you're grounded, centered, and balanced; and one, you're back!

## Journal Prompt: Roman Lararium

If you're near your altar, you may wish to reflect about what you experienced today and the feelings the Lararium brought forth. Take a few minutes to process your journey and document important details.

1. Were you able to visit the hearth of a traditional Roman home?

2. Describe the Lararium, or sacred altar, within the home.

3. What goddesses or other deities did you notice were being worshiped there?

Record any other thoughts or discussions with your guide that you want to remember down the road of life.

## Summing Up

Connecting to sacred ceremonies and worship within different venues in the ancient world can prove quite interesting and revealing. You may have experienced deep soul remembrances of things you've done in the past or became entertained or fascinated by ideas and concepts you never considered before. Either way, actively engaging with different parts of the world can bring a sense of oneness and remind you of how much people around the world have in common.

## Chapter Thirteen
# Past-Life and Genealogical Regressions to Discover the Goddess

At a soul level, somewhere along the line, you've likely encountered deities and goddesses in your past lives, or your ancestors worked with deities in their spiritual practices through the centuries. Now you will have the opportunity to find out exactly how deep your soul connection goes with various goddesses.

In the previous chapter, you explored goddesses within the context of the places I suggested to you in the ancient goddess journeys. This time, you will have more control over what you experience, and that will all depend on the intentions you set before and during the regressions. To take these journeys, you will make choices to either consciously set an intention to discover your connections to ancient Greece, for example, or you could simply ask that whatever information is for your highest good at this moment in time can emerge. Either is okay. It all depends on you and what you want to experience. Setting intentions can help you notice if you've had a past-life or ancestral connection to a specific place.

Typically, if you feel guided to explore a specific area, that might be because you lived a past life there, although that's not always the case. Once in awhile, you may be surprised to learn that even though you asked about ancient Greece, you may not have lived there in past lives, and you may not have any ancestral connections there either. Regressions are always revealing and can provide surprising answers. If you leave your focus more open-ended to allow for highest good, that is also informative and brings forth concepts, ideas, and thoughts that you may have never considered before. One thing is for certain—either way, you will receive what is best for you at this moment in your life. Your higher self and soul will see to that.

If you can't decide which group of goddesses you want to explore, go back through the first section of this book, or glance back at your journal and review your notes. Within those notes, as I've been reminding you throughout our time together, you likely left yourself huge clues about the inner workings of your soul, and that information will get you going in the right direction. Should you set intentions or ask for highest good? Why not try both? You can always do these journeys more than once and receive totally new outcomes. Take some time to record the journey, consider your intentions, and then prepare yourself for a wonderful experience.

## Past-Life Regression

For best results, I recommend retreating to your sacred space as you do for any guided journey work. This is especially true for past-life regression, which is quite a bit longer than the other journeys you've done up to this point. Make sure you settle in and prepare with all the items that will make you feel supported and fully nurtured, including your favorite music, blankets, candles, essential oils, or whatever else you like. All those items help set the stage to bring comfort to your soul so you can go deeper into the journey. Are you ready to go on a regression to discover your personal soul connections with the Goddess? Awesome!

### EXERCISE: GODDESS PAST-LIFE REGRESSION

Settle in your sacred space. Sit with your feet flat on the floor and your hands in your lap. Close your eyes and breathe, breathing in love and peace and joy and happiness, and exhaling any tensions and concerns. Continue breathing in love and light through your nose, exhaling tension. Call in any guides, ascended masters, or beings of light who wish to join you today. Thank them for being here and let them know that you request only your highest will to be done. Feel the energies of peace, healing, and relaxation fill your body, mind, and spirit. Very good. Notice that with every breath you take, you're becoming more and more relaxed.

Imagine there's a beam of pure white light coming down through the top of your head. Feel this loving light moving down, down, down, into your forehead, moving into your eyes, your nose, and down into your mouth and jaw. Allow this loving light to move into each vertebra in your neck and travel down into your shoulders, moving into your arms, your elbows, your wrists, hands, and fingers.

Breathe in peace and harmony and exhale tensions. Allow the white light to continue moving down, down, down into your spine, moving through your shoulder blades, into your heart center, moving into your stomach, your lungs, and going all the way down to the base of your spine. Continue to breathe. Breathing in love and peace and joy, and exhaling any tensions. Feel that light moving down through the base of your spine and into your legs, moving into your thighs, knees, calves, ankles, heels, and toes and down into the soles of your feet. Feel the light traveling through the soles of your feet and moving down, down, down, into the core of the earth.

Allow that light to become stronger and stronger as the light heals and relaxes you. Allow the light to help you release any tensions and concerns as the light becomes stronger and stronger. The light becomes so strong now, it begins to pour out of your heart center, creating a beautiful golden ball of healing light that surrounds your body by about three feet in all directions. Feel yourself floating inside this golden healing light, safe and secure, totally carefree, and know that within this golden ball of light, only that which is of your highest good can come through.

Now imagine there's a doorway in front of you. See this door, feel it, or just have an inner knowing that the door is there. In a moment, when I count to three, you will open the door and step inside your beautiful space where you feel safe and totally secure. Ready? One, two, and three; open the door now. Walk or float into this sacred space. Be there now, inside this beautiful place. Take a moment to feel the loving and supportive energy of this space where you are safe, secure, and totally carefree.

As you continue to enjoy the loving and supportive energies of your special place, I want you to imagine your beautiful angel or spirit guide floats down from above to join you. You can see your special guide, feel their presence, or allow yourself to have an inner knowing that your guide is there. As you greet your special guide who has been with your soul since the very beginning of time, remember that they know every single thing about you, and your soul, and your soul's journey. Feel the amazing unconditional love and high regard your guide has for you. Very nice.

Take a moment now and speak with your loving guide about your intentions for today. Let them know that you are here to go on a journey into your past lifetimes to explore lives where you worked with or worshiped goddesses. Take your time to speak with them now and receive any input from your guide that will be helpful for you to know before you begin your journey today.

PAUSE HERE.

Very nice. Know that your guide has heard your request. Imagine your guide informs you that they plan to help you connect to clothes you've worn in prior lifetimes. When you're ready, take your guide by the hand, and the two of you will walk or float across the room. As you do, you'll notice a set of five steps leading down to a lower level. In a moment, you and your guide will go down those steps. With each step you go down, you will feel more and more relaxed and at ease, more relaxed than you've ever felt before. Ready? Five, so relaxed; four, sinking into a state of full and total relaxation; three, so peaceful and serene; two, sinking further into yourself; one, and you're there. Be there now on this lower level. Notice there's a door right in front of you and your guide is opening that door now.

As you look inside to see what's behind that door, you find yourself gazing inside a huge room, and within that room, you immediately notice a long rack of clothing that begins quite close to you and extends far off into the distance. Your guide explains that these are all the clothes you have ever worn before, so this room and these clothes feel very safe, secure, and familiar to you. Take your guide by the hand, and the two of you will begin now to float. As you float closer to these clothes, you can see or sense all the items you have in your current closet. Go ahead now and continue with your guide, floating past your current wardrobe, moving down the line as you move farther and farther along this rack of clothing. Know that the farther back you float, the older the clothes will be. You begin now to notice items you used to own, and then you sense things you had as a child, a baby, and you can sense that rack of clothes is full and continues on and on for as far as the eye can see.

Imagine now that you can once again ask your guide to take you all the way back to the earliest time or the most significant time that would be most for your highest good at this moment in your soul journey when your soul encountered or worked with Goddess energy. Your guide will help you find the appropriate clothes that relate to that period and important event. Still holding your guide's hand, continue floating on and on, farther and farther and farther. Continue to notice that the farther back you go, the more relaxed you feel. Very good. In a moment, when I count to three, you will arrive at the appropriate clothing that your guide would like to share with you today. Ready? One, walking past the clothes; two, farther and farther and farther into the closet, you're almost there; and three, you're there. Be there now. Some clothing lights up. Your guide takes them off the rack and hands them to you. Try them on now. Imagine at the end of the closet, there's a mirror there.

What kind of clothes are you wearing? Are you a man or a woman? What do you look like? Imagine you can glance down and notice what kind of shoes you're wearing. If you can't see anything, imagine you can have an inner knowing about what you're wearing, or your guide can tell you about these clothes. Receive this information easily in any way you can.

How do you feel? How old are you? Notice anything else that may be important. Ask your guide for any clarification.

PAUSE HERE.

Notice now that the mirror you're looking into has a doorknob on it. In a moment, when I count to three, you will open that door and step out, into that life, wearing those clothes. Ready? One, two, and three; turn the doorknob, open that door, and step out into that lifetime. Be there now. Notice what's happening. What year is this, the first thought that comes into your mind? Where are you? Are you alone or with other people? How do you feel? What's happening? Notice everything you can about this moment.

PAUSE HERE.

Imagine you can fast-forward from this moment to the next most significant event of this lifetime where you are with other people and be there now. Notice what happens next. Where are you now? What's happening? Why are these events important? As you experience the energy of the other people there, do you notice anyone who either looks or feels like somebody you know from your current life? Maybe, maybe not, but if you do, who is this? Notice the first thought that pops into your mind. How does your relationship with this person in this other lifetime relate to the things you're doing together in your current life? What lessons are the two of you learning together as souls that you've been exploring over the course of many lifetimes? Very good.

If there's nobody in these events you've known in your current lifetime, notice the relationships you have with the people you're with and what you're doing. How do you feel around them? How are these events impacting your current lifetime? Very good.

Next, imagine you can fast-forward to the next most significant event in this lifetime where you are engaged in some form of worship. Be there now. Notice what's happening. What are you doing? What goddesses or other deities are you encountering there? How do you feel?

Take your time and allow yourself to move through any and all rituals or practices.

PAUSE HERE.

As you become more aware of the practices you engaged in during these early times, how do they relate to your current lifetime? What lessons did you learn through these beliefs? How can this information help and improve your current incarnation?

Take your time to understand all you need to know and notice any other important events of your life so that you will better understand why this lifetime is so important for you to notice at this moment in your soul's history. Again, notice how this information will help you in your current life's future.

PAUSE HERE.

When you're ready, imagine you can fast-forward to the very last day of your life. Be there now, still surrounded by a protective golden bubble of light; notice how it is that you pass into spirit and do that now. You're lifting up, up, up, out of that body, out of that life, floating higher and higher and higher, into that peaceful space between lives. Floating in the clouds now, peaceful and relaxed, imagine a cord of light connects you with that lifetime and all of the experiences there, both good and bad. Your guide is now holding a big pair of golden scissors. When I count to three, your guide will cut the cord between you and this early life-time. Ready? One, two, and three, and cut! The cord is cut, and your guide is sending a loving and healing light to you and all who were with you in that early time, blessing everyone and sending them healing and love. Very good. Turn to your guide and allow them to help you learn more about this experience by answering some important questions. What lessons did you learn in the life you just visited? How will you use the information you learned today about your past spiritual practices to assist you in your current life? Take your time and ask your guide to help you clarify any other areas you need to better understand.

PAUSE HERE.

When you're sure you've received what you came for, take your guide by the hand and the two of you will float down through the clouds and find yourselves back inside the room with the clothing rack. Your guide takes the clothes you're wearing and hangs them up, putting them away. The two of you walk or float past all your many clothes that you've worn throughout the ages, passing by the items you wore in your current life-time as a baby, as a child; you're moving quickly now, all the way back to your current wardrobe. Your guide opens the door to the room, and you find yourself back by the steps. See the five steps you walked down when you began this journey. Go ahead now and walk up those five steps, knowing that with each step you climb, you will begin moving closer to your current life reality and waking consciousness. Five, climbing up a step; four, so relaxed; three, moving peacefully toward your current life; two, feeling filled with inner peace; and one, you're back at the top of the steps. Be there now, back in the peaceful and safe space where you began your journey. Take a moment to feel the supportive energy as you begin to look around your special sacred space. Thank your guide and ask any further questions you might have about what you experienced today. Feel free to ask anything that will give you more insights. You could ask your guide about your soul's purpose and how that applies to the life you just visited. Or you may have another question. Your guide would like to assist with anything you need. Go ahead now and allow your guide to give you clarification either by telling you things, showing you, or helping you have an inner knowing about what you need to learn.

PAUSE HERE.

Very good. Thank your guide for joining you today. Again, feel the unconditional love and high regard they have for you. Say goodbye and watch them float away. When you're ready, walk or float back to the door you first entered and go back out to where you began your journey.

Be there now, back where you started. In a moment, when I count back from five, you will return to full waking consciousness, feeling awake, refreshed, and better than you felt before. Ready? Five, you're grounded, centered, and balanced; four, you're continuing to process this information in your dreams tonight, so by tomorrow morning, you will be fully integrated into this new energy and awareness; three, you're driving safely and being completely safe in all your activities; two, grounded, centered, and balanced; and one, you're back!

Remember that you likely had many lifetimes with different deities, depending on what part of the world you visited today, so you can always do this again and receive new information.

## Journal Prompt: Processing Your Goddess Past-Life Regression

After such a powerful journey, I encourage you to record your thoughts in your journal, and feel free to use these prompts or write anything else that happened during the regression:

1. Where did you visit today?

2. What Goddess energy did you encounter from your former incarnations, if any?

3. What lessons can you bring forward to enhance and improve your current lifetime?

Write any other thoughts, ideas, or advice your guide shared with you and be sure to make detailed notes about the sights and sounds you experienced.

## Genealogical Regressions to Connect with Ancestral Goddesses

On the collective level, people are becoming more aware of exactly how connected we are to our own ancestors and why ancestral healing is important. Without a doubt, at some time in the past, your ancestors worshiped goddesses and other deities.

You are about to experience a Genealogical Regression where you will travel into the past to see, feel, and experience the things your ancestors did long before your birth. You will visit ancestors on your mother's and father's sides of your family. When we discuss the topic of parents, remember, that could vary depending on your unique situation. Parents could mean your birth parents, adoptive or foster parents, a grandparent, or anyone who acted as a caregiver for you during your lifetime. Important connections exist regardless of whether you're blood related to someone or not. As with any guided journey, your intention will determine the information you will receive. If you have several parental figures in your life, you could attempt to set an intention for the specific parental figure you'd like to meet, but you can also allow the parent to show up and see who appears. You can always go back and repeat the journey to address your birth parents and foster parents, for example. In these exercises, I'll help you consciously intend to discover information and have experiential encounters with times in the past when your ancestors worked with Goddess energies. You may encounter goddesses from ancient times, or you might discover deities from living religions. If your goddess is from a living religion, remember to approach her with care and respect, keeping in mind that your ancestors possibly worshiped these deities, so to meet with them in this space should be seen as a true honor.

The difference between this process and the past-life regression is that instead of gazing out of your own eyes and noticing that you are a completely different person, perhaps even a different gender, and you're living in ancient times, in the Genealogical Regression, you will float over events and see other people engaging in various activities, and you will come to recognize that some of the people you will encounter are your ancestors. The process will feel like you're voyeuristically floating over scenes where you'll be able to eavesdrop on your ancestors and gain real insights into their lives, feelings, and circumstances. You will be able to notice what you will and then identify how your ancestors' past behaviors and practices influenced your whole family through the generations and how that energy affects you on a personal level. You will also be able to send love, peace, and joy to all of those important souls who paved the way for you to be exactly who you are in your current life experience.

## Goddess Maternal Genealogical Regression

First up, you will explore your mom's side of the family and discover which, if any, goddesses or deities your family worshiped by speaking to the ancestors on her mother's and father's sides of the family.

### EXERCISE: GODDESS MATERNAL GENEALOGICAL REGRESSION

Go to your sacred space and take a seat. Sit with your feet flat on the floor and your hands in your lap. Close your eyes and breathe, breathing in love and peace and joy and happiness, and exhaling any tensions and concerns. Continue breathing in love and light through your nose, exhaling tension. Call in your guides, ascended masters, or beings of light who wish to join you today and ask them to help you connect with information that is for your highest and best.

Allow peace, healing, and relaxation to fill your body, mind, and spirit. Very good. Notice that with every breath you take, you're becoming more and more relaxed. Imagine there's a beam of pure white light coming down through the top of your head. Feel this loving light moving down, down, down, into your forehead, moving into your eyes, your nose, and down into your mouth and jaw. Allow this loving light to move into each vertebra in your neck and travel down into your shoulders, moving into your arms, your elbows, your wrists, hands, and fingers.

Allow the white light to continue moving down, down, down into your spine, moving through your shoulder blades, into your heart center, moving into your stomach, your lungs, flowing down to the base of your spine. Continue to breathe. Breathing in love and peace and joy, and exhaling any tensions. Feel that light moving down through the base of your spine and into your legs, moving into your thighs, knees, calves, ankles, heels, and toes and down into the soles of your feet. Feel the light moving through the top of your head, traveling down your spine and moving out the soles of your feet. Allow that light to become stronger and stronger as the light heals and relaxes you. Allow the light to help you release any tensions and concerns as the light becomes stronger and stronger. The light becomes so strong now, it begins to pour out your heart center, creating a beautiful golden ball of healing light that surrounds your body by about three feet in all directions. Feel yourself floating inside this golden healing light, safe and secure, totally carefree, and know that within this golden ball of light, only that which is of your highest good can come through.

Now imagine there's a doorway in front of you. See this door, feel it, or just have an inner knowing that the door is there. In a moment, when I count to three, you will open the door and step inside your beautiful space where you feel safe and totally secure. Ready? One, two, and three; open the door now. Walk or float into this sacred space. Be there now, inside this beautiful place. Take a moment to feel the loving and supportive energy of this space where you are safe, secure, and totally carefree.

As you continue to enjoy the loving and supportive energies of your special place, I want you to imagine your beautiful angel or spirit guide floats down from above to join you. Feel the amazing unconditional love and high regard your guide has for you.

Take a moment now and speak with your loving guide about your intentions for today. Let them know you would like to do an ancestral healing for your mother and her side of the family. As you discuss this, notice there's a door on the other side of your sacred space and that door is opening now, and here comes your mother. Notice this is her higher self, the highest aspect of her soul. Notice that she is smiling and so very happy to see you.

Imagine you can let your mom know that you would like to learn more about any ancient times when your ancestors worshiped goddesses or other deities in the past. Let her know that you would like to discover this connection for her mother's side of the family. As you mention this, imagine you and your mom take your guide by the hand and begin to float toward that door your mother came through. In just a moment, when I count to three, you and your mom and your guide will float through that door, and when you do, you will find yourselves floating over a light that looks like a ray of sunshine. That sunbeam represents time and your ancestral history. You will feel totally relaxed as you float over that sunbeam to a very early time in your family history. On the count of three, you will open that door. Ready? One, two, and three; opening that door now. You're there, floating over that sunbeam. Know that you are floating over the current time and that the farther out you float, the earlier the time will be. Allow your guide to take you and your mom to a very early time in your ancestral history when your ancestors worshiped deities. Ready? Floating out now, over the light, farther and farther and farther, out, out, out to a very early time that will be for your highest good. On the count of three, you will arrive. Ready? One, two, and three; you're there. Imagine you and your guide and mom can float down, down, down, over those events where you can float above them, and notice what's happening.

What year is this? Notice the first thought that floats into your mind. Where are you in the world? What's happening? Which ancestor or ancestors do you see? What deities are they worshiping or what are their spiritual practices? Take your time to notice all you can.

PAUSE HERE.

Very good; now imagine the three of you can lift, up, up, up, higher and higher, and float over these early events. Your guide is sending love and light to all your ancestors at this very early time. Notice the energy there is getting lighter and lighter and lighter, brighter and brighter and brighter. Very nice.

Imagine now you can ask your guide some important questions. How has this experience of your ancestors affected your current life-time? What did your ancestors learn in these early times? How can you best honor their legacy? What can you take away from this experience to use in your current lifetime? What will you let go of or leave behind?

Notice there's an energetic cord of light that is now connecting you and your mom with these early times. Your guide is bringing out a pair of golden scissors. In a moment, when I count to three, your guide will cut that cord. Ready? One, two, and three, cut! A beautiful healing light is pouring down over all people in these early events, and that light is healing your ancestors, and all events are getting lighter and lighter, brighter and brighter. That light is now moving through your mother, and she is becoming lighter, and you are now also feeling lighter than ever before. Allow that light to lift you all higher and higher, up, up, up until you are once again floating over the sunbeam below you. Go ahead now and take your guide by the hand as the three of you float all the way back toward the present day and back into your sacred space. As you float, imagine you can send love and healing light to all your ancestors between this very early time and right now. Ready? One, floating toward today; two, sending that healing and light to your ancestors; and three, you're back, floating through the door. You arrive inside your sacred space. Take a moment to speak with your mom and your guide about anything important.

PAUSE HERE.

Now imagine you can do the same process, only this time, when the three of you float through that door, you will be traveling into the past to your mom's father's side of the family to visit any experiences where they worshiped goddesses or other deities. Float back toward the door now and open it. Hold your guide's hand as you, Mom, and your guide float all the way back in time, over that sunbeam to the earliest time or to a significant time when your family members worked with the Goddess. On the count of three, you will arrive at this early family event. Ready? One, two, and three, and be there now. Float down, down, down and hover over these events. What's happening? Where are you? What year is this? What ancestors do you notice? How are these early relatives worshiping the Goddess or other spiritual energies? Take your time to notice all you can.

PAUSE HERE.

Now imagine the three of you can lift up, up, up, and float over those early events. How are these early spiritual practices affecting your family overall? How have they affected your mother? How have you been impacted by these practices? What lessons did your family learn in these early times? How can you invest this information in your future? Take your time to receive any and all information.

PAUSE HERE.

As you continue to learn more, allow a healing and loving light to emerge and pour over all the people involved in these early events. Notice your guide with the golden scissors, and in a moment, your guide will cut the cords between you and all involved. Ready? One, two, and three, cut! A beautiful healing light is pouring down from above and healing everyone there, and all those very early events are becoming lighter and lighter, brighter and brighter. You notice your mom becoming lighter, and you are now also becoming lighter and feeling better than ever before. As this light continues to transform all people, you and your mom and guide lift up, up, up, higher and higher, floating above these early events. You all begin to float back toward today, but only as quickly as you can extend this loving light to everyone in your entire family between that early time and now. Ready? Three, floating toward today; two, moving quickly and sending peace and love and light to all; and one, you're back! Float back into your sacred space and take a moment to speak to your mom and your guide about any special or important information you learned today.

PAUSE HERE.

Very good. Thank your mom for joining you today and imagine she says goodbye and walks or floats back through the door. Thank your guide and watch them float away. When you're ready, walk or float back to the door you first entered and go back out to where you began your journey. Be there now, back where you started. In a moment, when I count back from five, you will return to full waking consciousness, feeling awake, refreshed, and better than you felt before. Ready? Five, you're grounded, centered, and balanced; four, you're continuing to process this information in your dreams tonight, so by tomorrow morning you will be fully integrated into this new energy and awareness; three, you're driving safely and being completely safe in all your activities; two, grounded, centered, and balanced; and one, you're back!

## JOURNAL PROMPT: GODDESS MATERNAL GENEALOGICAL REGRESSION

Take as long as you need to meditate, sit quietly, and reflect on the healing you did with your mother and ancestors today. When you're ready, take a moment and record your thoughts in your journal.

1. How did it feel to meet with your mother's higher self?

2. Describe what happened when you met with both sides of her family.

3. What goddesses did you encounter, if any, and what did you learn?

Make notes about any generational healing that took place and how the goddesses or deities you encountered influenced your entire family line. Remember, too, that you can come back later and do this journey again for greater insight. Meanwhile, I hope you felt the beneficial energy of connecting with your ancestors at such a deep level and gained insights into your path.

## Goddess Paternal Genealogical Regression

Now that you've discovered the information about your mother's side of the family, it's time to do another Genealogical Regression to get in touch with your father's side. Please note, to avoid repetition, this script will be shorter. Basically, you will walk through your same relaxation, go into your sacred space again just like you've done before, only this time, you will be meeting with your dad, exploring his lineage on both his mother's and father's sides of the family.

### EXERCISE: GODDESS PATERNAL GENEALOGICAL REGRESSION

Return to your sacred space. Sit with your feet flat on the floor and your hands in your lap. Close your eyes and breathe, breathing in love and peace and joy and happiness, and exhaling any tensions and concerns. Continue breathing in love and light through your nose, exhaling tension. Call in any guides, ascended masters, or beings of light who wish to join you today. Thank them for being here and know your highest good will be done. Continue to imagine healing energy moving through your body with each breath you take. Feel the energies of peace, healing, and relaxation fill your body, mind, and spirit. Very good.

Surround yourself with protective golden light. See your familiar doorway in front of you and walk through that door now. Your guide is already there waiting for you. Take a moment now and speak with your loving guide about your intentions for today. Let them know you would like to do an ancestral healing for your father and his side of the family. As you discuss this, notice there's a door on the other side of your sacred space, and that door is opening now, and here comes your father. Notice this is his higher self, the highest aspect of his soul. Notice he is happy to see you.

Imagine you can let your dad know that you would like to explore times when your ancestors worshiped goddesses or other deities. Tell him you would like to explore that connection for his mother's side of the family. As you mention this, imagine you and your dad take your guide by the hand and begin to float toward that door your dad came through. In just a moment, when I count to three, you and your dad and guide will float through that door over that light that looks like a ray of sunshine and represents time and your ancestral history. On the count of three, you will open that door. Ready? One, two, and three; opening that door now. You're there, floating over that sunbeam. Know that you are floating over the current time and that the farther out you float, the earlier the time will be. Allow your guide to take you and your dad to a very early time when your ancestors worshiped deities. Ready? Floating out now, over the light, farther and farther and farther, out, out, out to a very early time that will be most for your highest good. On the count of three, you will arrive. Ready? One, two, and three; you're there. Be there now. Imagine you and your dad and guide can float down, down, down, over those events where you can float above them, and notice what's happening.

What year is this? Notice the first thought that floats into your mind. Where are you in the world? What's happening? Which ancestor or ancestors do you see? What deities are they worshiping or what are their spiritual practices? Take your time to notice all you can.

PAUSE HERE.

Very good. Now imagine the three of you can lift, up, up, up, higher and higher, and float over these early events. Your guide is sending love and light to all your ancestors at this very early time. Notice the energy there is getting lighter and lighter and lighter, brighter and brighter and brighter. Very nice.

Imagine now you can ask your guide some important questions. How has this experience of your ancestors affected your current lifetime? What did your ancestors learn in these early times? How can you best honor their legacy? What can you take away from this experience to use in your current lifetime? What will you let go of or leave behind?

Notice there's an energetic cord of light that is now connecting you and your dad with these early times. Your guide is bringing out a pair of golden scissors. In a moment, when I count to three, your guide will cut that cord. Ready? One, two, and three, cut! A beautiful healing light is pouring down, and that light is healing your ancestors, and all events are getting lighter and lighter, brighter and brighter. That light is now moving through your dad, and he is becoming lighter, and you are now also feeling lighter than ever before. Allow that light to lift you all higher and higher, up, up, up until you are once again floating over the sunbeam below you. Go ahead now and take your guide by the hand as the three of you float all the way back toward the present day and back into your sacred space. As you float, imagine you can send love and healing light to all your ancestors between this very early time and right now. Ready? One, floating toward today; two, sending that healing and light to your ancestors; and three, you're back, floating through the door. You arrive inside your sacred space. Take a moment to speak with your dad and your guide about anything important.

PAUSE HERE.

Next, the three of you will float through that door and go into the past to your dad's father's side of the family to visit any experiences where they worshiped the Goddess or other deities. Float back toward the door now and open the door. Notice that sunbeam below you that now represents time on your dad's father's side of the family. Hold your guide's hand as you and your dad and guide float all the way back in time, over that sunbeam to the earliest time or to a significant time when your family members worked with the Goddess. On the count of three, you will arrive at this early family event. Ready? One, two, and three, and be there now. Float down, down, down and hover over these events. What's happening? Where are you? What year is this? What ancestors do you notice? How are these early relatives worshiping the Goddess or other spiritual energies? Take your time to notice all you can.

PAUSE HERE.

Now imagine the three of you can lift up, up, up, and float over those early events. How are these early spiritual practices affecting your family overall? How has your dad been affected? What lessons did your family learn in these early times? How has this energy influenced you? How can you invest this information in your future? Take your time to receive any and all information.

PAUSE HERE.

As you continue to learn more, allow a healing and loving light to emerge and pour over all the people involved in these early events. Notice your guide with the golden scissors, and in a moment your guide will cut the cords between you and all involved. Ready? One, two, and three, cut! A beautiful healing light is pouring down from above and healing everyone there, and all those very early events are becoming lighter and lighter, brighter and brighter. You notice your dad becoming lighter, and you are now also becoming lighter and feeling better than ever before. As this light continues to transform all people, you and your dad and guide lift up, up, up, higher and higher, floating above these early events. You all begin now to float back toward today, but only as quickly as you can extend this loving light to everyone in your entire family between that early time and now. Ready? Three, floating toward today; two, moving quickly and sending peace and love and light to all; and one, you're back! Float back into your sacred space and take a moment to speak to your dad and your guide about any special or important information you learned today.

PAUSE HERE.

Very good. Thank your dad for joining you today. Imagine Dad says goodbye and walks or floats back through the door. Thank your guide for assisting you. When you're ready, walk or float back out to where you began. Be there now. In a moment, when I count back from five, you will return to full waking consciousness, feeling awake, refreshed, and better than you felt before. Ready? Five, you're grounded, centered, and balanced; four, you're continuing to process this information in your dreams tonight, so by tomorrow morning, you will be fully integrated into this new energy and awareness; three, you're driving safely and being completely safe in all your activities; two, grounded, centered, and balanced; and one, you're back!

## Journal Prompt: Goddess Paternal Genealogical Regression

Reflect for as long as you need on your journey and the ancestors you encountered. Take a moment and record your thoughts in your journal about anything you experienced. Consider the following:

1. Describe your meeting with your father and his family.

2. What goddesses did you encounter, if any?

3. How did that early time in your ancestral history affect the family?

Take any other notes or write down any other ideas or thoughts and consider keeping your journal nearby in case you have any other ideas come to you in your dreams over the next few days. I hope you received some valuable information about your early ancestral history that will help you in the future.

## Meeting Your Ancestor

Now you will take another helpful journey to meet with a specific ancestor who can share information. Rather than sending light to events, you will have a chance to have a one-on-one conversation with an ancestor. As with any of these journeys, your intention is important. Would you like to ask for highest good and see who shows up? Do you prefer to consider a specific ancestor whom you perhaps researched on Ancestry.com or someone your family told you about whom you would like to learn more about? It's all up to you, and again, you could do more than one journey to experience both.

### EXERCISE: MEETING YOUR ANCESTOR

Sit quietly and reflect on the intention you want to set for this journey. Prepare your sacred space accordingly and retreat there at a time when you won't be disturbed. Sit with your feet flat on the floor and your hands in your lap, close your eyes, and breathe. Allow the familiar beam of pure white light to move down through the top of your head. Feel this loving light moving down, down, down, into your forehead, moving into your eyes, your nose, and down into your mouth and jaw. Allow this loving light to move into each vertebra in your neck and travel down into your shoulders, moving into your arms, your elbows, your wrists, hands and fingers, moving down, down, down into your spine, moving through your shoulder blades, into your heart center, moving into your stomach, your lungs, and going all the way down to the base of your spine. Continue to breathe. Breathing in love and peace and joy, and exhaling any tensions. Feel that light moving down through the base of your spine and into your legs, into your thighs, knees, calves, ankles, heels, and toes and down into the soles of your feet.

Feel the light moving through the top of your head, traveling down your spine, and moving out the soles of your feet. The light becomes so strong, it begins to pour out of your heart center, creating a beautiful golden ball of healing light that surrounds your body by about three feet in all directions. Feel yourself floating inside this golden healing light, safe and secure, totally carefree, and know that within this golden ball of light, only that which is of your highest good can come through.

Now imagine there's a doorway in front of you. See this door, feel it, or just have an inner knowing that the door is there. In a moment, when I count to three, you will open the door and step inside your beautiful space where you feel safe and totally secure. Ready? One, two, and three; open the door now. Walk or float into this sacred space. Be there now, inside this beautiful place. Take a moment to feel the loving and supportive energy of this space where you are safe, secure, and totally carefree.

Right now, your beautiful angel or spirit guide floats down from above to join you. Feel the amazing unconditional love and high regard your guide has for you.

Take a moment now and speak with your loving guide about your intentions for today. Let them know you would like to meet with an ancestor who would be most for your highest good to meet at this time, an ancestor who will share a powerful message with you today.

As you make this request, you notice a door is opening and someone is walking through that door now. This is your ancestor. See them, feel their presence, or just have an inner knowing they're there. Say hello. Who is this and what do they have to share with you today? Can they share any information about the family connection to any goddesses or deities? Take your time to receive messages or ask questions.

PAUSE HERE.

When you're ready, thank your ancestor for being here today. Imagine they turn around and walk back through the door.

Go ahead now and allow your guide to give you any further clarification. PAUSE HERE.

When you're ready, thank your guide for joining you today. Say goodbye and watch them float away. Walk or float back to the door you first entered and go back out to where you began your journey. Be there now, back where you started. In a moment, when I count back from five, you will return to full waking consciousness, feeling awake, refreshed, and better than you felt before. Ready? Five, you're grounded, centered, and balanced; four, you're continuing to process this information in your dreams tonight, so by tomorrow morning, you will be fully integrated into this new energy and awareness; three, you're driving safely and being completely safe in all your activities; two, grounded, centered, and balanced; and one, you're back!

## Journal Prompt: Meeting Your Ancestor

Take a moment and record your thoughts in your journal.

1. What ancestor did you meet today? Take note of any details about them, including their name or where they come from.

2. Did they give you information about any goddesses or deities your family worked with or worshiped in the past?

3. How did their practices influence you and other generations of your family?

Make any additional notes or record anything else they said that you will want to recall down the road.

Remember, every time you do a regression, you may get a new answer and have totally different experiences. Everything that emerges does so in the time when it is most useful, so when you're ready or feel guided, do the regression again and find out more about your past lives or ancestral past.

## Summing Up

Ancestral healing is a great practice to do for helping ourselves personally as well as our family and planet as a whole. As we continue to expand our understanding of the interconnectivity we share with all people around the world and with those who are linked to us directly through our past-life connections and DNA, our new insights will undoubtedly benefit humanity for generations to come. The more consciously you honor your own soul's journey and acknowledge the sacrifices of your forebears and discover more about your unique journey in your own past-life experiences, the more easily you can invest that wisdom into creating a brighter future for all people.

# Conclusion

Goddess *discovered*. *Discovered* in the past tense suggests that something is complete, accomplished, absolute. The material contained within this book brought one great discovery to me—how little I know. Opening doors to new worlds and cultures is a mind-expanding and lifelong endeavor. This journey makes me want to know, learn, and discover even more about our world and the beautiful souls who inhabit our amazing planet.

The need for caution mentioned throughout regarding respect and regard shown to different belief systems and peoples throughout the world brings me a deep sense of gratitude to be alive at such an incredible moment in history when our collective determination to give equality and voice to marginalized people can become a reality.

I am also reminded of a story I hadn't considered in years about my profession in the field of past-life regression that speaks to this point. In 2006, I traveled to India to speak at an international gathering of past-life regression practitioners. Within the walls of our conference, I met people from around the world who engaged in the techniques of guiding people into their past lives. Meeting everyone and sharing those deep discussions remains one of the most incredible experiences of my life. Strangely, however, when I ventured around India after the conference to do some traveling, people wanted to know what brought me there. I told them about my work, and every single person I met had never heard of such a thing as a past-life regression. Some seemed to find the idea fascinating, while others dismissed the possibility of being able to clear one's karma by simply going on a guided imagery journey. Throughout my career I have been quite clear that

I am not espousing any belief system in my work, nor am I attempting to perform any aspects of Hinduism or any other belief system or religion that follows the doctrine of reincarnation. I've repeatedly stressed that fact to clients, students and in media interviews for over twenty years now. Still, I am always asked about whether somebody needs to believe in past lives to benefit from a regression. My answer is and always will be *no*. Regression is a process, not a religion. It is a healing method. I happen to believe in reincarnation, of course, yet the technique of visually encountering scenes to help you make sense of your current situation is a healing method and not a religion or doctrine.

Likewise, now that my Genealogical Regression process is out there in the public purview like never before, I must state again that the healing modality of consciously loving our forebears and ancestors and sending them love and light has absolutely nothing to do with the belief and veneration of ancestors that occurs either in living religions or in practices from ancient times. Again, the method is a healing modality.

The collective sense of divinity inherent within consciousness has been carried over from one generation to the next by our earliest ancestors. Worshiping goddesses, deities, or gods is *part of our DNA*. Consider our human instincts to breathe, to survive, to find and forage food, to take care of our young…all primal instincts brought forth from the earliest times in human history. When we discover the Goddess, we acknowledge the humanity and collective spirituality of all who have gone before us. The renaissance of thinking about our divinity may actually be part of our ancestral heritage that is awakening within us at this particular moment in history. By remembering how our collective ancestors worshiped the deity long ago, we forge a new path of understanding to carry us into a brighter future.

My hope for you, dear reader, is that *The Goddess Discovered* helped you gain your own insights about your soul, your ancestors, and the cultures and peoples around the world. Everyone is different, and with so much material covered here, I know each person will walk away with what they need and enjoy. I pray the journey helped you on your path. It certainly changed my life for the better. With that, I send you love and light and I wish you the full support of the Goddess as you continue your journey through life.

# Bibliography

Abrams, Abiola. *African Goddess Initiation: Sacred Rituals for Self-Love, Prosperity and Joy.* Carlsbad, CA: Hay House Publishing, 2021.

Adkins, Lesley, and Roy A. Adkins. *Handbook to Life in Ancient Rome.* Oxford: Oxford University Press, 1998.

Aguilar-Moreno, Manuel. *Handbook to Life in the Aztec World.* New York: Oxford University Press, 2006.

Aldana, Carlos Lopez. *Mexico's Famous Archaeological Relics: The Popocatepetl and Iztaccihuatl Volcanoes Legend.* Mexico City: National Museum, 1949.

Allen, James P. *The Egyptian Coffin Texts: Middle Kingdom Copies of Pyramid Texts.* Vol. 8 of Oriental Institute Publications, vol. 132. Chicago: The Oriental Institute of Chicago, 2006.

Allen, Stephen, and Wayne Reynolds. *Celtic Warrior 300 BC–AD 100.* Oxford: Osprey Publishing, 2001.

Amnesty.org. "Why Saying 'Aborigine' Isn't OK: 8 Facts About Indigenous People in Australia." Amnesty International, August 9, 2015. https://www.amnesty.org/en/latest/campaigns/2015/08/why-saying-aborigine-isnt-ok-8-facts-about-indigenous-people-in-australia/.

Andean Lodges. "Andean Deities: What Was the Importance of the Sun, the Earth and the Moon to the Inca Culture?" Andean Lodges, November 27, 2019. https://andeanlodges.com/en/andean-deities-what-was-the-importance-of-the-sun-the-earth-and-the-moon-to-the-inca-culture/.

Anderson, Johannes C. *Myths and Legends of the Polynesians*. New York: Dover Publications, 1995.

Angelsname. "Meaning of Tombe." Angelsname. https://angelsname.com /meaning/ainu-mythology/girl/tombe.

Anthony, Andrew. "So Is It Nature Not Nurture After All?" *Guardian*, September 29, 2018. https://www.theguardian.com/science/2018/sep/29 /so-is-it-nature-not-nurture-after-all-genetics-robert-plomin-polygenic -testing.

Archaeology World Team. "Massive 1,100-Year-Old Maya Site Discovered in Georgia's Mountains?" Archaeology World, August 10, 2020. https:// archaeology-world.com/massive-1100-year-old-maya-site-discovered-in -georgias-mountains/.

Art Institute of Chicago. "Denarius (Coin) Depicting Goddess Venus." Art Institue Chicago. https://www.artic.edu/artworks/142606/denarius -coin-depicting-the-goddess-venus.

Asante, Molefi Kete, and Ama Mazama. *Encyclopedia of African Religion*. Thousand Oaks, CA: Sage Publications, 2009.

Ash, Anna, John Giacon, and Amanda Lissarrague. *Gamilaraay, Yuwaalaraay & Yuwaalayaay Dictionary*. Alice Springs, AUS: IAD Press, 2003.

Asher-Greve, Julia M., and Joan Goodnick Westenholz. *Goddesses in Context: On Divine Powers, Roles, Relationships and Gender in Mesopotamian Textual and Visual Sources*. Zurich, Switzerland: University of Zurich, 2013.

Ashkenazy, Michael. *Handbook of Japanese Mythology*. Santa Barbara, CA: ABC-Clio, 2003.

Aston, W. G., and Terence Barrow. *Nihongi: Chronicles of Japan from the Earliest Times to AD 697*. North Clarendon, VT: Tuttle Publishing, 1972.

Athenaeus. *The Deipnosophists or Banquet of the Learned of Athenaeus*. London: Henry G. Bohn, 1854.

Atkinson, Brett. *Malta & Gozo*. 8th ed. Fort Mill, SC: Lonely Planet Global Limited, 2021.

Auset, Brandi. *The Goddess Guide: Exploring the Attributes and Correspondences of the Divine Feminine*. Woodbury, MN: Llewellyn Worldwide, 2009.

Averbeck, Richard E. "Myth, Ritual, and Order in 'Enki and the World Order.'" *Journal of the American Oriental Society* 123, no. 4 (October–December 2003): 757–71.

Bancroft, Hubert Howe. *The Native Races of the Pacific States of North America*. Vol. 3 of *Myths and Languages*. New York: D. Appleton and Company, 1875.

Bane, Theresa. *Encyclopedia of Spirits and Ghosts in World Mythology*. Jefferson, NC: McFarland & Company, 2016.

Barcellos, Gustavo. *Friendship and Its Paradoxes: Essays from the VI Latin American Congress of Jungian Psychology*. Newcastle Upon Tyne, UK: Cambridge Scholars Publishing, 2017.

Bard, Kathryn. *An Introduction to the Archaeology of Ancient Egypt*. West Sussex, UK: John Wiley & Sons, 2015.

Barnes, Rev. William B. D. "On the Welsh Triads: With a Confirmation of an Ancient One from Other Sources." *Fraser's Magazine for Town and Country* LXXIV (October 1866): 536.

Barnett, Mary. *Gods and Myths of Ancient Egypt: The Archaeology and Mythology of Ancient Peoples*. Kent, UK: Grange Books, 1999.

Batchelor, John. *An Ainu-English-Japanese Dictionary*. London: Methodist Publishing House, 1905.

Batchelor, John. *The Ainu of Japan*. London: The Religious Tract Society, 1892.

Bechstein, Ludwig. *Beutsches Sagenbuch*. Leipzig, Germany: G. Wigand, 1853.

Beckwith, Martha. *Hawaiian Mythology*. New Haven, CT: Yale University Press, 1940.

Behind the Name. "Hina." Behind the Name. https://www.behindthename.com/name/hina.

Behind the Name. "Hine." Behind the Name. https://www.behindthename.com/name/hine.

Bellows, Henry Adams. *The Poetic Edda: Translated from the Icelandic with an Introduction and Notes*. New York: Princeton University Press, 1936.

Bernal, Ignacio. *The Olmec World*. Translated by Doris Heyden and Fernando Horcasitas. Berkeley, CA: University of California Press, 1969.

Berndt, Ronald Murray. *Australian Aboriginal Religion*. Leiden, The Netherlands: E. J. Brill, 1974.

Besom, Thomas. *Of Summits and Sacrifice: An Ethnohistoric Study of Inka Religious Practices*. Austin, TX: University of Texas Press, 2009.

Best, Elsdon. *Memoirs of the Polynesian Society: The Māori*. Wellington, NZ: The Polynesian Society, 1941.

Biebuyck, Daniel, and Kahombo C. Mateene. *The Mwindo Epic: From the Banyanga (Congo Republic)*. Berkeley, CA: University of California Press, 1969.

Biggs, Patricia. "Hopi." Arizona State University. https://grcahistory.org/history/native-cultures/hopi/.

Bingham, Ann, and Jeremy Roberts. *South and Meso-American Mythology A to Z*. 2nd ed. New York: Chelsea House, 2010.

Bispham, Edward, and Daniele Miano. *Gods and Goddesses of Ancient Italy*. London: Routledge, 2019.

Blacket, William Stephens. *Researches Into the Lost Histories of America*. London: Trubner & Co., 1883.

Blakemore, Erin. "Aboriginal Australians: Aboriginal Australians Could Be the Oldest Population of Humans Living Outside Africa, Where One Theory Says They Migrated fromin Boats 70,000 Years Ago." *National Geographic*, January 31, 2019. https://www.nationalgeographic.com/culture/article/aboriginal-australians.

Blamires, Steve. *Magic of the Celtic Otherworld: Irish History, Lore and Rituals*. Woodbury, MN: Llewellyn Worldwide, 2005.

Bloomfield, Maurice. *The Sacred Books of the East: Hymns of the Arharva-Veda Together with Extracts from the Ritual Books and the Commentaries*. London: Henry Frowde, 1897.

Blumberg, Antonia. "11 Powerful Goddesses from Around the World to Invoke in Your Life: Get Familiar with These Impressive Deities." *Huffington Post*, February 8, 2016. https://www.huffpost.com/entry/goddesses-from-around-the-world_n_56b8f607e4b08069c7a852d1.

Bolin, Inge. *Rituals of Respect: The Secret of Survival in the High Peruvian Andes*. Austin, TX: University of Texas Press, 2002.

Borza, Eugene N. *In the Shadow of Olympus: The Emergence of Macedon*. Princeton, NJ: Princeton University Press, 1990.

Breasted, James Henry. *A History of Egypt: From the Earliest Times to the Persian Conquest*. Lancaster, PA: Charles Scribner's Sons, 1905.

Brice, Lee L. *Warfare in the Roman Republic: From the Etruscan Wars to the Battle of Actium*. Santa Barbara, CA: ABC-CLIO, 2014.

Brinton, Daniel G. *Essays of an Americanist: I. Ethnologic and Archaeologic; II. Mythology and Folk Lore; III. Graphic Systems and Literature; IV. Linguistic*. Philadelphia, PA: Porter & Coates, 1890.

Brodeur, Arthur Gilchrist, trans. *The Prose Edda by Snorri Sturluson*. New York: The American Scandinavian Foundation, 1916.

Bromwich, Rachel, and Daniel Simon Evans. *Culhwch and Olwen: An Edition and Study of the Oldest Arthurian Tale*. Cardiff, UK: University of Wales Press, 1992.

Brown, Joseph Epes. *The Sacred Pipe: Black Elk's Account of the Seven Rites of the Oglala Sioux*. Norman, OK: University of Oklahoma Press, 1989.

Bruder, Edith, and Tudor Parfitt. *African Zion: Studies in Black Judaism*. Newcastle Upon Tyne, UK: Cambridge Scholars Publishing, 2012.

Buchler, Ira R., and Kenneth Maddock. *The Rainbow Serpent: A Chromatic Piece*. The Hague, Netherlands: Mouton Publishers, 1978.

Budge, E. A. Wallis. *The Egyptian Book of the Dead: The Papyrus of Ani in the British Museum*. New York: Dover Publications, 1967.

Budge, E. A. Wallis. *The Gods of the Egyptians: Studies in Egyptian Mythology*. Vol. 1. New York: Dover Publications, 1969.

Budge, E. A. Wallis. *The Gods of the Egyptians: Studies in Egyptian Mythology*. Vol. 2. New York: Dover Publications, 1969.

Budson, Andrew E. "Why Is Music Good for the Brain?" *Harvard Health Blog*, October 7, 2020. https://www.health.harvard.edu/blog/why-is-music-good-for-the-brain-2020100721062.

Burkhart, Louise M. *Before Guadalupe: The Virgin Mary in Early Colonial Nahuatl Literature*. Albany, NY: Institute for Mesoamerican Studies, 2001.

Butler, Samuel, trans. *The Iliad of Homer*. N.p.: Lions Gate Classics, 2013.

Byrne, Aisling. *Otherworlds: Fantasy and History in Medieval Literature*. Oxford Scholarship Online, January 2016. https://oxford.university pressscholarship.com/view/10.1093/acprof:oso/9780198746003 .001.0001/acprof-9780198746003-chapter-1.

Cahill, Suzanne E. *Transcendence & Divine Passion: The Queen Mother of the West in Medieval China*. Stanford, CA: Stanford University Press, 1993.

Cali, Joseph, and John Dougill. *Shinto Shrines: A Guide to the Sacred Sites of Japan's Ancient Religion*. Honolulu: University of Hawai'i Press, 2012.

Campbell, Joseph. *The Hero with a Thousand Faces*. 3rd ed. Novato, CA: New World Library, 2008.

Campbell, Trenton. *Gods and Goddesses of Ancient China*. New York: Britannica Educational Publishing, 2015.

Carrasco, David, and Scott Sessions. *Cave, City, and Eagle's Nest: An Interpretive Journey Through the Mapa de Cuauhtinchan No. 2*. Albuquerque, NM: University of New Mexico Press, 2007.

Carroll, Barbara. *Gods, Goddesses, and Saints: A Solitary Practice of Chanting and Meditation*. N.p.: Outskirt Press, 2016.

Center for Disease Control. "What Is Epigenetics?" CDC, last reviewed August 15, 2022. https://www.cdc.gov/genomics/disease/epigenetics.htm.

Chamberlain, Basil Hall. *A Translation of the "Ko-ji-ki" or "Records of Ancient Matters."* N.p.: Asiatic Society of Japan, 1919.

Charlton, David. *E. T. A. Hoffman's Musical Writings: Kreisleriana, the Poet and the Composer, Music Criticism*. Cambridge: Cambridge University Press, 1989.

Church, Alfred John, and William Jackson Brodribb. *The Works of Tacitus*. London: Macmillan, 1864–1877.

Clarke, Adam. *A Concise View of the Succession of Sacred Literature, in a Chronological Arrangement of Their Authors and Their Works, from the Invention of Alphabetical Characters to the Year of Our Lord 1445*. London: T. S. Clarke Publishers, 1830.

Cleary, Thomas. *The Flower Ornament Scripture: A Translation of the Avatamsaka Sutra*. Boston: Shambhala Publications, 1984.

Cock-Starkey, Claire. *Lore of the Wild: Folklore & Wisdom from Nature*. Beverly, MA: Quarto Group Wide Eyed Editions, 2021.

Cole Babbitt, Frank. *The Greek Questions of Plutarch*. Cambridge, MA: Harvard University Press, 1936.

Cape Breton University. "The Mi'kmaq." Cape Breton University. https://www.cbu.ca/indigenous-affairs/mikmaq-resource-centre/the-mikmaq/.

Conger, Cristin. "Were Ancient Egyptians the First Feminists? Women's Rights in Ancient Egypt." How Stuff Works. https://history.howstuffworks.com/history-vs-myth/first-feminist1.htm.

Conze, Edward. *Perfect Wisdom: The Short Prajnaparamita Texts*. Devon, UK: Buddhist Publishing Group, 1973.

Cook, P. D. MacKenzie. *Epona: Hidden Goddess of the Celts*. London: BM Avalonia, 2016.

Cotterell, Arthur. *A Dictionary of World Mythology*. Oxford: Oxford University Press, 1986.

Coulter, Charles Russell, and Patricia Turner. *Encyclopedia of Ancient Deities*. Chicago: Fitzroy Dearborn Publishers, 2000.

Courlander, Harold. *The Fourth World of the Hopis*. New York: Crown Publishers, 1971.

Courlander, Harold. *The Fourth World of the Hopis: The Epic Story of the Hopi Indians as Preserved in Their Legends and Traditions*. Albuquerque, NM: University of New Mexico Press, 1987.

Courlander, Harold, and Ousmane Sako. *The Heart of the Ngoni: Heroes of the African Kingdom of Segu*. New York: Crown Publishing, 1982.

Craig, Robert D. *Dictionary of Polynesian Mythology*. Westport, CT: Greenwood Press, 1989.

Crawford, Gary. "Origins of the Ainu." Nova Online, November 2000. https://www.pbs.org/wgbh/nova/hokkaido/ainu.html.

Crüsemann, Nicola, Margarete van Ess, Markus Hilgert, Beate Salje, and Timothy Potts. *Uruk: First City of the Ancient World*. Los Angeles: J. Paul Getty Museum, 2013.

Cunningham, Scott. *Hawaiian Religion & Magic*. Woodbury, MN: Llewellyn Publications, 1994.

Daly, Kathleen N., and Marian Rengel. *Greek & Roman Mythology A to Z Revised Edition*. New York: Facts on File, 2004.

Daniel, Gabriel. *The Discourses of Cleander and Eudoxus Upon the Provincial Letters*. N.p.: Cullen, 1701.

Das, Rasamandala. *The Complete Illustrated Guide to Hinduism: A Comprehensive Guide to Hindu History and Philosophy, Its Traditions and Practices, Rituals and Beliefs, with More Than 470 Magnificent Photographs*. Leicestershire, UK: Anness Publishing, 2012.

Dasa, Pandit. "The 33 Million Gods of Hinduism: Why Hindus Worship So Many Gods and Goddesses Is a Real Mystery for Most People. In the West the Concept of Polytheism Is Nothing More Than Fantasy or Mythology Worthy of Comic Book Material." *Huffington Post*, August 6, 2012. https://www.huffpost.com/entry/the-33-million-demigods -o_b_1737207.

Dashorst, Patricia, et al. "Intergenerational Consequences of the Holocaust on Offspring Mental Health: A Systematic Review of Associated Factors and Mechanisms." *European Journal of Psychotraumatology* 10, no. 1 (August 30, 2019): 1654065. doi:10.1080/20008198.2019.1654065.

Dayman, Lucy. "15 Best Shinto Shrines You Have to Visit." Japan Objects, November 20, 2020. https://japanobjects.com/features/shinto-shrines.

Delaere, Christopher, and José M. Capriles. "The Context and Meaning of an Intact Inca Underwater Offering from Lake Titicaca." *Antiquity* 94, no. 376 (2020): 1030–41. doi:10.15184/aqy.2020.121.

Department of Ancient Near Eastern Art. "The Akkadian Period (ca. 2350–2150 B.C.)." In *Heilbrunn Timeline of Art History*. New York: The Metropolitan Museum of Art, 2000. http://www.metmuseum.org/toah /hd/akka/hd_akka.htm.

Department of Asian Art. "Jōmon Culture (ca. 10,500–ca. 300 B.C.)." New York: The Metropolitan Museum of Art, 2002. https://www.met museum.org/toah/hd/jomo/hd_jomo.htm.

Department of the Arts of Africa, Oceania, and the Americas. "Tahiti." In *Heilbrunn Timeline of Art History*. New York: The Metropolitan Museum of Art, 2000. http://www.metmuseum.org/toah/hd/tahi/hd_tahi.htm.

Descoeudres, Jean-Paul, Derek Harrison, and Penelope Mary Allison. *Pompeii Revisited: The Life and Death of a Roman Town*. Sydney: Meditarch, 1994.

Dimock, Edward C. "The Goddess of Snakes in Medieval Bengali Literature." *History of Religions* 1, no. 2 (1962): 307–21. http://www.jstor.org/stable /1062059.

Dods, Marcus. *The Works of Aurelius Augustine, Bishop of Hippo*. Edinburgh, Scotland: T&T Clark, 1871.

Doniger, W. "Shiva." *Encyclopedia Britannica*, May 6, 2021. https://www .britannica.com/topic/Shiva.

Dooling, D. M. *The Sons of the Wind: The Sacred Stories of the Lakota from the James R. Walker Collection*. Norman, OK: University of Oklahoma Press, 1984.

Dorling Kindersley. *Cultural Treasures of the World: From the Relics of Ancient Empires to Modern-Day Icons*. London: Penguin Random House, 2022.

Dowman, Keith. *Masters of Mahamudra: Songs and Histories of the Eighty-Four Buddhist Siddhas*. Albany, NY: State University of New York Press, 1985.

Dudhane, Rahul. "How Many Gods Are There in Hinduism?" Hinduism Facts, November 18, 2021. https://www.hinduismfacts.org/how-many -gods-are-there-in-hinduism/.

Dunn, Joseph. *The Ancient Irish Epic Tale Táin Bó Cúailnge "The Cualnge Cattle-Raid."* London: David Nutt, 1914.

Dutt, Manmatha Nath. *A Prose English Translation of Harivamsha*. Project Gutenberg, April 25, 2020.

Dutton, Bertha P. *American Indians of the Southwest*. Albuquerque, NM: University of New Mexico Press, 1983.

Editors of Hinduism Today. *What Is Hinduism? Modern Adventures into a Profound Global Faith*. India: Himalayan Academy, 2007.

Eng, Khoo Boo. *Understanding Chinese Culture in Relation to Tao*. Singapore: Partridge Publishing, 2019.

Espak, Peeter. *The God Enki in Sumerian Royal Ideology and Mythology*. Tartu, Estonia: Tartu University Press, 2014.

Evelyn-White, Hugh G. *Hesiod: The Homeric Hymns and Homerica*. New York: The MacMillan Co., 1914.

Evelyn-White, Hugh G. *The Theogony of Hesiod*. Cambridge, MA: Harvard University Press, 1914.

Falkner, David E. *The Mythology of the Night Sky: Greek, Roman, and Other Celestial Lore*. 2nd ed. Cham, Switzerland: The Patrick Moore Practical Astronomy Series, 2020.

Fears, J. Rufus. "The Cult of Virtues and Roman Imperial Ideology." In *Aufstieg und Niedergang der römischen Welt*, 827–948. Edited by Wolfgang Haase and Hildegard Temporini. Berlin: Walter de Gruyter, 1994.

Fee, Christopher R., and Jeffrey B. Webb. *American Myths, Legends and Tall Tales: An Encyclopedia of American Folklore*. Vol. 1, *A–F*. Santa Barbara, CA: ABC-CLIO, 2016.

Flammini, Diego. "10 Interesting Facts About Potatoes." Farms. https://www.farms.com/ag-industry-news/10-interesting-facts-about-potatoes/10.

Florida State Parks. "Crystal River Archaeological Park." Florida State Parks. https://www.floridastateparks.org/parks-and-trails/crystal-river-archaeological-state-park.

Ford, Clyde W. *The Hero with an African Face: Mythic Wisdom of Traditional Africa*. New York: Bantam Books, 1999.

Ford, Patrick K. *The Mabinogi and Other Medieval Welsh Tales*. Oakland, CA: University of California Press, 2019.

Fowler, W. Warde. *The Roman Festivals of the Period of the Republic: An Introduction to the Study of the Religion of the Romans*. New York: MacMillan and Co., 1899.

Franklin, Anna. *Magical Celebrations: Midsummer of the Summer Solstice.* Woodbury, MN: Llewellyn Publications, 2003.

Frazer, James George. *Apollodorus the Library in Two Volumes.* New York: GP Putnam's Sons, 1921.

Frazer, James George. *The Golden Bough: A Study in Magic and Religion.* 3rd ed. London: MacMillan and Co., 1911.

Freitag, Barbara. *Sheela-Na-Gigs: Unraveling an Enigma.* London: Routledge, 2004.

Gahlin, Lucia. *Gods & Myths of Ancient Egypt: An Illustrated Guide to the Mythology, Religion & Culture.* London: Anness Publishing, 2014.

Gaiman, Neil. *Norse Mythology.* London: W. W. Norton & Company, 2017.

Gates, William. *Friar Diego de Landa's Yucatan Before and After the Conquest.* Baltimore, MD: The Maya Society, 1937.

George, Enzo. *Newgrange Burial Chamber.* New York: Gareth Stevens Publishing, 2018.

Gombrich, Richard F. *How Buddhism Began: The Conditioned Genesis of the Early Teachings.* 2nd ed. London: The Athlone Press, 1996.

Gómez, R., et al. "Genographic Consortium: Y Chromosome Diversity in *Aztlan* Descendants and Its Implications for the History of Central Mexico." *iScience* 24, no. 5 (April 30, 2021): 102487. doi: 10.1016/j.isci.2021.102487.

Goodenough, Simon. *Egyptian Mythology.* New York: New Line Books, 2006.

Goulbourne, Harry. *Race and Ethnicity: Critical Concepts in Sociology.* Vol. 2, *Solidarities and Communities.* London: Routledge, 2001.

Graham, Mark W. "Toward a Late Roman Cosmology of Space and Frontiers." In *News and Frontier Consciousness in the Late Roman Empire,* 27–50. Ann Arbor, MI: University of Michigan Press, 2006. http://www.jstor.org/stable/j.ctv3znzhj.8.

Grajetzki, Wolfram. *Burial Customs in Ancient Egypt: Life in Death for Rich and Poor.* London: Gerald Duckworth & Co., 2003.

Granet, Marcel. *Chinese Civilization.* New York: Routledge, 1951.

Graves, Robert, and Felix Guirand. *New Larousse Encyclopedia of Mythology*. London: Hamlyn Publishing, 1968.

Gray, David. "Buddhism in Tibet." Oxford Bibliographies, September 13, 2010. https://www.oxfordbibliographies.com/view/document/obo-9780195393521/obo-9780195393521-0166.xml.

Gray, Louis Herbert, and George Foot Moore. *The Mythology of All Races in Thirteen Volumes*. Vol. 3, *Celtic*. Boston: Marshall Jones Company, 1918.

Green, C. M. C. *Roman Religion and the Cult of Diana at Aricia*. Cambridge: Cambridge University Press, 2007.

Green, Miranda. *Celtic Goddesses: Warriors, Virgins and Mothers*. New York: George Braziller, 1996.

Greenleaf, Richard E. "The Mexican Inquisition and the Indians: Sources for the Ethnohistorian." *The Americas* 34, no. 3 (January 1978): 315–44.

Gries, Helen. *The Ishtar Gate of Babylon: From Fragment to Monument*. Regensburg, Germany: Schnell & Steiner, 2022.

Griffis, William Elliot. *The Mikado's Empire in Two Volumes*. Vol. 1, *History of Japan from 660 B.C. to 1872 A.D.* New York: Harper & Brothers Publishers, 1903.

Griffith, Ralph T. H., trans. *Complete Rigveda Book 1*. Sacred Texts. https://www.sacred-texts.com/hin/rigveda/rv01013.htm.

Griffith, Ralph T. H., trans. *The Hymns of the Rig Veda*. N.p.: E. J. Lazarus and Co., 1889.

Griffith, Ralph T. H., trans. *The Hymns of the Rig Veda*. 2nd ed. N.p.: E. J. Lazarus and Co., 1897.

Grimal, Pierre. *The Penguin Dictionary of Classical Mythology*. New York: Penguin Books, 1992.

Grinnell, George Bird, and John Dunbar. *Pawnee Hero Stories and Folk Tales with Notes on the Origin, Customs and Character of the Pawnee People*. New York: Charles Shribner's Sons, 1893.

Gu, Sharron. *A Cultural History of the Chinese Language*. Jefferson, NC: McFarland & Company, 2012.

Guest, Lady Charlotte. *The Mabinogion from the Welsh of the Llyfr Coch O Hergest.* London: Bernard Quaritch, 1877.

Gwynn, Edward. *Poems from the Dindshenchas: Text, Translation and Vocabulary.* Vols. 7–9. Dublin: The Academy House, 1900.

Hall, David A. *The Buddhist Goddess Marishiten: A Study of the Evolution and Impact of Her Cult on the Japanese Warrior.* Boston: Brill Academic Publishers, 2013.

Hamilton, H. C., and W. Falconer. *Geography of Strabo: In Three Volumes.* Vol. 1. London: Henry G. Bohn, 1854.

Harish, R. "Hymn to a Forest Nymph in the Rig Veda." Speaking Tree, June 15, 2020. https://www.speakingtree.in/blog/hymn-to-a-forest-nymph -in-the-rig-veda.

Harris, Karen. "Hawaii's Goddess of Snow, Poli'ahu." History Daily. https:// historydaily.org/hawaiis-goddess-of-snow-poliahu.

Harrison, Jane. *The Little Books of Modern Knowledge: Myths of Greece and Rome.* New York: Doubleday, Doran & Company, 1928.

Harvard Art Museum. "Paper God: Daoist Goddess Who Cures Rashes and Measles." Harvard Art Museum's Collections Online, June 19, 2022. https://hvrd.art/o/206623.

Hathaway, Nancy. *The Friendly Guide to Mythology: A Mortal's Guide to the Fantastical Realm of Gods, Goddesses, Monsters, and Heroes.* New York: Penguin Books, 2001.

Hawley, John S., and Donna M. Wulff. *Devi: Goddesses of India.* Oakland, CA: University of California Press, 1996.

Haywood, John. *The Ancient World: Earliest Times to 1 BC.* Vol. 1. New York: Oxford University Press, 1999.

Heijmans, BT, et al. "Persistent Epigenetic Differences Associated with Prenatal Exposure to Famine in Humans." *Proc Natl Acad Sci USA* 105, no. 44 (November 4, 2008):17046–9. doi: 10.1073/pnas.0806560105.

Henry, Teuira, and J. M. Orsmond. *Ancient Tahiti.* Honolulu: Bernice P. Bishop Museum Bulletin, 1928.

Herbert, Jean. *Shinto: At the Fountainhead of Japan.* London: Routledge, 1967.

Herzfeld, Michael, and Margot D. Lenhart. *Semiotics 1980*. Bloomington, IN: Indiana University Semiotic Society of America, 1980.

Hess, Richard, and David Toshio Tsumura. *I Studied Inscriptions from Before the Flood: Ancient Near Eastern, Literary, and Linguistic Approaches to Genesis 1–11*. Winona Lake, IN: Eisenbrauns, 1994.

History.com Editors. "Babylonia." A&E Television Networks, February 2, 2018. https://www.history.com/topics/ancient-middle-east/babylonia.

History.com Editors. "Teotihuacan." A&E Television Networks, August 21, 2018. https://www.history.com/topics/ancient-americas/teotihuacan.

Hodge, Frederick Webb. *Smithsonian Institution Bureau of American Ethnology: Annual Report of the Bureau of American Ethnology to the Secretary of the Smithsonian Institution*. Washington, DC: Smithsonian Institution Bureau of American Ethnology, 1918.

Holcombe, Charles. *A History of East Asia: From the Origins of Civilization to the Twenty-First Century*. Cambridge: Cambridge University Press, 2017.

Holland, Eileen. *Holland's Grimoire of Magical Correspondence: A Ritual Handbook*. Franklin Lakes, NJ: Career Press, 2006.

Holstein, Justus Frederick. *Rites and Ritual Acts as Prescribed by the Roman Religion According to the Commentary of Servius on Vergil's Aeneid*. New York: Voelcker Bros., 1916.

Hornum, Michael. *Nemesis: The Roman State, and the Games*. Leiden, The Netherlands: E. J. Brill, 1993.

Hsun, Lu. *A Brief History of Chinese Fiction*. Honolulu: University Press of the Pacific, 1982.

Hudson, S. A. M. *UXB Malta: The Most Bombed Place on Earth—Royal Engineers Bomb Disposal 1940–44*. Gloucestershire, UK: The History Press Unlimited, 2011.

Hughes, Kristoffer. *The Book of Celtic Magic: Transformative Teachings from the Cauldron of Awen*. Woodbury, MN: Llewellyn Worldwide, 2014.

Ikram, Salima. *Death and Burial in Ancient Egypt*. Cairo: The American University in Cairo Press, 2015.

Indian Health Service. "Navajo Nation History: The People." Indian Health Service. https://www.ihs.gov/navajo/navajonation/#:~:text=The%20 Navajo%20people%20call%20themselves,their%20story%20on%20 the%20creation.

Isaacs, Jennifer. *Australian Dreaming: 40,000 Years of Aboriginal History*. New South Wales, AUS: New Holland Publishers, 2005.

Jablow, Alta. "Gassire's Lute: A Reconstruction of Soninke Bardic Art." *Research in African Literatures* 15, no. 4 (1984): 519–29. http://www .jstor.org/stable/3819348.

Jackson, H. J. *Those Who Write for Immortality: Romantic Reputations and the Dream of Lasting Fame*. New Haven, CT: Yale University Press, 2015.

Jacob, Poppy. "A Brief History of the Mabinogion." Culture Trip, September 4, 2017. https://theculturetrip.com/europe/united-kingdom/wales /articles/a-brief-history-of-the-mabinogion/.

Jestice, Phyllis G. *Holy People of the World: A Cross-Cultural Encyclopedia*. Vol. 3. Santa Barbara, CA: ABC-CLIO, 2004.

John, Igor Bertram. *The Mabinogion*. London: David Nutt Publishing, 1901.

Johnson, Samuel. *The History of the Yorubas: From the Earliest Times to the Beginning of the British Protectorate*. London: George Routledge & Sons, 1921.

Jones, Constance A., and James D. Ryan. *Encyclopedia of Hinduism*. New York: Facts on File, 2007.

Jones, David M. *The Complete Illustrated History of the Inca Empire: A Comprehensive Encyclopedia of the Incas and Other Ancient Peoples of South America, with More Than 1000 Photographs*. Dayton, OH: Lorenz Books, 2012.

Jones, Lindsay. *Encyclopedia of Religion*. 2nd ed. Farmington Hills, MI: Thomas Gale, 2005.

Jordan, Michael. *Dictionary of Gods and Goddesses*. 2nd ed. New York: Facts on File, 2004.

Jowett, Benjamin. *Gorgias by Plato, 380 BC*. New York: Scribner's Sons, 1871.

Jowett, Benjamin. *The Republic by Plato, 360 BC*. New York: Scribner's Sons, 1871.

Jung, Carl G., Aniela Jaffe, Richard Winston, and Clara Winston. *Memories, Dreams, Reflections*. Revised ed. New York: Vintage Books, 1973.

Jung, Carl Gustav. *The Archetypes and the Collective Unconscious*. New York: Bollengen Foundation and Princeton University Press, 1969.

Kaehr, Shelley. *Egyptian Energy Healing: The Nine of Heliopolis*. Dallas: Out of This World Publishing, 2020.

Kaehr, Shelley. *Egyptian Energy Healing: Memphis Triad*. Dallas: Out of This World Publishing, 2020.

Karlsdóttir, Alice. *Norse Goddess Magic: Trancework, Mythology and Ritual*. Rochester, VT: Inner Traditions/Bear, 2015.

Keay, John. *India: A History*. New York: Harper Collins, 2000.

Kidd, I. G. *Posidonius*. Cambridge: Cambridge University Press, 1988.

King, L. W. *Enuma Elish: The Epic of Creation*. London: Luzac and Co., 1902.

King, Leonard W. *Enuma Elish: The Seven Tablets of Creation; The Babylonian and Assyrian Legends Concerning the Creation of the World and of Mankind*. New York: Cosimo Classics, 2010.

Kinsley, David R. *Hindu Goddesses: Visions of the Divine Feminine in the Hindu Religious Tradition*. Los Angeles: University of California Press, 1988.

Kinsley, David. *Hindu Goddesses: Vision of the Divine Feminine in the Hindu Religious Tradition*. Delhi: Motilal Banarsidass Publishers, 1998.

Kinsley, David R. *Tantric Visions of the Divine Feminine: The Ten Mahavidyas*. Berkeley, CA: University of California Press, 1997.

Kinsley, David R. *The Goddesses' Mirror: Visions of the Divine from East and West*. Albany, NY: State University of New York Press, 1989.

Klasanova, Lyudmila. "Chinnamunda." Teahouse, May 17, 2021. https://teahouse.buddhistdoor.net/chinnamunda/.

Klasanova, Lyudmila. "Simhamukha, the Lion-Faced Dakini." Teahouse, November 5, 2020. https://teahouse.buddhistdoor.net/simhamukha-the-lion-faced-dakini/.

Klieger, P. Christiaan. "Tara—An Example of Buddhist-Hindu Syncretism." *The Tibet Journal* 7, no. 3 (1982): 46–52. http://www.jstor.org/stable/43302175.

Knappert, Jan. *Pacific Mythology: An Encyclopedia of Myth and Legend*. New York: Harper Collins, 1992.

Kohn, Livia. *Daoism Handbook*. Leiden, The Netherlands: Brill, 2018.

Komjathy, Louis. *Daoism: A Guide for the Perplexed*. London: Bloomsbury Publishing, 2014.

Koshikidake, Shokai, and Martin Faulks. *Shugendo: The Way of the Mountain Monks*. Japan: Faulks Books, 2015.

Kramer, Samuel Noah, and John Maier. *Myths of Enki, the Crafty God*. Oxford: Oxford University Press, 1989.

Krober, Karl. *Artistry in Native American Myths*. Lincoln, NE: University of Nebraska Press, 1998.

Kroeber, A. L. *Handbook of the Indians of California*. Washington, DC: Smithsonian Institution Bureau of American Ethnology, 1925.

Kroger, Joseph, and Patrizia Granziera. *Aztec Goddesses and Christian Madonnas: Images of the Divine Feminine in Mexico*. New York: Routledge, 2016.

Kuiper, Kathleen. *Mesopotamia: The World's Earliest Civilization*. New York: Britannica Educational Publishing, 2011.

Kulkarni, Atul. *Satya Yuga: Dawn of Golden Age by Shivanda Bharati*. Bengaluru, India: Hamsa International, 2012.

Kuno, Meyer. *Aislinge Meic Conglinne: The Vision of Mac Conglinne, a Middle-Irish Wonder Tale*. Dublin: Royal Irish Academy, 1892.

Kyle, Donald G. *Athletics in Ancient Athens*. 2nd revised ed. Leiden, The Netherlands: E. J. Brill, 1993.

Lagerwey, John, and Marc Kalinowski. *Early Chinese Religion: Part One: Shang Through Han (1250 BC–220 AD)*. Leiden, The Netherlands: Brill NV, 2009.

Laing, Lloyd, and Jennifer Laing. *Celtic Britain and Ireland, AD 200–800: The Myth of the Dark Ages*. New York: Saint Martin's Press, 1990.

Lama, Dalai, and Geshe Thupten Jinpa. *Introduction to Buddhism: Teachings on the Four Noble Truths, the Eight Verses on Training the Mind, and the*

*Lamp for the Path to Enlightenment.* Boulder, CO: Shambhala Publishing, 2018.

Lange, Dierk. *Hausa History in the Context of the Ancient Near Eastern World.* http://dierklange.com/pdf/fulltexts/hausa/08_Sources-Bayajidda -legend.pdf.

Larrington, Carolyne. *The Poetic Edda.* Oxford: Oxford University Press, 2004.

Laugrand, Frederick, and Jarich Oosten. *The Sea Woman: Sedna in Inuit Shamanism and Art in the Eastern Arctic.* Fairbanks, AK: University of Alaska Press, 2008.

Lazreg, Marnia. "The Reproduction of Colonial Ideology: The Case of the Kabyle Berbers." *Arab Studies Quarterly* 5, no. 4 (1983): 380–95. http:// www.jstor.org/stable/41857696.

Leahy, A. H. *Heroic Romances of Ireland.* Vol. 2. London: David Nutt, 1906.

Leela, S. R., and Dr. Jayanthi Manohar. *Umasahasram English Translation by Vasishtha Kavyakantha Ganapati Muni.* N.p.: Daksha and Pradip Dalal, Hanuman Jayanti, 2014.

Leeming, David. *The Oxford Companion to World Mythology.* New York: Oxford University Press, 2005.

Leeming, David, and Margaret Leeming. *A Dictionary of Creation Myths.* Oxford: Oxford University Press, 1994.

Legge, James. *Tao Te Ching by Lao-Tzu: Sacred Books of the East.* Vol. 39. Oxford: Clarendon Press, 1891.

Leslie, Julia. *Roles and Rituals for Hindu Women.* Delhi: Motilal Banarsidass Publishers, 1992.

Lewis, Mark Edward. *The Flood Myths of Early China.* Albany, NY: State University of New York Press, 2006.

Lienhardt, Godfrey. *Divinity and Experience: The Religion of the Dinka.* Oxford: Clarendon Press, 1961.

Lind, Michael. *Ancient Zapotec Religion: An Ethnohistorical and Archaeological Perspective.* Louisville, CO: University Press of Colorado, 2015.

Lindow, John. *Norse Mythology: A Guide to the Gods, Heroes, Rituals and Beliefs.* New York: Oxford University Press, 2001.

Lindsay, Alexander Crawford. *Etruscan Inscriptions Analysed*. London: John Murray, 1872.

Lisina, Elena. "Kannon: The Goddess of Mercy: Huge Kannon Statues in Japan." Japan Travel, December 5, 2019. https://en.japantravel.com/blog /kannon-the-goddess-of-mercy/60826.

Liusuwan, Nicholas. "Is Buddhism a Philosophy or a Religion?" *Huffington Post*, December 6, 2017. https://www.huffpost.com/entry/is-buddhism -a-philosophy_b_10176992.

Lloyd, John Edward. *A History of Wales from the Earliest Times to the Edwardian Conquest in Two Volumes*. Vol. 1. 2nd ed. London: Longmans, Green, and Co., 1912.

Loar, Julie. *Goddesses for Every Day: Exploring the Wisdom & Power of the Divine Feminine Around the World*. Novato, CA: New World Library, 2011.

Luce, T. J. *Livy: A Composition of His History*. Princeton, NJ: Princeton University Press, 1977.

Ludvik, Catherine. *Sarasvati: Riverine Goddess of Knowledge*. Boston: Brill's Indological Library, 2007.

Lynch, Patricia Ann. *African Mythology A to Z*. 2nd ed. New York: Chelsea House, 2010.

Macaulay, G. C. *The History of Herodotus*. London: Macmillan, 1890.

MacCullough, John Arnott. *The Religion of the Ancient Celts*. Edinburgh, Scotland: T&T Clark, 1911.

MacDonald, Margaret Read. *Pachamama Tales: Folklore from Argentina, Bolivia, Chile, Paraguay, Peru, and Uruguay*. Santa Barbara, CA: Libraries Unlimited, ABC-CLIO, 2014.

Macri, Martha J., and Gabrielle Vail. *The New Catalog of Maya Hieroglyphs*. Vol. 2, *Codical Texts*. Norman, OK: University of Oklahoma Press, 2009.

Mahathera, Narada. *The Buddha and His Teachings*. N.p.: Buddhist Publication Society, 1988.

Malory, Sir Thomas. *Le Morte d'Arthur*. New York: JM Dent & Sons, 1906.

Maori Dictionary. "Rarohenga." Te Aka Māori Dictionary. https://maori dictionary.co.nz/search?idiom=&phrase=&proverb=&loan=&hist LoanWords=&keywords=Rarohenga.

Marchant, Jo. "Inside the Tombs of Saqqara: Dramatic New Discoveries in the Ancient Egyptian Burial Ground." *Smithsonian Magazine*, July 2021. https://www.smithsonianmag.com/history/inside-tombs-saqqara -180977932/.

Margoles, Michelle. *Mame Coumba Bang: A Living Myth and Evolving Legend: Sengal: Arts and Culture.* N.p.: Carleton College, 2007. https:// digitalcollections.sit.edu/isp_collection/105/.

Marsh, Richard. *The Legends and Lands of Ireland.* New York: Sterling Publishing, 2004.

Martell, Hazel Mary. *The Kingfisher Book of the Ancient World from the Ice Age to the Fall of Rome.* New York: Kingfisher Laurousse Kingfisher Chambers, 1995.

Martin, Roger William. *Tree-Kangaroos of Australia and New Guinea.* Australia: CSIRO Publishing, 2005.

Matthews, John, Caitlin Matthews, and Virginia Chandler. *Arthurian Magic: A Practical Guide to the Wisdom of Camelot.* Woodbury, MN: Llewellyn Worldwide, 2017.

McElroy, D. R. *A Handbook of Folklore, Myths, and Legends from Around the World.* New York: Wellfleet Press, 2020.

McIntyre, Gwynaeth, and Sarah McCallum. *Uncovering Anna Perenna: A Focused Study of Roman Myth and Culture.* London: Bloomsbury Publishing, 2019.

McMahon, Keith. *Misers, Shrews and Polygamists: Sexuality and Male-Female Relations in Eighteenth Century Chinese Fiction.* Durham, NC: Duke University Press, 1995.

Mercer, Samuel A. B. *The Pyramid Texts.* New York: Longmans, Green & Co., 1952.

Metropolitan Museum of Art. "The Goddess Kurukulla." The Met. https:// www.metmuseum.org/art/collection/search/665918.

Mierzwicki, Tony. *Practicing Greek Polytheism Today*. Woodbury, MN: Llewellyn Worldwide, 2018.

Mi'kmaq Spirit. "The Coming of Nukumi." Mikmaw Spirit. https://www.muiniskw.org/pgCulture3a.htm.

Milbrath, Susan. *Star Gods of the Maya: Astronomy in Art, Folklore, and Calendars*. Austin: University of Texas Press, 2000.

Miller, Barbara Stoler. *Jayadeva's Gitagovinda: Love Song of the Dark Lord*. N.p.: Columbia University Press, 1977.

Miri, Adhid. "From Babylon to Berlin: The Ishtar Gate in the Pergamon Museum." Chaldean News, August 27, 2020. https://www.chaldean news.com/features-1/2020/8/27/from-babylon-to-berlin.

Monaghan, Patricia. *The Encyclopedia of Celtic Mythology and Folklore*. New York: Facts on File, 2004.

Monaghan, Patricia. *Encyclopedia of Goddesses and Heroines: Africa, Eastern Mediterranean, Asia*. Vol. 1. Santa Barbara, CA: Greenwood, ABC-CLIO, 2009.

Monaghan, Patricia. *Encyclopedia of Goddesses & Heroines*. Novato, CA: New World Library, 2014.

Monaghan, Patricia. *The New Book of Goddesses & Heroines*. Woodbury, MN: Llewellyn Publications, 1997.

Monaghan, Patricia. *Women in Myth and Legend*. London: Junction Books, 1981.

Moorey, Theresa. *Understand Chinese Mythology*. London: Hodder Education, 2012.

Mortimer, W. Golden. *Peru: History of Coca: "The Divine Plant" of the Incas*. New York: J. H. Vail & Company, 1901.

Myers, Elisabeth R. "Algeria's Amazigh Problem: Escalation of the Kabylia Conflict (Part 1 of 2)." Inside Arabia, March 16, 2022. https://inside arabia.com/algerias-amazigh-problem-escalation-of-the-kabylia-conflict -part-1-of-2/.

Mythopia. "Goddesses of Hawaiian Mythology." Medium, March 9, 2019. https://medium.com/@mythopia/goddesses-of-hawaiian-mythology -2d2daddc52c6.

Nagar, Shanti Lal. *Brahmavaivarta Purana*. Delhi: Parimal Publications, 2003.

Nandakumar, Mali. "Female Deities in Vajrayana Buddhism." IndicaToday, October 1, 2018. https://www.indica.today/long-reads/female-deities -vajrayana-buddhism/.

National Geographic Society. "Olmec Civilization: The Role of the Olmec in Mesoamerican Society Is a Matter of Hot Debate between Archae- ologists and Anthropologists." National Geographic, August 11, 2020. https://www.nationalgeographic.org/encyclopedia/olmec-civilization/.

National Geographic Staff. "What Was 'Lucy'? Fast Facts on an Early Human Ancestor." National Geographic, September 19, 2006. https:// www.nationalgeographic.com/history/article/lucy-facts-on-early-human -ancestor.

Ní Bhrolcháin, Muireann. "The Manuscript Tradition of the Banshenchas." *Ériu* 33 (1982): 109–35. http://www.jstor.org/stable/30007585.

Nicholson, Henry B. *Topiltzin Quetzalcoatl: The Once and Future Lord of the Toltecs*. Boulder, CO: University Press of Colorado, 2001.

Nosselt, Friedrich August. *Mythology Greek and Roman*. Translated by A. W. Hall. London: Kerby & Endean, 1885.

O'Brien, Barbara. "History of Buddhism in China: The First Thousand Years." Learn Religions, September 8, 2021. http://learnreligions.com /buddhism-in-china-the-first-thousand-years-450147.

O hOgain, Daithi. *Myth, Legend & Romance: An Encyclopaedia of Irish Folk Tradition*. London: Chapmans Publishers Prentiss Hall Press, 1991.

Oloruntoba, Samuel Ojo, and Toyin Falola. *The Palgrave Handbook of Africa and the Changing Global Order*. Cham, Switzerland: Palgrave Macmillan, 2022.

Oneida Indian Nation. "Godasiyo, the Woman Chief." Oneida Indian Nation. https://www.oneidaindiannation.com/godasiyo-the-woman -chief/#:~:text=Godasiyo%20was%20a%20wise%20and,villagers%20 or%20being%20understood%20themselves.

Ovid. *Metamorphoses*. Translated by John Dryden. Edited by Sir Samuel Garth. Hertfordshire, UK: Wordsworth Classics of World Literature, 1998.

Ovid. *Ovid's Fasti with Notes and an Introduction by Thomas Keightley*. Dublin: Richard Milliken and Son, 1833.

Palmer, H. R. "52. 'Bori' Among the Hausas." *Man* 14 (1914): 113–7. https://doi.org/10.2307/2787459.

Parry, John Jay. *The Vita Merlini: Latin Text by Geoffrey of Monmouth, Bishop of St. Asaph, (1100?–1154)*. Urbana, IL: The University of Illinois, 1925.

Patel, Sanjay. *The Little Book of Hindu Deities: From the Goddess of Wealth to the Sacred Cow*. New York: Penguin Plume, 2006.

Philippi, Donald L. *Kojiki*. Tokyo: University of Tokyo Press, 1968.

Picken, Stuart D. B. *Historical Dictionary of Shinto*. 2nd ed. Plymouth, UK: The Scarecrow Press, 2011.

Pinch, Geraldine. *Egyptian Mythology: A Guide to the Gods, Goddesses, and Traditions of Ancient Egypt*. Oxford: Oxford University Press, 2002.

Ponchia, Simonetta, and Mikko Luukko. *The Standard Babylonian Myth of Nergal and Ereškigal: Introduction, Cuneiform Text and Transliteration with a Translation, Glossary and Commentary*. N.p.: Neo-Assyrian Text Corpus Project, 2013.

Poole, Reginald Stewart. *Catalogue of the Coins of Alexandria and the Nomes by British Museum Department of Coins and Medals*. London: British Museum, 1892.

Porció, Tibor. *The One with the White Parasol: Four Sitātapatrā Texts in the Derge Kanjur and a Dunhuang Text*. Vienna, Austria: University of Vienna, 2000.

Preston, Richard J. "Nehiyawak (Cree)." In *The Canadian Encyclopedia*. N.p.: Historica Canada, 2012.

Preston-Matto, Lahney. *Aislinge Meic Conglinne: The Vision of Mac Conglinne*. New York: Syracuse University Press, 2010.

Raines, John C., and Daniel C. Maguire. *What Men Owe to Women: Men's Voices from World Religions*. Albany, NY: State University of New York Press, 2001.

Read, Herbert, Michael Fordham, Gerhard Adler, and William McGuire. *The Collected Works of C. G. Jung.* Vol. 1. New York: Bollingen Foundation, 1957.

Read, Kay Almere, and Jason J. Gonzales. *Mesoamerican Mythology: A Guide to the Gods, Heroes, Rituals, and Beliefs of Mexico and Central America.* New York: Oxford University Press, 2002.

Redford, Donald B. *The Ancient Gods Speak: A Guide to Egyptian Religion.* Oxford: Oxford University Press, 2002.

Reid, Margaret. *The Changing Face of Guanyin in East Asian Religions.* N.p.: University of Canterbury, 1997.

Reider, Noriko. *Seven Demon Stories from Japan.* Louisville, CO: Utah State University Press, 2016.

Roberts, Peter Alan, with Tulku Yeshi. "The Basket's Display: Karandavyuha: The Noble Mahāyāna Sutra." *Aryakarandavyuhanamamhayanasutra Toh* 116, no. 51(2013): 200a–247b.

Roller, Duane W. *The Geography of Strabo: An English Translation, with Introduction and Notes.* Cambridge: Cambridge University Press, 2014.

Rollin, Tracy. *Santa Muerte: The History, Rituals, and Magic of Our Lady of the Holy Death.* Newburyport, MA: Weiser Books, 2017.

Roman, Luke, and Monica Roman. *Encyclopedia of Greek and Roman Mythology.* New York: Facts on File, 2010.

Roscher, W. H. *Detailed Encyclopedia of Greek and Roman Mythology.* Edited by W. H. Roscher. Leipzig, Germany: B. G. Teubner, 1884.

Rose, Carol. *Giants, Monsters & Dragons: An Encyclopedia of Folklore, Legend and Myth.* N.p.: W. W. Norton & Company, 2000.

Rostworowski de Diez Canseco, Maria, and Harry B. Iceland. *History of the Inca Realm.* Cambridge: Cambridge University Press, 1999.

Rouse, W. H. D. *Apocolocyntosis of Lucius Annaeus Seneca the Younger.* London: William Heinemann, 1913.

Rowe, John Howland. *Inca Culture at the Time of the Spanish Conquest.* Washington, DC: United States Government Printing Office, 1946.

Ruckstuhl, Katharina, Irma A. Velasquez Nimatuj, and John-Andrew McNeish. *The Routledge Handbook of Indigenous Development*. New York: Routledge, 2023.

Russo, Carla Herreria. "The Mysterious Reason Tourists Keep Mailing Rocks Back to Hawaii." *Huffington Post*, October 20, 2016. https://www.huffpost.com/entry/peles-curse-lava-rocks-hawaii_n_5800337 de4b05eff5582c5c7.

Sawyer, Peter. *The Oxford Illustrated History of the Vikings*. New York: Oxford University Press, 1997.

Scheub, Harold. *Dictionary of African Mythology*. Oxford: Oxford University Press, 2000.

Scheub, Harold. *Trickster and Hero: Two Characters in the Oral and Written Traditions of the World*. Madison, WI: The University of Wisconsin Press, 2012.

Sciolino, Elaine. "In Dijon, Where Mustard Rules, You Can Also Meet an Ancient Goddess." *The New York Times*, October 5, 2019. https://www.nytimes.com/2019/10/05/arts/dijon-museum-architecture.html.

Sciolino, Elaine. *The Seine: The River That Made Paris*. New York: W. W. Norton & Company, 2019.

Seler, Eduard. *The Tolamatl of the Aubin Collection: An Old Mexican Picture Manuscript in the Paris National Library*. United Kingdom: A. H. Keane, 1901.

Seligman, C. G., and Brenda Z. Seligman. *Pagan Tribes of the Nilotic Sudan*. London: G. Routledge & Sons, 1932.

Sellar, A. M. *Bede's Ecclesiastical History of England: A Revised Translation*. London: George Bell and Sons, 1907.

Sengupta, Hindol. *Being Hindu: Understanding a Peaceful Path in a Violent World*. London: Rowman & Littlefield, 2018.

Shakespeare, William. *Romeo & Juliet*. London: The Nassau Press, 1895.

Sharer, Robert J., and Loa P. Traxler. *The Ancient Maya*. 6th ed. Stanford, CA: Stanford University Press, 2006.

Sharma, Arvind, and Katherine K. Young. *The Annual Review of Women in World Religions.* Vol. 4. Albany, NY: State University of New York Press, 1996.

Shaw, Miranda Eberle. *Buddhist Goddesses of India.* Princeton, NJ: Princeton University Press, 2006.

Shearar, Cheryl. *Understanding Northwest Coast Art: A Guide to Crests, Beings and Symbols.* Vancouver, BC: Douglas and McIntyre, 2013.

Sheard, K. M. *Llewellyn's Complete Book of Names: For Pagans, Witches, Wiccans, Druids, Heathens, Mages, Shamans & Independent Thinkers of All Sorts Who Are Curious About Names from Every Place and Every Time.* Woodbury, MN: Llewellyn Publications, 2011.

Shortland, Edward. *Māori Religion and Mythology.* London: Longmans, Green and Co., 1882.

Simon, W. "A Dictionary of Chinese Buddhist Terms with Sanskrit and English Equivalents and a Sanskrit-Pali Index." *Bulletin of the School of Oriental and African Studies* 9, no. 4 (1939): 1070–2. doi:10.1017 /S0041977X00135323.

Skilton, Andrew. *A Concise History of Buddhism.* Cambridge: Windhorse Publications, 1994.

Skye, Michelle. *Goddess Alive! Inviting Celtic and Norse Goddesses into Your Life.* Woodbury, MN: Llewellyn Worldwide, 2007.

Small, Ernest. *Top 100 Food Plants: The World's Most Important Culinary Crops.* Ontario: National Research Council of Canada, NRC Press, 2009.

Smith, Derek G. "Religion and Spirituality of Indigenous Peoples in Canada." *The Canadian Encyclopedia*, December 4, 2011. https://www.the canadianencyclopedia.ca/en/article/religion-of-aboriginal-people.

Smith, William. *A Dictionary of Greek and Roman Biography and Mythology.* London: John Murray, 1848.

Smith, William. *Dictionary of Greek and Roman Biography and Mythology.* Vol. 1. Oxford: Oxford University Press, 1844.

Smithsonian Magazine. "First City in the New World? Peru's Caral Suggests Civilization Emerged in the Americas 1,000 Years Earlier Than Experts

Believed." *Smithsonian Magazine*, August 2002. https://www.smithsonian
mag.com/history/first-city-in-the-new-world-66643778/.

Smithsonian Institution. "The Impact of Words and Tips for Using Appropriate Terminology: Am I Using the Right Word?" National Museum of
the American Indian. https://americanindian.si.edu/nk360
/informational/impact-words-tips.

Smithsonian Institution. "Nymph of the Luo River." Smithsonian National
Museum of Asian Art. https://asia.si.edu/learn/for-educators/teaching
-china-with-the-smithsonian/explore-by-object/nymph-of-the-luo
-river/.

Spaeth, Barbara Stanley. *The Roman Goddess Ceres*. Austin, TX: University
of Texas Press, 1996.

Specktor, Brandon. "Sorry, but Your Name Is Probably Illegal in Iceland."
Readers Digest, April 3, 2017. https://www.rd.com/article/icelandic
-baby-names/.

Spence, Lewis. *The Myths of Mexico and Peru*. London: George Harrap,
1913.

Spence, Lewis. *The Popol Vuh: The Mythic and Heroic Sagas of the Kiches of
Central America*. London: David Nutt Publishing, 1908.

Steele, Paul R., and Catherine J. Allen. *Handbook of Inca Mythology*. Santa
Barbara, CA: ABC-CLIO, 2004.

Stevens, Edward T. *Flint Chips: A Guide to Pre-Historic Archaeology, as Illustrated by the Collection in the Blackmore Museum, Salisbury*. London: Bell
and Daldy, 1870.

Stevens, Jenny. "Big Vagina Energy: The Return of the Sheela Na Gig." *The
Guardian*, March 8, 2021. https://www.theguardian.com/world/2021
/mar/08/big-vagina-energy-the-return-of-the-sheela-na-gig.

Stokes, Whitley. *Sanas Chormaic: Cormac's Glossary by Cormac, King of
Cashel, 836–908*. Translated and annotated by John O'Donovan. Cal-
cutta, India: Irish Archaeological and Celtic Society, 1868.

Stone, Andrea J. *Images from the Underworld: Naj Tunich and the Tradition of
Maya Cave Painting*. Austin, TX: University of Texas Press, 1995.

Study.com Editors. "Egyptian Women: Royalty, Privileges & Tradition." Study. https://study.com/academy/lesson/egyptian-women-royalty -privileges-tradition.html.

Sullivan, Bruce M. *The A to Z of Hinduism*. Kent, England: Scarecrow Press, 2001.

Sullivan, Thelma D. *Fray Bernardino de Sahagún, Primeros Memoriales*. Edited by Thelma D. Sullivan, et al. Norman, OK: University of Oklahoma Press, 1997.

Suzuki, Daisetz Teitaro. *Essays in Zen Buddhism*. London: Rider and Company, 1950.

Tagare, G. V. *The Vayu Purana*. Delhi: Shri Jainendra Press, 1987.

Tahara, Kaori. "The Saga of the Ainu language." The UNESCO Courier, October 2009. https://en.unesco.org/courier/numero-especial -octubre-2009/saga-ainu-language.

Tanaka, Stefan. *Japan's Orient: Rendering Pasts into History*. Los Angeles: University of California Press, 1993.

Taube, Karl Andreas. *The Major Gods of Ancient Yucatan*. Washington, DC: Dumbarton Oaks Research Library and Collection, 1992.

Tavárez, David. *Nicachi Songs: Zapotec Ritual Texts and Postclassic Ritual Knowledge in Colonial Oaxaca*. N.p.: Foundation for the Advancement of Mesoamerican Studies, 2005.

Tavárez, David. *Social Reproduction of Late Postclassic Ritual Practices in Early Colonial Central Mexico*. N.p.: Foundation for the Advancement of Mesoamerican Studies, 2000.

Tavarez, David. *The Invisible War: Indigenous Devotions, Discipline, and Dissent in Colonial Mexico*. Stanford, CA: Stanford University Press, 2011.

Te Ahukaramu, Charles Royal. "First Peoples in Māori Tradition—Tāne, Hineahuone and Hine." Te Ara—The Encyclopedia of New Zealand. https://teara.govt.nz/en/first-peoples-in-maori-tradition/page-2.

Thomas, Douglas, and Temilola Alanamu. *African Religions: Beliefs and Practices through History*. Santa Barbara, CA: ABC-CLIO, 2019.

Thompson, J. Eric S. *Maya History and Religion*. Vol. 99. Norman, OK: University of Oklahoma Press, 1990.

Tin, Daw Mya. *The Dhammapada*. Onalaska, WA: Pariyatti Publishing, 1984.

Townsend, Camilla. *Fifth Sun: A New History of the Aztecs*. New York: Oxford University Press, 2019.

Townsend, George Fyler. *Aesop's Fables*. Chicago: Belford, Clarke & Co., 1887.

Tremain, Cara G. "Patterns in the Dresden Codex." *The PARI Journal* 14, no. 1 (2013):6–12.

Trobe, Kala. *Invoke the Goddess: Connecting to the Hindu, Greek & Egyptian Deities*. Woodbury, MN: Llewellyn Worldwide, 2019.

Tsing, Anna Lowenhaupt, Nils Bubandt, Elaine Gan, and Heather Anne Swanson. *Arts of Living on a Damaged Planet: Ghosts and Monsters of the Anthropocene*. Minneapolis: University of Minnesota Press, 2017.

Tyler, Hamilton A. *Pueblo Gods and Myths*. Norman, OK: University of Oklahoma Press, 1964.

UNESCO World Heritage. "Delos." UNESCO. https://whc.unesco.org/en/list/530/.

UNESCO World Heritage. "Hal Saflieni Hypogeum." UNESCO. https://whc.unesco.org/en/list/130/.

UNESCO World Heritage. "Pre-Hispanic City of Teotihuacan." UNESCO. https://whc.unesco.org/en/list/414/.

UNESCO World Heritage. "Taj Mahal." UNESCO. https://whc.unesco.org/en/list/252/.

United Nations. "Who Are Indigenous Peoples?" United Nations Permanent Forum on Indigenous Issues. https://www.un.org/esa/socdev/unpfii/documents/5session_factsheet1.pdf.

Urton, Gary. *Inca Myths: The Legendary Past*. Austin, TX: British Museum Press & University of Texas Press, 1999.

Van De Mieroop, Marc. *A History of the Ancient Near East, ca. 3000–323 BC*. 3rd ed. Oxford: John Wiley & Sons, 2016.

Various Authors. *Routledge Library Editions: Myth*. 1st ed. London: Taylor & Francis, 2015.

Veldhuis, Nick. *Religion, Literature and Scholarship: The Sumerian Composition Nanse and the Birds with a Catalogue of Sumerian Bird Names*. Leiden, The Netherlands: Styx/Koninklijke Brill NV, 2004.

Verlag, Peter Delius. *National Geographic Essential Visual History of the World*. Washington, DC: National Geographic Society, 2007.

Vijnanananda, Swami. *Srimad Devi Bhagavatam (Devi Purana)*. N.p.: Sahaji, 2004.

Vyasa, Veda. *Padma Purana in English*. Internet Archive. https://archive.org/details/purana-padma-purana-eng/mode/1up.

Vyasa, Veda. *Vishnu Purana: English Translation with Sanskrit Text*. N.p.: Opensource, 2021.

Walker, Glenn. "Spider Rock." Indigenous Peoples Literature, 1996. http://www.indigenouspeople.net/spiderro.htm.

Wallis, Faith. *Bede: The Reckoning of Time*. Vol. 29. Liverpool: Liverpool University Press, 1999.

Walsh, Colleen. "What the Nose Knows: Experts Discuss the Science of Smell and How Scent, Emotion, and Memory Are Intertwined—and Exploited." *The Harvard Gazette*, February 27, 2020. https://news.harvard.edu/gazette/story/2020/02/how-scent-emotion-and-memory-are-intertwined-and-exploited/.

Watson, Burton. *Han Fei Tzu: Basic Writing*. New York: Columbia University Press, 1964.

Watterson, Barbara. *The Gods of Ancient Egypt*. Gloucestershire, UK: Sutton Publishing, 1999.

Wells, Peter S. *The Barbarians Speak: How the Conquered Peoples Shaped Roman Europe*. Princeton, NJ: Princeton University Press, 1999.

Werner, Alice. *Myths and Legends of the Bantu*. London: George G. Harrap & Co., 1933.

Werner, E. T. C. *Myths & Legends of China*. London: George G. Harrap & Co., 1922.

Wernerian Club and Philemon Holland. *Pliny's Natural History in Thirty-Seven Books*. Vol. 1. London: George Barclay, 1847.

White, William. *Roman Gods & Goddesses*. New York: Britannica Educational Publishing, 2014.

Whitehead, Henry. *The Village Gods of South India*. London: Oxford University Press, 1916.

Wilkinson, Richard H. *The Complete Gods and Goddesses of Ancient Egypt*. London: Thames & Hudson, 2017.

Williams, George. *Religions of the World: Shinto*. New York: Chelsea House Publishers, 2005.

Witschey, Walter R. T., and Clifford T. Brown. *Historical Dictionary of Mesoamerica*. Plymouth, UK: The Scarecrow Press, 2012.

Wolkstein, Diane, and Samuel Noah Kramer. *Inanna, Queen of Heaven and Earth: Her Stories and Hymns from Sumer*. New York: Harper & Row, 1983.

Wood, Stephanie. "Matalcueye." *Online Nahuatl Dictionary*. Edited by Stephanie Wood. Eugene, OR: Wired Humanities Projects, 2000.

Yang, Lihui, Deming An, and Jessica Anderson Turner. *Handbook of Chinese Mythology*. Oxford: Oxford University Press, 2005.

Yingming, Hong. *Xian Fo Qi Zong: The Sacred Traces of Taoist Immortals and Priests, Buddhas and Zen Masters*. N.p.: DeepLogic, 2018.

Yong, Ced. "108 Chinese Mythological Gods and Characters to Know About." Owlcation. https://owlcation.com/humanities/chinese-mythological-gods-characters.

Yong, Ced. "120 Shinto Gods and Goddesses to Know About." Owlcation. https://owlcation.com/humanities/shinto-gods-goddesses-kojiki-nihon-shoki.

Yonge, C. D. *The Treatises of M. T. Cicero: On the Nature of the Gods; On Divination; On Fate; On the Republic; On the Laws; and on Standing for the Consulship*. London: Henry G. Bohn, 1853.

Yu, Chun-fang. *Kuan-Yin: The Chinese Transformation of Avalokiteshvara*. New York: The Institute for Advanced Studies of World Religions, 2001.

ZaraMama. "Gourmet Popping Corn." ZaraMama. https://www.zaramama.com/.

## To Write to the Author

If you wish to contact the author or would like more information about this book, please write to the author in care of Llewellyn Worldwide Ltd. and we will forward your request. Both the author and the publisher appreciate hearing from you and learning of your enjoyment of this book and how it has helped you. Llewellyn Worldwide Ltd. cannot guarantee that every letter written to the author can be answered, but all will be forwarded. Please write to:

Shelley A. Kaehr, PhD
℅ Llewellyn Worldwide
2143 Wooddale Drive
Woodbury, MN 55125-2989
Please enclose a Self-addressed stamped envelope for reply,
or $1.00 to cover costs. If outside the U.S.A., enclose
an international postal reply coupon.

Many of Llewellyn's authors have websites with additional information and resources. For more information, please visit our website at http://www.llewellyn.com.